Holland

Present-day
Sydney

Port Jackson

Coalcliff

Jervis Bay
Cape St George

Bateman Bay

Twofold Bay

Cape Howe

Mallacoota Inlet

Point Hicks

Present-day
Melbourne

Ninety-
Mile
Beach

Tasman Sea

Wilsons Promontory

Flinders Island

Bass Strait

Furneaux
Group

Preservation Island

*Van Diemen's
Land*

nt-day
ide

■ Wreck site
----- Route to Port Jackson

Wreck of the
Sydney Cove

Wreck of the Sydney Cove

MAX JEFFREYS

NEW
HOLLAND

Published in Australia in 1997 by
New Holland Publishers Pty Ltd
3/2 Aquatic Drive
Frenchs Forest
NSW 2086 Australia

Typeset by Midland Typesetters
Printed in Australia by the Australian Print Group
Cover design by Arne Falkenmire
Cartography by Mark Seabrook

National Library of Australia Cataloguing-in-Publication Data

Jeffreys, Max.
    Wreck of the Sydney Cove.

ISBN 1 86436 302 9

1. Sydney Cove (Ship). 2. Shipwrecks – Tasmania – Furneaux Islands. I. Title.

910.916576

PICTURE CREDITS

Cover
Background: 1663 map of Terra Australis Incognita by Thévenot, National Library of Australia.
Spine inset and front cover: Painting of the ship *Borrowdale* (detail) by Francis Holman. Reproduced courtesy of the Australian National Maritime Museum.
Front cover inset: Portrait of John Hunter by Daniel Orme after Dighton (artist), Rex Nan Kivell Collection, National Library of Australia.

Internal
p. xii watercolour of Sydney Town by Edward Dayes, 1797, National Library of Australia; **p. 24** *Complete Encyclopedia of Illustration*, J.G. Heck, Park Lane, New York, 1979; **p. 56** illustration by Bronwyn Rennex; *p. 140* Coo-ee Historical Picture Library; **p. 248** 'Waterfall on the coast of Wattamolle, about 600ft' c.1843–46 (detail) by Robert Westmacott, Image Library, State Library of New South Wales. Illustration on chapter opener pages by John Bastock.

CONTENTS

ILLUSTRATIONS

MAPS

ACKNOWLEDGEMENTS

A number of people have assisted, sometimes unwittingly, in the re-creation of this epic. I was sailing to Sydney with friends Pauline and Graham Carson aboard their yacht *Silver Gull II*, when I first read of the *Sydney Cove* incident in a navigational text. Pauline and Graham were kind enough to read an early draft and make positive comments, as did Graham's father.

Pat Parsons, Russel Jackson, Tsibin Tchen and the Reverend Graeme Perkins, also a keen sailor, added further useful comments. Leo Milner, late of Calcutta, provided notes on life in Bengal. I obtained valuable help from Linda Clark of the Queen Victoria Museum in Launceston; Mike Nash of the Tasmanian Parks and Wildlife Service, Hobart; and the staff of the Mitchell Library in Sydney and the libraries at Monash and Melbourne universities. To all of these people I express my thanks.

My mother played a part when, long ago, she said, 'One day you'll write a book.' It is due primarily to my wife Diane, however, that the completed work came to fruition. For me, the research and writing were satisfaction itself. But she saw its publication prospects, particularly in the year of the wreck's bicentenary, and so encouraged me to seek out a willing publisher. Thank you, Diane – and thanks also to Averill Chase, Publishing Manager at New Holland Publishers, who also recognised the story's potential.

For Diane and Daniel

A view of the town of Sydney in 1797 by Edward Dayes.

PREFACE

In 1797, Great Britain was again besieged by her enemies and threatened with invasion, while her empire crumbled in the face of local rebellion and foreign influences. America was already lost. India, beset by internal strife and the commercial and military ambitions of other countries, was becoming increasingly unstable. The strategic tip of Africa, vital for Britain's eastern trade routes, was subject to similar rivalries and defensive manoeuvrings, while the many island outposts and far-flung harbours within her influence constantly changed hands in response to political intrigues and commercial dealings within the Old World.

Europe was in turmoil. Having thrown off the *Ancien Regime*, France was in the grip of revolutionary fervour, with all its attendant strife and uncertainty. Civil war had been narrowly averted through the diversions of a series of revolutionary wars, which had subjugated most of her neighbours, converting former enemies into friends and allies as a prelude to France's own expansionist zeal. France and England were locked in yet another bitter conflict, one that would ultimately embroil all Europe. In 1797 Napoleon Bonaparte was a rising, though still little known, commander, with a number of military and political successes to his credit.

England's Royal Navy had already dealt the first of several major blows against Napoleon and his allies, however, by soundly defeating a Spanish fleet off Cape St Vincent in February 1797. Six months later it had similarly dealt with the Dutch off Camperdown. Meanwhile Rear-Admiral Horatio Nelson's star, already ascending as a result of his actions at Cape St Vincent, was to come into full prominence against the French themselves at the Battle of the Nile the following year.

In 1797 France was emerging as a formidable land power, but it was Great Britain who held supreme command of the oceans. Despite the storm clouds that were gathering over Europe, Britain's supremacy on the high seas still allowed exploration and trade away from the toils of war. There were new colonies to be established and nurtured in promising lands on the far side of the globe. A new empire might help to offset the humiliating losses sustained by the old one.

Port Jackson was one such colony, having been established in 1788 as the first settlement on the eastern coast of New Holland, later to be known as Australia. For many reasons this remote penal enclave was still struggling for survival nine years after its founding. The area's earlier promise had not been fulfilled: the climate, land and native population had all proved adverse and the needs of the colonists were still being largely met by the Mother Country. In those first discouraging years, Port Jackson – or Sydney as it was soon to be known – was supplied by a motley collection of ships with a diverse assortment of cargoes and crews. They persistently braved the still largely unknown and perilous southern waters to bring cargoes from Britain, India and the Cape, from China, the Indies, and America.

This is the story of one such ship, the *Sydney Cove*, and of the men who sailed in her – and of the first significant overland journey within the unknown continent. The *Sydney Cove* was a British East Indiaman owned by Campbell, Clarke and Co., a Scottish firm trading from Bengal. Her last voyage was a speculative one, carrying rum and other spirits, and sundry other commodities from Calcutta to Port Jackson. She never reached Port Jackson, foundering amongst the Furneaux Islands of Bass Strait. The story is based on a diary kept by one of the survivors, and is a little known tale of trial and endurance, death and survival in Australia's earliest days. Although the story has been dramatised, it is based on real life events.

Captain Guy Hamilton, Hugh Thompson, William Clarke, the carpenter (unnamed), Mr Leishman, John Thistle and Archibald Armstrong were all living people. So, of course, were Captain James Cook, Captain Tobias Furneaux, Governor John Hunter, Dr George Bass, Lieutenant Matthew Flinders, Judge-Advocate David Collins, and Robert and John Campbell. Their identities are preserved in various historical records from around 200 years ago. All other names and characters, however, including that of Job Duggan, are by necessity inventions, because records of the crew's names are incomplete – though most of the people to whom they are attached made their own special contribution to this remarkable adventure.

1
A GALE OF
EXTREME VIOLENCE ...

24TH JANUARY, 1797. Fresh'ning winds from sou'west, increasing in strength. Squalls and rising seas – another gale imminent. 76 days out from Fort William, with no position'l observations possible for sev'ral days since. Leak for'rard still gives cause for some concern, tho' kept in hand by thrum'd sail of the 13th, still beneath the bow; and continual manning of the pumps.
FROM THE SHIP'S LOG

*I*n the creaking gloom of his dimly lit Great Cabin, Captain Guy Hamilton of the British East Indiaman *Sydney Cove* carefully wiped his goose-quill, snapped the lid of his ink-pot, and lightly sanded his log entry for the previous day. A typical entry, he mused as he reread it critically, slowly thumbing tobacco into a well-used clay pipe. Bland, factual and to the point.

In its lack of emotion and detachment, it was like the hundreds of others he had penned over the years. Stark, summary comments on the heavy bound vellum. There was no room for personal feelings, and so the entries lacked the spontaneity of the actual events. They told nothing of the pleasure of a carefully sought landfall, of the satisfaction of a successfully completed voyage, or of the uncertainty and occasional fear when facing the unknown. They failed to convey the stress of never-ending storms that drove the ship, as now, towards a distant, unfamiliar landfall across an unrelenting sea.

The ship shuddered as yet another mighty wave burst against her starboard quarter, followed by the muted rattle of solid spray on the dead-lighted gallery windows, and the soft rush of a flooding wash across the timbered deck above. He dipped a taper into the lamp, transferred the flame to his pipe, and drew heavily on its contents to bring them to life.

With an old sailor's instinct he could already sense the mounting turbulence and the gathering storm as his craft battled against the pursuing waves, thrusting aside the heaping tide that ceaselessly hove and threatened.

No written words could adequately express the sullen swell and surge of the awakening sea beyond the close limits of his cabin, nor the manic shriek and unceasing bluster of winds from the Roaring Forties which swept tempestuously over the decks and kept the rigging alive with endless wailing. Only mariners could understand the untamed might of the unencumbered seas of these latitudes, and the awesome emptiness of the globe's uncharted, unexplored vastness. Even that understanding depended on the extent of a man's seafaring experiences, tested by the moods of the many oceans.

Guy Hamilton had departed the Clyde and his native Scotland for a life at sea in 1727, a mere boy of ten, after which he spent many more years afloat than ashore. Now, 70 years later, he was in command of the *Sydney Cove*, bound from Bengal to Port Jackson on the recently settled coast of New Holland, across one of the world's wildest and loneliest oceans.

A heavier boom caused the ship to lurch and poise, before continuing a rolling downward slide. A gimballed oil-lamp on the bulkhead flickered smokily, its yellow light casting distorted shadows across the panelled walls as the timbers of the old ship shifted and groaned in protest. He listened and strained, attuned through long years under canvas to his ship's every mood, wary of each fresh shift in wind or weather that might presage another storm.

Somewhere a loose object fell and rolled, a victim of the constant working of ropes and lashings. And deep intuition, an indefinable gut feeling backed by the mercury weather glass, warned now of worse to come – one more wearying gale to add to the others that had plagued the voyage since the middle of December.

The voyage had started well enough. It was a measure of the esteem and trust of his employers, Messrs Campbell, Clarke and Co. of Calcutta, that he and his ship had been selected for the company's first speculative trade venture, with a cargo of saleable liquor to the new colony. Change was afoot, and what until recently had been a largely empty expanse on the charts, despite its discovery more than 150 years before, was at last being viewed with sufficient interest to encourage one or two experimental trade contacts.

Merchants from America and India were also beginning to eye the new settlement with some degree of favour, notwithstanding its forbidding penal status. Free migrants were already taking up land options, and their needs could only benefit anyone willing to stock a supply ship and risk the unknown. Campbell, Clarke and Co. were therefore eager to establish an early footing in the belief that there would be greater commercial prospects in the reasonably foreseeable future.

The ship left the crowded Calcutta wharves and waterways on the morning of 10 November 1796. After threading her way down the turbid Hooghli River amidst a throng of busy dhows, trim launches and bulking East Indiamen, she dropped her pilot and pressed south into the Bay of Bengal to pick up the seasonal monsoon winds blowing from the north-east at that time of year.

Captain Hamilton's voyage plan saw them maintaining their southerly heading across the Equator, then south-easterly to the Tropic of Capricorn for four or five weeks, standing well off the New Holland coasts (called de Witts and Leeuwin Lands by early Dutch explorers) to avoid contrary winds and currents. In the southern Indian Ocean he intended to pick up the ever-present westerlies, which would speed them eastwards below the known shores of *Terra Australis* to Van Diemen's Land and beyond.

For over a month *Sydney Cove* progressed steadily across the empty ocean. Though occasionally becalmed in the doldrums, there were also boisterous days under full sail, the distance slipping away across the deep blue sea, his ship fine and full beneath him. It was sailing at its best, a heart-lifting feeling he had so often appreciated. He rejoiced with a quiet pride and pleasure, a gleam in his eye while his craft surged purposefully through the waves with all available canvas. Her courses bellied taut and broad, her topgallants seemingly swept the drifting clouds, and her studding sails spread like wings on either hand, intent on catching every ounce of power from the slanting breeze.

In mid-December, however, they had been overtaken by a severe gale and heavy seas which had persisted, despite the season and latitude. At the same time a leak was discovered near the bow, and this had grown progressively worse with the labouring of the ship, reduced at times to bare poles beneath the fury of wind and waves.

Every plank and frame worked minutely against its neighbours under the wrench and twist of the storms. As the inflow of water increased, it was discovered that a butt-end had started behind timbers under the starboard bow. Though the forehold was partially unstowed in an attempt to reach the seat of the leak, it proved to be inaccessible from within the ship, and putting a man over the side in such violent weather was out of the question.

Now, with the persistent leak, another rising gale and a rapidly falling weatherglass, he had cause to recall a conversation earlier in the day with Hugh Thompson, his chief officer. The captain had grumbled freely in peeved accents.

'Six weeks, Mister, wi' one damn' gale after another!' he had said. 'An' worse tae come as we gang south, ah'm a'thinkin'. What's wi' us, ah'm askin'? In a' ma seventy years at sea ah've niver afore seen the likes! The North Atlantic in winter, aye, ah'd grant ye,' he conceded, 'but here we should be sailin' fair i' the tropics the noo, wi' summer tae boot!'

He glowered in uncharacteristic frustration. 'The Frenchies and Spaniards or lesser brigands ah cuid deal wi', but day after day like this, an' so far tae go yet! Is there tae be no respite? Bad enough the way it is, but neither can ah tell jist where we are wi'out sight o' the sun, an' yon leak's

4

a bother ah dinna need! What's tae do below, Chief? If ye've better news, man, be quick an' tell me!'

Hugh Thompson shook his head. 'Sorry sir, we're still taking in four to six inches an hour, even with the thrummed sail and the spell we've had, depending on the state o' the sea. Seems likely to stay that way – at least 'til the weather abates some. We might then put a boat over the side, though it'll be a while yet, I'd say.'

The old man nodded without enthusiasm. 'Aye, Chief, ye may well be right. But thank God the thrummin's stayed longer i' place than that we positioned afore Hogmanay! We might kill half the crew at the pumps otherwise – though ah have tae say it's a sterling job they're doin', an' they're more willin' than ah'd expeckit!'

The lascar crew were lithe agile men from Bengal, born to the sea and well-respected as seamen. They scrambled aloft with admirable nimbleness, swarming like monkeys in the maze of rigging as the need arose, regardless of the weather. They were relatively close to home, unlike their European counterparts, and worked cheerfully in the comfort of their accustomed climate. With few excesses and an almost fatalistic acceptance of their lot, the old captain acknowledged that his crew were a satisfying mix, and he had little need to discipline them with colt, lash, or belaying pin.

But early attempts to slow the leak by hauling spare sails beneath the bow had come to nought as the sails flayed to pieces. The crew had therefore to work long hours at the pumps in growing discomfort – apparently for the remainder of the voyage.

On this seventy-seventh day at sea, 25 January, a canny feeling in Captain Hamilton's belly told him that the weather was worsening after the slight but welcome relief of the last few days. It had become noticeably colder during the lull, in which they had reached the latitudes that marked the known southern limits of *Terra Australis*.

Watchkeepers shivered at their posts at night, and during the day hugged themselves for warmth in the fitful and all too infrequent sunshine. Daytime brought only the sight of leaden seas stretching away endlessly to merge with equally leaden clouds. Night held nothing save an impenetrable blackness, relieved only by occasional phosphorescence in the wash and wake, or rarely by a fleeting star sight, hazy and unconnected.

A knock at his cabin door broke into his musings. In answer to his bidding a wind-blown seaman stood in the doorway, damp and dishevelled. He spoke with a marked Dutch accent: 'Mr Thompson's compliments, sir, an' he said to tell you d' light's jus' starting to come up, an' we got a heavy sea rising on d' wind.'

'Aye, thank 'ee laddie. Ah'm a'ready that much aware frae the risin' feel o' things here, an' the weather glass's been fallin' off some time.' He nodded towards the instrument where it swayed in its brackets. 'There's something in the makin' oot yon. Tell Mr Thompson ah'd like tae see him doon here for a word when he's free.'

After the messenger had gone, the old man listened to the sounds of the ship, drawing slowly on his pipe before returning to his interrupted thoughts. There was an edge of uncertainty in the captain's frown as he gazed unseeing at the logbook entry in the flickering lamplight, while his mind roved the ship and the dark oceans beyond.

He was beginning to feel slightly uneasy as the *Sydney Cove* approached the Roaring Forties – a sensation he had rarely felt since his first command. Captain Hamilton was worried, though he would not have admitted it, even to himself. His concern centred on the fact that he didn't know his ship's position in the ocean's empty expanses, nor the proximity of New Holland's inhospitable coastline and offshore reefs.

It was only two decades since James Cook's voyages had led to men being able to plot both latitude and longitude with any certainty and so fix their positions with precision. Although Captain Hamilton carried the recently perfected chronometer, a necessity now in unknown waters off little-known coasts, inclement weather had hidden the sun from his sextant for most of the second month of the voyage, and star sightings had been so elusive and incomplete as to be useless.

MAP 1. *New Holland, as it was known after the voyage of Lieutenant James Cook, 1770, showing the approximate track of the Sydney Cove from Calcutta to the wreck site.*

Compass rose labels: North, South, East, West

New Holland labels:
G.F. de Witts Land
The Land of Eendracht
Shark's Bay
The Land of Lyons
The Land of Peter Nuyts
Arnheim's Land
York Cape
Carpentaria
New Holland
Cape Flattery
Cape Tribulation
Cape Grenville
Cape Bedford
Cape Sandwich
Cape Cleveland
Cumberland Isles
Cape Maryfold
Cape Capricorn
Northumberland Isles
Sandy Cape
Cape Morton
Cape Byron
NEW SOUTH WALES, DISC. 1770
Port Jackson
Botany Bay
Cape St George
Bateman Bay
Cape Banks
Cape Dromedary
Cape Howe
Point Hicks
Smoaky Cape
Van Diemen's Land
Sydney Cove driven ashore 8 Feb'y 1797

Latitude: 10°S, 20°S, 30°S, 40°S
Longitude: 110°E, 120°E, 130°E, 140°E, 150°E, 160°E

The rising seas pounded his ship loudly and shudderingly as he drew the tentative but invaluable charts towards him. The charts of the day were limited in their availability and rudimentary in terms of accuracy, and therefore limited in their contribution to the ship's safety. The material that he had gathered was not reassuring.

Whilst he possessed a hand-drawn copy of Cook's 1770 map of the New South Wales coast, with enough detail to help him find Port Jackson, and a sketch of Furneaux's islands off Van Diemen's Land to help identify landfalls there, the long coast east of Leeuwin Land had only been lightly marked by Dutch adventurers more than 150 years earlier. The southern coast of the island continent was incomplete, and even the marked sightings required confirmation. James Cook had not passed this way on his voyages, and it remained a void of uncertainty.

The lack of sun sights coupled with dubious charts meant he had no firm idea of where he was in relation to the hidden coast, but he knew that fairly soon he would have to turn eastwards towards Van Diemen's Land, still at least two thousand miles away. What lay between there and his ship's present position was almost totally unknown.

The ship's bell tolled the hour distantly. The sea continued its muted booming against the ship's creaking timbers and a greyness paled the larboard ports of his cabin. Soon it would be time to go back on deck for his final rounds before turning in. He worried about their position, but earlier, as he had paced the heaving quarterdeck in his thick boat cloak, instinct and the feel of the wind had told him it was too early to turn.

He laid aside the pipe that had now gone cold, glancing up as Hugh Thompson knocked before entering, pausing to set aside his dripping cape. Slowly and wearily the captain rubbed his smarting eyes, feeling an ache in his limbs that he had not known since the Atlantic chills nearly seven years before. His age was beginning to tell at last in the trials of the voyage. Not for the first time he wondered how much longer he could remain at sea, how many years of life were ahead of him.

God had indeed been kind to an old man. He was still sailing in command of his own ship when most of his contemporaries were long dead. Fortune had given him a comfortable billet while most of Europe was in turmoil. Many a younger man had been forced to leave the sea before his prime but not Guy Hamilton. Fatigue notwithstanding, his step was firm, his hand steady and his eye clear, but for how long? He sighed and turned to Hugh Thompson, who waited expectantly.

'If ah'm tae be honest wi' ma'sel', Chief, sometimes ah'm thinkin' ah'm too old the noo, for this kind o' life. Why does a man need tae be stayin' up all hours, in all kinds o' Godforsaken weather, searchin' for one more Godforsaken spot on a map? What's it all for?'

He spoke his thoughts frankly, not seeking a response. 'Maybe it's time ah retired tae mah wee croft i' the Western Isles, for a' the years left tae me? Time ah moved out o' the way of upcomin' folks like yoursel', eh?'

He was not usually given to such open introspection, but the last few weeks had been an unprecedented trial. 'This may well be mah last voyage,' he went on, 'tae the last place ah hav'nae been before. 'Tis seven years the noo since ah was last away home, when ah thought then o' retirin'. Aye, seven years – an' now ah'm turned eighty, too long,' he murmured, 'maybe much too long.'

He shook himself from his reverie, brisk once more. 'But – before that, we've tae somehow find Port Jackson! What we really need are better maps an' a few sun sights – neither o' which we have at present. So – let's try some intelligent guesswork i'stead, which is why ah called ye doon.'

He reached for his log and dragged the soiled, salt-stained charts back into the dimness of the light, their lack of clarity and attendant detail shouting uncertainty. Each of their spidery lines was familiar, but he scanned them intensely, as though hoping to see his ship marked against them.

'Afore long we need tae mak' a decision to turn wi' the westerlies,' he said, 'though not knowin' where we are for certain could become critical. A turn too soon could fetch us up on reefs off New Holland, here – aboot as far removed frae Port Jackson as it's possible tae be. The coast's dry, barren an' almost featureless in these parts by all accounts, tae be avoided like the plague. Too many earlier wrecks in a dangerous area – which is why they located the first settlement over east, in New South Wales. Besides that, o' course, Cook himself had been there.'

Hugh Thompson nodded, indicating the vast expanse of the Southern Ocean. 'But delayin' the decision, o' the other hand, could carry us too far south, with a risk of meeting driftin' icebergs like those off Newfoundland and Nova Scotia.' James Cook had recorded iceberg sightings in these latitudes on his own voyages, taller and more massive than any to be found in the North Atlantic.

'Aye, they'd be a hazard we can well do wi'out,' the old man responded, remembering the colder, familiar bite of the winds on deck, which had added to his sense of unease. 'We're still headin' south in unseasonable weather, not sure how far we travel each day in these winds an' seas. Icebergs, indeed! It's a dilemma, Mister, but one we have tae resolve soon.'

The captain shook his head doubtfully, fingering his beard in concentration, his eyes smarting from fatigue and the lamp smoke. 'These sightings an' recordings are on'y as good as the observer's navigation,' he mused, 'which ye ken yersel' sometimes leaves a lot tae be desired. What we've got here tells us on'y that an extensive coast's been seen in these latitudes, wi' a few landmarks hopefully noted within a league or two of their actual locations.'

Hugh Thompson pursed his lips. 'Aye, an' another dilemma's in the detail that's missing – the rocks an' reefs and off-shore islands which are almost certain to be there, out in that muck,' he observed, thinking of what had not been seen, but which might nevertheless lurk somewhere ahead in the grey, windswept wastes.

'Well, there or no', we've some calculations tae do,' the skipper declared, opening the log. 'Dead reckoning, Mister, by guess or by God! Let's ge' doon tae it!'

His own careful recordings, even without sextant readings, gave him a roughly approximate position by dead reckoning. Such calculations were often little better than informed guesses, their efficacy waning as the veiled days wore on. Dead reckoning, he readily acknowledged, had caused the loss of many worthy men, in oceans and latitudes far better known than these. But it was all they had for the moment. Quietly he bent his head over the charts, his lips moving silently in a seaman's prayer.

The dark morning was paling reluctantly as Hugh Thompson stamped his feet in the lee of the mizzenmast and drew his damp clothing more closely to him. The building sea to leeward was revealed as a shifting mass of mountains and valleys streaked with foam that bespoke a monstrous power. He hunched down further into his tarpaulin cape, sensing yet another salt-laden jet winging towards him as the ship lurched beneath his feet, the sound of the wave bursting on the quarterdeck reaching him an instant before its sodden, searching aftermath.

He cursed ineffectually, his mouthings automatic, unthinking. He felt water shift inside his seaboots, and thought again of his dry cabin below decks, its relative warmth and the blessed sanctuary it would soon offer. 'In not more'n a half hour,' he mused thankfully, 'and not a moment before time.'

He was a tall man, broadly built, grizzle-bearded and weatherbeaten from years before the mast in all climes, at all tasks as he rose from ship's boy to chief officer. The bulk of the mizzen was hard put to shelter his dripping figure and he cursed again, spitting salt, as more airborne spray found his hiding place and swirled about it.

Bristol born, a year off forty and a hardy seaman, he nevertheless enjoyed such scant comforts as his calling offered and the only one in view at the end of this long, wet night watch was that of his personal cubby just below his feet, with a thick towel and a stiff tot of rum. And then into the blankets.

A halyard slatted briefly, loosened by the constant straining in the rising seas. He peered into the gloom, seemingly at nothing, but his shouted order against the wind was answered at once by shadowy figures hurrying across the streaming space to put the errant mischief to rights.

The sea shifted darkly beyond the bulwarks. He looked around once more, then up across the soaring silhouettes of masts, spars and furled sails, of the rod-straight standing rigging which guyed the masts in pyramid shafts, and of running gear climbing at crisscross angles and slants into the greying sky amongst the upperworks. There they were lost from sight beyond his spray-assailed vision. Rain fell across his hood and cape while the wind keened shrilly in a brief squall that swept the decks and set the taut sails drumming.

A foul night by any standard, and worse to come if he read the signs right. Since late yesterday the wind on the starboard beam had been steadily gathering strength and for the past two hours the steepening waves had been making their presence felt. More bad weather, as if they hadn't already had their fair share.

Staring, he could just discern ragged patches of racing cloud, darkening against a flannel sky which hung low and threatening. Though he could barely see them, he knew that waves would already be cresting everywhere, with spume breaking from their wind-blown tops.

He moved back towards the helmsman at the spoked wheel, a blacker bulk against the shadowed quarterdeck and the massive outlined helm, and peered into the compass box. Its faint light glimmered through glass obscured by soot from the lamp within and salt upon its surface. He wiped it clear with a broad hand and noted the heading. South-east by south, and a stiff gale rising to starboard. Everything pointed to a full storm in the offing, the first real harbinger of the notorious Roaring Forties.

'Are you awake there, John Saul?' He addressed his harsh enquiry to the helmsman. As chief officer and principal overseer he was not normally a harsh man, unless circumstances warranted it.

'Aye, Chief, I'd not be dozin' in this weather! Nothing like a good blow an' a few loose gallons o' cold brine to keep away the cobwebs.' The West Country tones of the man clinging to the wheel rose like a growl in his throat, though he remained unperturbed. A seaman in his mid-fifties, he knew his job and that no rebuke was intended. John Saul *would* be awake at the wheel any night, which was why he was there now. His skills were instinctive, steering strongly on the feel of the wind and the thrust of the wheel against his body. A good man on a rough night, such as this one.

The growl came again. 'I'd say she'll be buildin' up for a real hard blow afore too long, Chief, the way she's shapin' now. Got the feel o' the seas south o' the Cape, three days out from Table Bay, she has. An' they didn't call that place the Cape o' Storms for nothin'.'

Hugh Thompson braced himself against the heel of the ship as another heavy wave crashed against the quarter, climbing high above the deck before splattering its breadth across them on the face of the wind. He heard the helmsman grunt with the effort of holding her against the sea until the pressures eased. His own memories of passages round the Cape of Good Hope were stirred by John Saul's remarks.

'We'd best be havin' a second man on the wheel at the next change o' watch, Chief,' the helmsman shouted. 'She's heavier on the weather this last hour. There'll be four needed to hold her afore this day's through, unless I'm much mistaken.'

Leaning close to catch the words over the howling wind Hugh Thompson yelled his agreement, reflecting his own feelings. He scanned the sails, dark and full against the swiftly moving rack of clouds. At last light the previous day they had furled and secured the topgallants, the lighter sails set at the top of each mast, together with the driver on the aftermast. During the night, with wind and sea rising, the captain had prudently ordered the main course to be handed completely as a precaution against worsening conditions and the danger of being caught by a squall with too much sail in total darkness.

Such prudence had paid dividends on many occasions, and the captain was respected for it. There came a point where the utility of keeping sails bent in adverse conditions fell below the increasing risks to ship, crew, and rigging. A canny sailing master would recognise that point and take necessary action.

They were sailing now under topsails and reefed foresail, but still running near to six knots. Heavy gusts were more frequent, a constant banshee wail coming from the rigging, while the ship heeled against the mounting onslaught. Very soon they would have to take in the remaining course, or risk storm damage and a shredded sail – at the very least. The captain's bulky figure emerged from below as though in response to the chief officer's thoughts, struggling against the pitch and roll of the ship, and the searching blast of the wind.

There were no acknowledgements between the captain and those on deck. Guy Hamilton had already been up many times that night. He stood hunched in silence by the larboard quarterdeck rail, gazing out at the heaving seas around them, now clearly menacing in the grey dawn light.

Hugh Thompson marvelled at the Old Man's ability to weather the storms in spite of his earlier sentiments. He stared at the skipper's back, waiting for the inevitable decision. Taking in all that he saw with an experienced eye, the old Scot swung about and addressed him: 'Twenty-four hours more, Mister, an' then we'll mak' our turn, sights or no'. Frae the pace we've been makin' ower these few days past, we're surely well beyont yon sou'west corner the noo, as we agreed, an' these winds are feeling fair like the Forties tae me!'

'When we change ower watches shortly,' he continued, 'have the foresail taken in an' well-secured and single reefs in all tops'ls. Nay, belay that,' he countered, staring aloft at the low, fast-moving clouds. 'See they put in double reefs to save 'emsel's goin' up there again, later. We can shake 'em out if needs be, if the wind eases some, though ah doubt it will wi'outen a brisk ol' blaw furst. Something nasty's buildin',' he added with certainty, 'an' up yon'll be nae place tae be in a few hours, ah'm a-thinking. Perhaps runnin' afore the wind'll ease things later. Ah'll turn in for a wee while after ma rounds below. Ah need tae have anither look at wha' the leak doon there's doin'.'

He turned to go, but his concern was clearly visible. 'Get Mr Leishman tae check all the lashin's aloft an' below as soon as it's light enough tae see by. Winds like these'll pu' the sails an' hatch covers off i' no time unless they're a' well secure. An' after the turn, post two lookouts an' mak' sure they stay awake. Ah can do wi'out reefs under ma keel this weather!'

Thompson nodded assent. 'Aye, sir. I'll also go round all the hatches on my way down, just to be sure. I couldn't be wetter than I am now.' He reflected that the deck wasn't any place for a man to be, either, knowing that in these conditions more men were washed from the decks than were lost from the rigging. But for his own peace of mind he would still go down and check the vulnerable coamings and covers, making sure their battens and wedges were firm. A broached cover at the height of a gale would cause a vessel to rapidly flood with little chance of tackling the damage before she started to founder.

The nearest help was thousands of miles away and they had only their own resources and precautions to fall back on. In this region their loss would pass almost unrecorded, yet another unfortunate mishap on the high seas. The oceans in this mood were merciless and unforgiving and seldom offered second chances. Prevention, therefore, was better than cure – as he had learned from the Old Man.

Guy Hamilton heaved himself across the canting deck, towards the larboard companionway. At the top of the ladder he paused. 'Tell Mr Leishman tae call me if needs be,' he shouted over the wind. 'In any case be sure he calls me afore noon.' Then he was gone, the chief officer's acknowledgement hanging on the air. The skipper would, he knew, be up and prowling again long before noon with a sea and sky as ominous as these.

He smiled to himself. The skipper was like an old hen with a brood, but his smile faded as he recalled some other masters of his youth who would never have cared, whatever the weather. He gazed after the captain.

Despite the Old Man's age, Thompson reminded himself, he is still as sharp as a switch, and without doubt one of the most able seamen alive. Many a younger captain paled in comparison, including a number he had known himself. If anyone could successfully see this perilous voyage through, the skipper could. Captain Hamilton was the sort of man you'd confidently follow to the ends of the earth – which was exactly what they were doing. He laughed aloud at his own observation, and turned back to the helmsman. In the rising light of day, John Saul winked in return, understanding.

The climb down into the depths of the ship, negotiating steep ladders which gave access to the fetid lower holds, was like descending into the bowels of a dank mine. The dull boom and roar of the sea beyond the timbers were accentuated in the close atmosphere, the continual rattle of the bilge pump chains added sharpness to the din, while the light from the lamps held by two lascars flickered and danced amongst a host of leaping shadows. The decks trembled and shook, little constrained beneath the rope-lashed heaps of cargo, while the entire scene tilted, swayed and creaked incessantly to the pitch and roll of the storm-tossed vessel.

The group crouching attentively in the dimly lit forehold resembled a distorted mediaeval nativity, with the captain, his two lascar assistants and the young supercargo, William Clarke, focussing their attention on the bald head of the ship's carpenter, presently working at the level of the deck.

Here and there in the gloom, where they had cleared a space at the very bottom of the hold, they had wedged loose cargo items where they could not run amuck. The inflow of water was causing renewed concern, and its continuous to-and-fro rush between frames was audible above all other sounds.

Under pressure from the storm-racked seas the working of the surrounding timbers had again increased the severity of the leak. Each movement brought forth a glistening swirl of water into the hole where the carpenter laboured, trying in vain to reach the seat of the threatening leak in order to stem it.

''Tis no good, I'm tellin' ye,' the man shouted over the clamour, throwing down a sodden plug of oakum in frustrated disgust. ''Tis still away out o' my reach an' that o' any man here, just as I said it was before!'

He glanced around malevolently, perspiration beading his face in the lamplight despite the forbidding chill of the atmosphere and the coldness of the swirling waters in which he stood. He was a heavily built belligerent Irishman, cramped in an impossibly small work area, and now more than usually illtempered after being roused from his slumbers to ply his skills, even though his own wellbeing was as much at risk as everyone else's.

'The throuble's hard behind one o' these frames here, too low down t' reach,' he said, stabbing a finger with certain finality. 'Short o' takin' all the bows apart from inside hereabouts, there's nothin' more to be done that'll be of any help until she's beached. Meanwhile ye've upwards o' two feet o' water swilling about the bilges an' not gettin' no less!'

His hostile glance fixed on one of the lascars near him. 'Until we find a place a man might better put t'ings t' rights in, with room t' move an' all,' he went on thickly, still addressing his remarks to Guy Hamilton, 'I'd be thinkin' o' turnin' more o' these heathen beggars to the pumps, with a rope's end behind 'em if necessary!'

The faces of the Indian sailors remained impassive, though they understood the man's accented English well enough. 'Let them do somethin' to save their miserable skins for once, I say, for sure they'd be the first to drown if we go, no matter how many o' their pagan gods they pray to!'

The captain frowned in anger, having recognised the man's undisguised truculence early in the voyage. Forced by necessity to sign him on as a late replacement for a better man carried away in a fever, with time for only the scantiest of recommendations, he knew that the abrasive manner and abusive comments could only create disharmony and resentment amongst native crew members unless they were sharply suppressed. He had therefore always been quick to check overt unfairness and injustice. Malcontent in a crowded vessel could grow like a brewer's ferment.

'Enough o' that, Duggan,' Hamilton snapped, his jaw angrily set, 'Ah'll not be hearin' talk o' that kind aboard my ships! Any time, d'ye hear?

17

You stick to yer ain work an' leave me tae mind mine, an' ah'll thank ye tae keep your uncalled for remarks tae yersel'!' Age had not diminished the captain's authority, and the carpenter glowered sullenly under the sharp lash of his tongue. The old Scot turned to the young man who had been standing quietly by during the brief confrontation.

'Mr Clarke, ye'll oblige me by kindly seein' all this cargo properly restowed an' secured, wi' all perishable articles up high,' he said crisply. 'I intend tae put extra hands o' the pumps while this storm lasts, but we'd best safeguard aught that's likely tae spoil through wettin' if we chance take in more o' the sea than we can handle. Maybe the fothering's come adrift again, or slippit, ah shouldn'ae wonder. If that's so, we'll need tae haul it back or replace it as soon as things ease. That may be a wee while yet so, in the meantime, whan ye're finished on yon restowin', would ye go roon' what else ye can get at, an' shift it up high if it's likely tae suffer ... '

Muffled shouts and the sound of running feet on the deck above interrupted the skipper's instructions to the young supercargo. The urgency of more indistinguishable shouting and other running feet brought a questioning frown to his face as the old man swung round and started hurriedly towards the nearest ladder, all other matters forgotten, his lantern-bearers following closely. A voice at the lower hatch, high-pitched with tension, halted them halfway, its message chilling in impact.

'*Captain!* Cap'n Hamilton, sir, please come quickly! It's Mr Leishman, sir, gone overboard from the main tops'l yard! The sea's runnin' dreadful high, sir, an' – an' we can't see him! Come quickly, sir, come quick!'

The captain hurried towards the quarterdeck and the taffrail, while men standing on the yards and in the rigging stared vainly aft into the cauldron of the sea. But Mr Leishman, the second officer, was never to be seen again.

In reefing the main topsail under Captain Hamilton's last instructions, he had been aloft with others of the relieving watch to hand the heavy canvas when a flogging sail had unbalanced him momentarily, the yard and footrope jerking tautly under the strain of the wildly convulsing folds. The sail bellied and flapped as the sailors aloft struggled to control it with the restraining buntlines. An instant later, Leishman was pitched clear onto the lower yard before vanishing with a cry into the boiling foam below.

As soon as they heard '*Man overboard!*' the watch crew ran to their stations, expecting a rapid turnabout. Others at the rails and higher vantage points strove to catch a glimpse of the tiny figure drifting quickly down their broken wake before it was lost in the welter of spray and heaving cross-seas. On seeing the second officer fall, Hugh Thompson instantly despatched a man to rouse the captain before raising the dreaded cry. Striding quickly to the bulwarks on the starboard quarter, he glimpsed his comrade briefly in the raging turbulence to windward before a fountain of spray climbed high above the deck, blocking his vision and temporarily blinding him. When next he could see, the man was gone, with nothing to mark his passing.

All seamen knew the risks of their calling in conditions such as these. A feeble grip, a moment's inattention, or a wet or icy footing whilst working high on the yards could spell disaster in an instant. They also knew the dangers of broaching, or capsizing a sailing ship entirely while trying to turn in piling seas and high winds. The prospects of rescuing anyone unlucky enough to be lost overboard, even in fair weather, were remote.

The howling winds pressed the *Sydney Cove* from abaft the beam and drove her on, even under minimal sail. She had insufficient canvas to claw back should a turn be ordered, which would still see them driven helplessly downwind. To raise more would be suicidal. The risks for all were too great. And there was no chance of being able to launch a rescue boat.

Guy Hamilton reached the quarterdeck, his chest heaving from exertion, blood racing in his temples, but too late. There was nothing to be done for their lost crew-mate. The captain leant by the rail, cursing his years while his head swam, cursing the vile weather and the Godforsaken sea while Hugh Thompson lent an arm for support against the ceaseless pitch and roll of the ship.

His anguish was barely audible above the raw power of the storm. 'A guid man gone, Mr Thompson, God rest his poor soul! An' all because ah reminded him tae be doubly sure aboot his job! As if ah needed tae! He should'na been up there, Mister, he should'na. An' ah should niver a' sent him!'

As he recovered from his unaccustomed dash to the upper deck, all the small anxieties rushed back to him with renewed concern. Another severe gale, a leaking ship, no sights of sun or stars for days on end, and that re-emerging, nagging uncertainty as to their whereabouts, except that there was a lee shore somewhere to larboard. Unconsciously he stared hard in that direction, searching vainly for answers.

And now the death of a valued officer. Though it was common for men to be swept from exposed decks, the old Scot had not lost a man from one of his ships for many a voyage, such were the pains he took to ensure the safety and wellbeing of those in his care. The loss was a blow, a stark reminder of the frailty of men who ventured into these wild extremes.

He glared balefully at the ragged grey clouds and the greyer, wind-whipped seas. One man gone, with another two thousand miles of the torments of the Roaring Forties to go. The horror stories of these latitudes were legion, and from his lifetime at sea Guy Hamilton knew most of them.

One man lost, the ship disabled, a crew hard-pressed, and they had barely touched the worst. Their situation was becoming perilous. The thought stayed with him as he stared out across the blind ocean, others scarce suppressed in the deepest recesses of his mind. How many more, Lord, before we're through and this passage is over? How many more, and who, and when?

2
A PERFECT
HURRICANE …

25TH JANUARY, 1797. Second mate, Mr Leishman, lost o'board in falling from main tops'l yard during the first hour of the morning watch. Sail was being reduc'd to d/reef'd tops'ls in face of increasing inclement weather. Full gale to near hurricane from SW, poor visibility. Later forc'd to bare poles following loss of fores'l, main tops'l and driver blown from their lashings. No success in attempting to caulk bow-leak from inboard.
FROM THE SHIP'S LOG

*A*ll day long the buffeting wind howled about them, shrieking through the bar-taut rigging, beating into every corner of the ship, filling the very air they breathed with flying spray and salt foam. The raging waves splintered upon the streaming timbers, their crests fragmenting as they rose above their neighbours.

The endless shrilling of the gale tore at nerves strung tight under the strain of survival, every movement fraught with danger as the ship heeled under the pounding of the seas, each moment painful in the ceaseless, mind-numbing battery of remorseless sound. There was no escape from the wrath of the elements, no small sanctuary to offer momentary relief.

The sea and the sky were as one, no horizon dividing waves and cloud. Curtained veils of rain swept interminably over the decks, sharp squalls mingled with spume and spray, drenching huddled watchkeepers. While several men ceaselessly manned the pumps, three men were now needed at the wheel, so much had the wind and sea blown up since the watch before dawn.

The amount of sail had been reduced, and only the close-reefed main- and fore-topsails clothed the yards above. By noon the captain was back on deck, weighing the storm and anxiously checking every aspect of his ship.

Heavy seas regularly flung themselves wildly across the decks as the Sydney Cove plunged into the barely yielding sea. The ship's waist was constantly awash and water ran both above and below decks, despite secure hatches and her closely shuttered ports. The lifelines rigged fore and aft on either beam had already saved more than one of the crew from broken limbs or worse.

Anyone venturing out from the secure cubbies they had found for themselves took their lives in their hands. There was relatively less to fear aloft, away from the reach of the sea, with lines to cling on to once they had climbed up the windward side, to be blown securely against the rigging rather than away from it. On deck, however, a sudden surge of tons of green water could carry a man away instantly.

The bitter cold added to their afflictions, whilst swathing rain interspersed with hail periodically swept the decks clear of salt, and even seemed to suppress the waves beneath the sheer weight of each thundering downpour. The voyage had become a nightmare of menacing seas, battering winds and unremitting noise, the violence of this latest onslaught being the culmination of more than six wearying weeks of constant toil and sleeplessness, of soaked clothing, and raw skin.

As the long day progressed it became clear to Hugh Thompson that concern for the state of the crew was weighing on the captain. Although the Old Man had been correct in sending the second officer aloft to check the sail lashings, the man's death troubled him, and he blamed himself for what might have been an unnecessary order.

'But such a check *was* necessary, sir,' Hugh Thompson urged reassuringly, 'and was part of his duties. Sails loose in this weather'd kill even more in tryin' to secure them, as you well know – even the entire ship in seas like these. It was an accident you couldn't't've foreseen – an act of God.'

The captain merely shook his head. 'Ye may be right, mister, but this passage is startin' to wear us all doon, an' we can ill afford anyone tae be sick or injured awa' from a post, let alone drowned. We'll be needin' all the hands we've got afore we're through, ah'm thinkin'. We're in a bad place, right enough. If this is summer i' these parts, thank God we're no' here i' the middle o' winter!'

'As it is,' he pointed out, 'the men are bruised and bone-weary a'ready. We all ken the miseries o' this trip well enough! We need tae watch 'em for exhaustion, rest 'em where we can, an' mak' sure they get reg'lar vittles o' sorts. They're guid men, but they're on'y human. A poorly crew ah dinna need the noo, sae gang easy on 'em where ye can. Soon, hopefully, we'll ha' sunshine tae raise their spirits – God knows, after a' this time, they need it!'

Then came a squall which burst upon them without warning. From out of the grey mists to starboard came even stronger blasts. Mountainous walls of water surged in from the hidden wastes of the oceans, as icy rain drove horizontally against exposed flesh, flailing on the roaring, breath-snatching wind like a thousand whips.

The *Sydney Cove* heeled dangerously under the combined pressures, her rolling bowsprit spearing deep into the boiling torrents. Tons of water cascaded aboard, and for a long moment the ship slewed and broached.

'*Hold the head!* Bring her round, damn you, before we're all lost!' Hugh Thompson's frantic curses were carried away on the gale, but the men at the wheel needed no urging to right the ship as she staggered under the burden.

Muscles bulged beneath sodden garments and veins stood out on dripping countenances as they struggled grimly. The deck canted to a seemingly impossible angle. From aloft a violent thrashing sent shudders through the straining stays and shrouds and into the very bowels of the stricken ship, alerting all to the escape of a sail from its bonds as the winds sought to press the helpless craft into final oblivion. Eye-stinging gusts and the deepening gloom prevented the crew from seeing which sails had broken free, but their danger was now at its height.

The storm-racked vessel wallowed for what seemed an eternity, totally

The Sydney Cove *heeled dangerously under the combined pressures.*

at the mercy of screaming, titanic forces. The men aboard her clawed vainly upwards from below decks, or clung desperately to the nearest solid, unmoving timbers until the monstrous pressures eased.

Infinitely slowly, the *Sydney Cove* turned before the storm, shedding the immense weight of water in streaming cascades. The winds beat violently across her stern with increased intensity as she swung, as though seeking to prevent any escape.

With sounds like musket fire, the starboard fore- and mainsheets were wrenched asunder, unable to withstand the strain as they were caught by the gale from another quarter. In an instant the rampant sails had filled to their full extent in short-lived freedom, before tearing themselves to pieces, bursting shudderingly into a thousand ragged fragments.

The dazed sailors on deck could do little as the cannon-like reports heralded troubles aloft, sheer survival demanding that they maintain their holds on precious life-preserving structures. Freed of the terrible weight of the sails, however, and once more on an even keel, the *Sydney Cove* pitched and soared as she began a runaway ride under bare poles down the steep and looming following seas.

In a lull that followed the squall, the captain was at last able to make himself heard, and he quickly took stock of the damage whilst the opportunity offered. The efforts of the crew restored life to chilled limbs.

'Mr Thompson, put as many men as ye need tae the pumps, an' keep them at it 'til we've got the leak in check. Push 'em tae it if ye have tae – some are leukin' a mite daze't frae weariness, tho' nae wonder. If this villainous weather keeps on we'll ha' scant respite, so let's keep one step ahead while we can.'

As the chief officer turned away, moving with practised certainty from one hand-grip to another, the old man beckoned to William Clarke. 'Go below, Mr Clarke, if ye please, an' check all the stowin's and lashin's wi' the carpenter, while this bit o' a calm lasts. Tak' one or two o' the men with ye, an' get word back tae me on how bad things are in the lower holds. Ah'm thinkin' we'll ha' taken a lot o' water in the last hour or so.'

The youngster nodded and turned to leave, but the captain detained him further, his lined face grey and strained but thoughtful. 'We'll nae doubt be havin' a lang night afore us unless ah sadly misjudge it, an' some o' the men seem pretty near exhausted. There's nae help for that, for 'tis only tae be expeckit i' these raw latitudes. Even so, we can mak' 'em a mite more comfy wi' stores an' sustenance. We've blankets aboard, an' Fearnaughts an' other extra claes for those as needs 'em – aye, an' a wee rum toddy might no' be amiss, for those that want it.'

He looked keenly into the young man's face, gauging him before continuing. 'Ah'm afraid ah'll be askin' ye tae act more in place o' puir Leishman for the rest o' the voyage, God rest his soul. At least as far as ye can,' he added, acknowledging the other's youth and lack of seamanship. 'Ah've a canny feelin' we might all be called on tae do the unexpeckit afore this jauntie's ower. Aye, mark well ma words! So – awa' wi' ye the noo, an' see tae it!'

A short while later the chief officer and one of the Indian seamen strode grim-faced onto the quarterdeck. The captain looked at both expectantly. Without wasting words, Hugh Thompson outlined the problem: 'The lascars refuse to work any longer on deck in these conditions, Cap'n, an' are saying many are sickly from the cold an' wet. I've seen some an' it's true they don't look any too well, but there's half a fathom o' water below, at least, an' getting no less. There's pumping to be done, an' quickly, but short o' me using a rope's end on 'em they're not prepared to come on deck. Azim here asked to speak to you.'

Captain Hamilton turned a glowering eye on the cape-clad Indian seaman, who flashed a white-toothed grin despite a glance from the old man that was matched only by the ferocity of the weather.

'Ye'd mutiny at a time like this, would ye?' the Captain grated, his voice as icy as the surging sea. 'Ye'd haul out an' endanger the ship? Dae ye ken wha' ye're aboot, ye rascals? Ye'd better have good reason for disobeyin' orders or, Lord help me, ah'll be havin' ye keel-hauled! Speak up an' be sharp about it!'

Unabashed, Azim Prakash spoke his piece in heavily accented but clear, occasionally hesitant English. The Indian was as lean as his fellows, but his unflinching stance and keen brown eyes told of assurance and intelligence well beyond the norm of such sailors.

'With all most respects, sah,' he began, glancing at Hugh Thompson, 'the men are not refusing their duties, only that they do not wish to be any longer out in this so terrible rain and cold. Today some men are come off watch so numbed, yes, that they are hardly able to be standing, and others they have had to – to pummel them, sah, in order to bring feelings to their bodies.'

'With so total respects, sah, I am asking only that we be allowed to work to empty the ship of water from below, sah, by chain of buckets perhaps, with only those outside at the pumps as needed, and changed very often. If you will permit, sah, I will all this arrange myself and the men will work harder, I am promising. In such cold weather like this the men otherwise cannot – cannot hardly do work, they are themselves so cold!'

'Please to understand, sah,' he went on earnestly, 'that these men have not before known the weather such as it is being now. I most humbly beg of you, most respectfully on their behalf, that you permit them some little more shelter, sah, so that they can work better and – and longer than they can otherwise.'

His imploring gaze did not waver from the captain's face. The old man's grimness had already waned as he understood and accepted the plea. The conditions on deck were rapidly becoming inhuman, and any means of prolonging the energies of the crew was welcome. He had never believed in beating men into submission as force only bred resentment. Each man depended entirely on his fellows on voyages like this, as they were far removed from any other form of help. And the state of the weather was undeniable.

Guy Hamilton nodded, but kept his voice deliberately sharp. 'So be it then, for jist this once! Ah'm no unreasonable an' we can do wi'oot ailing men on this passage, wi' things nae gettin' the better. See tae it they bale from the well, Mr Thompson, wi' the pumps kept going at all times! No more'n fifteen minutes pumpin' for each man, then a spell below.'

He looked hard at the Indian, steel again in his eye. 'Ah'm givin' Mr Thompson a free haun' tae see there's nae slackin' nor malingerin', an' he's likely tae be carryin' a belaying pin tae ginger things alang if he has tae! Ge' alang wi' ye, back tae work, an' if there's ony more sich nonsense as this, yourn'll be the first backside ah'll lay a seaboot tae!'

With a bobbing grin, the man scurried off, glad of the promised relief, delighted to be sailing under such a skipper as old Captain Hamilton. The Old Man's bark was worse than his bite. Few captains, he knew, would have even heard his request. But Mr Hamilton was a humane and considerate person.

In making his plea, the seaman had a special responsibility to his younger brother Rajendra, one of the men – though still only a boy – who had earlier come off watch in a state of shivering exhaustion. As the only two able-bodied males, their family in Bengal relied heavily on the seafaring brothers for subsistence. It was necessary therefore to take whatever steps were needed to ensure their survival.

The lull following the squall offered only relative calm, the eye of the storm. Before long the gale was once more roaring with renewed intensity. The creaming, spume-blown ocean was undiminished in its wild undulations, never once refraining from tossing the ship this way and that. By nightfall it was as if the winds had never ceased, a misery of blasting cold, bitter rain, and almost total darkness.

There was little opportunity during the interlude to replace the sails which had blown out. In any case, there was no point in risking the loss of further sails whilst the weather raged unchecked. Forlorn tatters of the burst foresail, new at the start of the voyage, and the main topsail were therefore left to decorate the yards in ragged streamers, neither being worth the risk of sending men aloft to clear them.

The remnants lent an abandoned air to the ship, with pieces occasionally being torn free and borne away on the wind, although the shreds of the driver were cleared from the mizzenmast to avoid encumbering the helmsmen. Soon the ship was hove to and left to her own devices in the plunging maelstrom, while her crew worked feverishly below decks to keep her afloat.

The welcome respite after the squall, brief though it was, served to confirm the slippage of the canvas thrumming passed beneath the hull two weeks earlier. Its chafed lines lay slack around the gunwales, with one riven edge floating loose amongst the heaving waves where nothing could be done to either retrieve or replace it. Releasing the fothering might only have made matters worse by increasing the risk of a still greater inflow. With little effective external constraint, the leak had visibly increased, until the additional baling began to take effect. Heartened by this new arrangement, the crew tackled the accumulating waters with a string of buckets broken out from the cargo, to the constant squeak and rattle of the pumps.

Self-preservation was paramount, and all were spurred on by the sight and sound of four feet of darkly glistening brine sluicing and gurgling in the bilges and lower hold. But the violent weather persisted, and there was no further let-up for those aboard. Each man slaved at his labours, fully aware of their growing plight and collective distress, but mostly absorbed in his own special burden of ache and anxiety, hunger and overwhelming tiredness. As the tedious night wore on, exhaustion began to take its toll as first one, and then another, staggered away from the pumps with the haggard features and heaving chests of almost total collapse.

Tragedy struck around midnight. Just before the change of watch an Indian seaman, older than most, clutched at his chest with a choking cry and fell to his knees. Two men came quickly to his aid, helping him to struggle half to his feet, but there was nothing they could do as his knees buckled once more with a final groan, and he fell to lie still upon the streaming deck.

In the bedlam of sound from the storm, pumps and swirling waters, no-one had heard the man's wheezing breath. In the almost total darkness, no-one had seen the involuntary rolling of the man's eyes, his growing pallor, or the other signs of stress and pain that had racked him where he stood.

The chief officer was called but he was as helpless as the rest in reviving the stricken crewman, who was carried below, thoroughly chilled and wet, to where he might recover in the rare shelter of a bunk. But he died before his bearers had staggered halfway.

Less than two hours later death carried John Saul away without a word. The trusty helmsman had taken his turn with the rest, adding his own strength to the pump handles where the energy of others was dwindling. His long spell at the wheel and little rest had tired him more than he knew. He was no longer young, and the vigour needed for working the pumps demanded more from his solid frame than did the wheel, more than he had given for many a long month. He collapsed suddenly like a felled oak, and was dead before anyone could reach him.

A second death in so short a span was an uncomprehending shock to minds already addled with strain and fatigue. Crewmates received news of this latest incident unemotionally, stoically, resignedly without a word – just a puzzled frown and a stunned shake of the head. Full realisation of the meaning and privation behind the fatalities would come later.

The sea meanwhile continued its inexorable flow, each plunge of the ship spurting the jetting liquid between the sprung timbers, each soaring rise a swallow. Somehow, desperation wrung new reserves of stamina, and as the bucket chain clanked its way to and from the deck in company with the thud and squeal of the pumps, the waters began slowly to diminish. Men stumbled and swore unthinkingly, fumbled buckets or the labour-sparing rhythm of the pumps and were breathlessly cursed by their fellows, but the battle with the inflow was slowly being won.

By early morning the gale had moderated a little, though the vast heaving of the oceans never ceased. The rain eased and the cloud lifted reluctantly. Blear-eyed men reported glimpses of fading stars through the scudding cloud-rack, but most of those still working below missed the significance of the reports, so far were they gone.

The well was finally cleared of water, and, although the rattle of the pumps continued to resound through the ship, the *Sydney Cove* floated higher once more, temporarily freed of her unwanted, life-threatening burden. The strengthening light brought figures on deck where the boarding seas and flying spray had abated, to haul the rigging into place, to clear the yards of their ragged remnants, and to bend on new sail. With the last threads of will and energy, the *Sydney Cove* was slowly and reluctantly coaxed into motion. Brute force and a dogged urge to live had saved the day.

The previous twelve hours had been a nightmare of prolonged tedium and harsh, mindless toil without rest or respite for anyone. Once relieved, aching backs, cramping muscles and the pain of raw and blistered palms assailed men as they fell recumbent to sleep the sleep of the dead.

It had been the blackest of black nights, of unrelenting tyranny from the elements that called on strengths which no man had known he possessed. The full light of day showed the final price of their night's survival, when men were called to replace the thrumming beneath the starboard bow, to further contain the leak.

They failed to rouse the frail Indian youth who had coughed his way through half the long night watch, wheezing consumptively, arms clasped across his chest for hours after being carried below, and who had finally slipped away in the midst of his sleeping shipmates without a murmur. No tears were shed, nor sorrow evident. Such deaths were an unavoidable fact of life at sea. His canvas-wrapped body was carried aft to lie alongside the others awaiting consignment to the deep when the day faded mournfully to a close.

For a week they drove eastwards under a sullen rain-laden sky and a peevish half-gale, which at least kept their canvas filled, though this was often reefed down when the pursuing westerlies howled about their ears and screamed again through the rigging. The following seas charged boisterously beneath and about them, a dead dark grey, ominously and eagerly foreboding. The ship rolled and pitched, heaving into every attitude without let up, making even rest amongst the toil-worn crew a labour. When not on watch the sailors wedged themselves into any secure corner they could find, to doze fitfully, fully clothed, until the next dread summons for duty on deck.

The long days of steady progress under gentle winds and blue skies in waters far to the north might never have been. Men spoke little in their discomfort, having long since exhausted the vagaries of the weather, the way of the ship, or the progress of the seemingly endless voyage.

Each day merged imperceptibly into the next. What variation there was lay between cold weariness on deck and damp discomfort below.

Conversation became superfluous, each man knowing the others' thoughts to be a reflection of his own.

Even the cry of '*Land ho!*' and the forward lookout's outflung arm on the first day of February failed to rouse the crew, so drained were they of energy and interest after weeks of seeking merely to survive. Most landfalls, especially those marking the last days of a passage, were normally greeted with a surge of excitement and a charging of the atmosphere aboard which brightened a man's eye and lightened his step. But the island they encountered in the mist was grey and anonymous, promising neither refuge nor respite. Neither was it marked on any chart they possessed.

The sun shone weakly above it through obscuring cloud, and provided a fleeting chance for both captain and chief officer to sight it as best they could with their sextants, more guess than good fortune placing them at latitude 40 degrees 1 minute south, longitude 143 degrees 48 minutes east, after calculations with times and angles on their crude charts and tables.

''Tis Van Diemen's Land we're at, Mister!', the old captain cried to the grinning Hugh Thompson, his own face alive with new knowledge after so many long days of doubt and gloom. 'At last we're free frae a' that damnable uncertainty, an' we've a guid firm coastline tae follow!'

In the suffused light and comparative calm of his cabin, his gnarled finger traced the line of the known coast across the outspread chart. The burden of worry he had carried for so long lightened momentarily, his voice and eyes containing an almost boyish excitement and eagerness.

Hugh Thompson nodded encouragingly, stepping dividers quickly up the indented line on the chart from the southern cape, calculating days. 'All being well and with a fair wind,' the chief officer said, 'we could make Port Jackson in little more than a week after turning north! And I'm not ashamed to say it, sir, but this is one voyage I'll be glad to see an end of!'

Guy Hamilton smiled grimly, recognising that this ocean and this voyage were by far the worst he had encountered in a career stretching back over seventy long years. 'Aye, Mister, this'd tak' some beating if they offered prizes for the wurst journey in the world! Ah vow the old North Atlantic an' Cape Horn'll top most things, most o' the time, as well ah ken frae hard experience, but ah'd say now yon wee stretch of ocean oot yonder,' he nodded towards the bulkhead, 'wuid win it over both any time!'

His levity faded a little as he studied the chart further, gauging the days ahead. 'Mind, we'll be on a lee shore running south frae here, an' who knows wha' it'll be when we roun' yon cape there. The winds an' currents may well shift a muckle once we're oot beyont Van Diemen's Land, an' aucht might happen ower sich a girt mass o' water there.'

His hand stretched over the eastern seas towards the charted islands of New Zealand 1,500 miles away. He glanced up at his chief officer, concern once more showing in the gathered lines of his determined face.

'We mayn't yet be oot o' the wuids, Chief, by a lang way. 'Twould be foolish the noo' – nay, unforgivable – tae lose oor grip on things sae close tae hame, ah'm thinkin'. Dinna ferget we're still in the Roarin' Forties, on the backside o' Van Diemen's Land, an' likely sae tae be for some time yet. Many's the mon who forgot that kind o' thing, an' that's a mistake on'y tae be made the once. Keep a tight ship, Mister, an' a sharp lookout, especially wi' a keen weather eye. We've still go' a tidy way tae go afore we can breathe easy, as headin' the way we are it may well get worse afore it gets better, if all we hear's true.'

Slowly the crew took some interest in the facts that away off the larboard beam lay Van Diemen's Land and that their final haven was less than two weeks away. But even this raised more questions in their tired minds. What lay between that distant port and themselves? In pushing south, as they were, what further hazards lay in store? Or could they now expect a restful shoreward run?

What would greet their arrival at the infant colony, and could they reasonably look forward to any special comforts and refreshment? Or would the penal settlement be as austere and forbidding as the cliffs and crags that loomed darkly on the beam, with no break to mar their line, no river, bay, or harbour in which they could escape the unrelenting winds for a while?

They saw a distant coast of steep heads and precipitous bluffs, rainswept ramparts showing no signs of habitation or humanity. It lay uninviting, hiding mysteries beyond its scrubby hills under a thick blanket of mist. It was a coast devoid of lights or beacons, a bleak and predatory coast without welcome or warning.

Its aspect inspired no joy, even after they had rounded the south-eastern cape two days later and turned their bowsprit northward. Brooding islands and headlands plunging sheer into the sea presented silent, cold grey faces to match the cold grey waves, a colourless scene of drear monotony totally bereft of the sun's life-giving warmth. And the untiring, endless wind blew as it seemed it always had, although now carrying them north to better climes.

'If ye're a prayin' man, Mr Thompson, a few choice phrases wouldn'a be much amiss the noo!' Guy Hamilton leaned against his chief officer, both hands gripping the quarterdeck rail, and yelled the words into his ear above the rising scream and buffet of the wind. 'The Almighty's oot in all o' this somewhere, an' that's aboot as close tae Him as ye'll ever be gettin', this side o' the grave!' As he spoke, the gale rose again to an unearthly roaring shriek. The seas reared green in a frenzied welter of foam that hurled itself against the ship, twisting and heeling her laden 400 tons like a toy, while the masts whirled and swayed dizzyingly against the leaden cloud.

Hugh Thompson squinted sideways to escape the needle-sting of the driving rain, his reply pitched high and barely audible above the uproar which shook the naked yards and beat around the upperworks with deep resonant vibrations. 'It's too bloody close for me if He is,' he shouted, gasping in the fierceness of the wind. 'This is more like the work of the Devil, I'd say, except hell'd be a damn sight warmer an' drier!'

Even those few words required immense effort, and conversation was becoming impossible. Hamilton merely nodded in agreement, the movement almost lost beneath his dripping cowl.

Both men ducked involuntarily as yet another comber arched high above the starboard quarter, smashed over them violently, and then swept headlong across the tilting deck, its sounds lost in the thunder, foam and fury of the raging gale and the maelstrom of turbulent, rain-lashed seas. Solid spray repeatedly burst and rattled like grapeshot against their tarred capes and seaboots as the ship plunged and rolled wildly. Every sheet, shroud and stay, each halyard, lift and ratline was set humming, vibrating, trembling. Every obstruction to the wind screamed and wailed as if under torture, while the ship laboured and groaned in protest, shuddering in every strained fibre and lurching, crashing and gyrating beneath the wall of wind and water that thrust broadside upon them, smashing across the beam and canting the *Sydney Cove* at such an angle that her swooping yardarms seemed to brush the leaping seas.

The air which scoured exposed faces and left hands chapped and raw was thick with salt-laden spindrift snatched from the foam-streaked waves. Salt water cascaded and swirled below the men in never-ending torrents, first one way then another in a contorted interplay of tide races. The smothering seas poured over, rushed through and broke around rails, capstans, companionways and coamings in the white hiss of each fearful flood, often submerging the ship to the collar of the mainmast as she repeatedly buried her beak, struggling valiantly against the press of countless tons of water in an effort to stay afloat before succumbing to the next massive onslaught.

The deck heeled to and fro, squirming and shifting under the wilful surge and dash of wave after wave. Men groaned below decks where the wild movements were accentuated, their prostrate forms uncaring that their quarters were being steadily reduced to a sodden shambles under the shifting broken mass of clothing, foodstuffs, personal possessions, ancient bilge water, drowned rats and other unspeakable debris. There was no escape.

In fact, the *Sydney Cove* was becoming helplessly embroiled in the whirling veils of a climatic monster, capable of creating hurricane force winds and dangerously high and violent seas. A rare phenomenon in these latitudes, these conditions were more common further north. No-one aboard imagined that the worst was yet to come.

William Clarke, supercargo and acting second officer, was a relative stranger to the sea. At 22 years of age, this was only his third voyage of any duration. His first, in the previous year, had been the passage from Scotland to India. Prior to this he had served for several years as a land-bound articled clerk, a junior in the family firm of Campbell, Clarke and Co. Ltd of Glasgow, at whose behest he had finally ventured forth for wider company experience. His second voyage had been to China aboard the company's vessel *Sydney Cove*, under Captain Hamilton, which was continuing on now to New Holland as part of his present journey, after returning briefly to Bengal from Canton.

On embarking as supercargo he had been informed by his uncle, one of the firm's senior partners, that this was to be an important discovery cruise that would extend his background and help him appreciate better the active side of merchant trading. He would also be able to examine at first hand both the trade potential in the new colony of Port Jackson and the prospects of establishing a base there in the future.

The young Scot huddled by the leeward shrouds of the mizzen mast, a hand clutching the rigging to steady himself where he stood apart from the other quarterdeck occupants, staring fearfully into the monstrous vortex of flying spray and stinging rain. Nausea had driven him up from below before he had succumbed, advice given to him earlier by the late second officer, Mr Leishman. On the open deck he could at least breathe fresh air, so long as he could stand the other discomforts and not be too daunted by the threatening elements.

From his wind-battered vantage point he had watched as the might of the storm crashed about him, awe-inspiring in its power and enormity. He had witnessed the foaming deluge of gigantic waves sweeping across the solid decking whilst the ship plunged and reared as she ran desperately before the wind. He marvelled at the steadfastness of the crew in the face of such inclemency, and at the stoicism with which they bore the worst that nature had to offer. And he admired the seemingly casual composure of the captain and chief officer as they conversed at the quarterdeck rail, their apparent unconcern offering comfort and assurance.

He glimpsed the bulky figure of the carpenter struggling hurriedly up the well deck ladder as another surging comber smote the ship, causing those on deck to stagger and fall as the ship lurched in response. *'The wheel!* Lend a hand there and *take hold of the bloody wheel!'* Hugh Thompson's frantic cry cut across the flailing wind as he leapt for the spokes to help the sole crewman left clinging to the dangerously straining helm. The ship yawed under the pressure of the following seas and the deck canted heavily to the new threat.

The bursting wave had flung aside all the other men at the wheel, smashing them flat with only their lifelines to secure them as they gasped and retched weakly in the receding waters. The chief officer's unsympathetic cries bellowed out above the lash of the storm and the driving rain as they fought for control over the slewing vessel, in defiance of the eager waves which bore down upon her exposed flanks.

'She'll broach if we don't catch her head! Bring her round! Give more weight and *bring her round!'* he called, heaving alongside the startled supercargo who found himself thrusting at the spoked wheel, and the captain who had also appeared there.

'Get those feeble bastards back on their feet! Mr Clarke, kick them into life if you have to, but get 'em over here again, quickly! Look lively now!'

The men struggled up amongst the tangle of lines and urgent abuse, fully aware of their dire position and the perils of being swamped in a broaching ship. As they slowly fought the ship to rights, the breathless accents of the carpenter cut even more urgently and fearfully through their straining efforts.

'Cap'n! Cap'n, sorr! We – we're leakin' badly again,' the man said with anguish on his face, his words tumbling in haste. 'There's water a'floodin' in down there like we're a'sinkin' fast, sorr! Somethin' – somethin's

broken away below, t'be sure, sorr, an' – an' can't be reached neither, like I always said. The fother'd sail we fixed's not workin' or – or's come adrift again, an' – an' yon leak's the worst than ever! What – what're we goin' t'do now so far from port, sorr, for – for there'd be nothin' – nothin' we can do excepting maybe dump some cargo to lighten ship!'

The man was near to panic, and like many big men of his type had only limited reserves of courage, resourcefulness or determination. Captain Hamilton rounded on him quickly with all the harshness he could muster, and struck the man a forceful blow on the chest.

'Stop yer blatherin' man an' pull yersel' taegether!' he shouted, glaring angrily. 'How wuid ah ken whit's goin' on, or whit tae do when ye canna mak' yersel' intelligible? Like as not we're no' sinkin' at a', sae jist tell me again, *slowly*, what it is yer sae fashed aboot! Mebbe then ah can mak' some sense on it!'

Down below, where the carpenter had to shout to make himself heard, the old skipper's lips tightened under his beard and his expression grew grim. The leak was being measured as a threatening twelve inches an hour. The inflow had increased visibly, but at the seat of the original leak there were no signs of anything further amiss. Clearly there was a second leak somewhere, but conditions were such as to preclude any hope of a search, even if anything could be done to rectify it should the new leak be discovered.

The captain quickly recognised their plight, and his decisions were swift and assertive. Those around him saw that there was only one possible course of action and they acted quickly on instructions.

'Mr Thompson, I want the number o' people on the pumps an' balin' tae be doubled immediately, tae keep us afloat as long as possible. Duggan here was aye right in sayin' we're sinkin',' he went on, pitching his voice above the boom of the seas and the creak of protesting timbers. 'We're takin' water in fast, sae we'll need tae lighten ship quickly. There's dead livestock swillin' aroon' tae go first, alang wi' throwin' much o' the heavy cargo an' ballast overboard where we can. Ah'll have Mr Clarke an' the carpenter see tae that shortly, wi' all spare hands. When ye've put the extra people where ah want 'em, ah'll see ye in mah cabin aboot the next moves.'

As the chief officer returned to deck level to do his captain's bidding, Guy Hamilton turned to the young supercargo and the ashen-faced carpenter.

'Mr Clarke, you an' the chippie here'll need tae go over the cargo an' ship's fittin's tae see wha' can be jettisoned. Anythin' that's bulky or weighty, or likely tae be spoilt in sea-water we'll get rid of at once. Ah'm sendin' ye doon enough men tae help pull it oot o' stowage and either cast it oot the larboard gun-ports if ye can, or cart it up on deck.'

He stared hard at both men, his flinty glance conveying all the authority of his office, and all the long years of managing men at sea. The carpenter looked away.

'Buckle doon the pair o' ye, since a lot'll depend on how much can be discarded, an' how soon. Ah'd pitch all o' yon rum overboard first if it was fully up tae me, but Campbell and Clarke'd be sore aboot it ah'm thinkin', if there's any chance o' gettin' it ashore as salvage. We'll save it wi' the livestock that's left while we have tae, for there's plenty else tae go. Keep some rice an' other staples in reserve though, wi' casks o' drinkin' water handy, jist in case.' His words carried unspoken but clear meanings.

'There's heaps o' cannon shot we'll no' be needin' against the Frenchies,' he went on, 'since they're the least o' mah worries! Ower the side wi' ony o' the guns ye might easily shift, an' powder as well, though some we'd maybe better save for the small arms an' muskets.'

He hesitated, seeking to sound optimistic. 'On'y keep wha' might be usefu' tae us on land, if we get – when we can find a sheltered anchorage fairly soon. Throw the rest overboard wi' what ballast, spare cordage an' extra blocks ye can reach, but mind in a' this that ye keep the ship in trim. Take frae both sides evenly, as ye go.'

Hugh Thompson was waiting in the captain's cabin when the old man arrived wet, drawn, and tiring rapidly from his exertions. Without removing any of his dripping clothing he hurried over to where the charts lay strapped on the table and rapidly summed up the situation for their mutual benefit.

'Frae the sound an' feel o' the wind an' weather oot yon, it's mah guess we're very close tae having a hurricane aroond our ears. The last one ah saw like this was in the Caribbean, ten years or more ago, screechin' like all the fiends in Hell, an' it put four big slavers up the beach, high an' dry.'

He looked squarely into the chief officer's face. 'We'll no' be makin' it tae Port Jackson this trip, Mister, for we're takin' in too much water. An' we're aye too far frae the settlement tae get much more mileage oot o' this ol' ship wi'oot killin' more o' the crew at the pumps. Throwin' the cargo an' armaments overboard's on'y tae buy us precious time, for it winna save us.'

'Time's runnin' oot fast,' he added with certainty, 'so we'd better be standin' in for the land an' maybe run ashore where best we can tae at least chance savin' the ship an' the people. Beachin's nigh oor on'y option the noo. This we have tae do, as ah'm sure ye feel as ah do we'd no' survive in open boats were we tae try an' abandon the ship here.'

Both men pored over the chart, gleaning what information they could from its scant detail. A rare fix earlier in the day, when the ragged clouds had momentarily revealed a hazy sun, placed them by timepiece reckoning in the latitude of 40 degrees 56 minutes south, longitude 149 degrees 40 minutes east of Greenwich, or 25 leagues or so east of the coast of Van Diemen's Land.

'This mornin' we were hereabouts,' the old man said, jabbing a finger at the chart, 'headin' north by nor'east. We're aboot here the noo,' he went on, pointing to a spot to the south-east of Furneaux's Islands and roughly seventy miles from the little-known Van Diemen's Land coast, 'wi' a few sea miles tae cover yet afore we're oot o' trouble. The odds are agin us, Chief, but we're also in God's guid hands.'

'Ah dinna like wha' ah've seen o' yon coast wi' sae many cliffs an' off-shore rocks. But if we gang north by west though, up taewards Cape Barren an' these islands here, there'd maybe be more of a chance tae beach

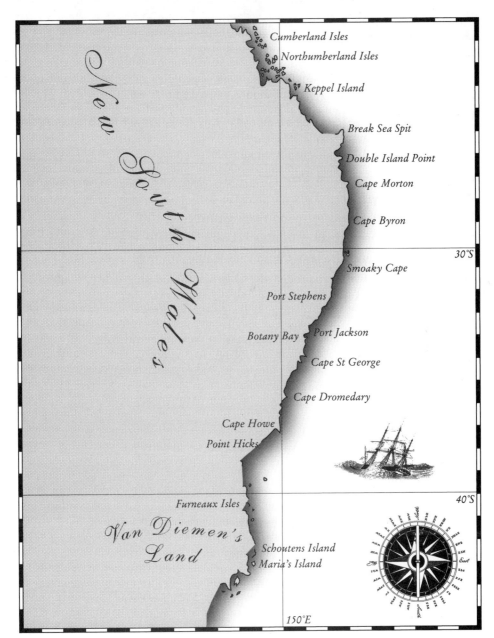

New South Wales

Cumberland Isles
Northumberland Isles
Keppel Island

Break Sea Spit
Double Island Point
Cape Morton

Cape Byron

30°S

Smoaky Cape

Port Stephens

Botany Bay — Port Jackson

Cape St George

Cape Dromedary

Cape Howe
Point Hicks

40°S

Furneaux Isles

Van Diemen's Land

Schoutens Island
Maria's Island

150°E

MAP 2. *Known coast of early New South Wales, south-east Australia, prior to 1797.*

41

the ship amongst them, an' then land the remains o' the cargo. Aye, an' we might even mak' a few repairs if we're tae be a' that lucky!'

His eyes twinkled and his face split in a rare, crooked smile, wholly enigmatic but oddly reassuring to Hugh Thompson. Was this what had kept the Old Man going for so long, the chief officer wondered? A simple faith and a sure feeling for one's destiny?

They quickly agreed on their plan of action, then once more forced their way on deck against the raging, remorseless elements. Disregarding the risk of blowing out sails in the still ferocious winds, they made as much sail as they could to speed their journey.

The pumps were clearly no longer coping with the renewed inflow of water, however, and the levels rose inexorably, hour by hour. More and more as evening drew into night the ship wallowed sluggishly, heavy on the helm, her bulk barely responsive. As the long night progressed towards morning with no let-up from the pitiless winds and dreadful seas, and only perpendicular rock and boiling surf in view as they closed the coast, their plight became ever more clearly a race against time.

3

ASHORE
TO THE ISLAND ...

8TH FEBRUARY, 1797. *40 degrees 56 minutes South, 149 degrees 40 minutes East. Winds near hurricane strength, dangerous seas, poor visibility. A fresh leak wrought by the storm requir'd some lesser cargo and a large quantity of shot and other sundries to be jettison'd. Ingress of waters beyond capacity of pumps requires that we close the land, with the likelihood of beaching to save the ship. Furneaux's Islands offer possible sanctuary.*
FROM THE SHIP'S LOG

*D*aybreak revealed a less wild sea and less threatening sky, while the nearby land offered some welcome protection from winds that had shifted during the night.

Though the sea was still scattered with whitecaps, the battering of the gales now sounded more like the moaning of the wind through the upper branches of a pine forest, high and distant. It was a sound which brought immense relief to the seamen, almost beyond exhaustion from the intense labour of the past night, trying valiantly to keep their stricken craft afloat an hour or two longer.

Sanctuary was still alluringly close, yet just as elusively distant. The land they saw not two miles to starboard, a large scrub-covered, shallow-peaked island the shape of a low-lying volcano, appeared dark and forbidding, its approaches barred by hump-backed rocks ringed by warning necklets of bursting waves and wind-torn spray. Beyond and to the north lay a larger island, its summits hidden in cloud but its fringes promising the greater possibility of sandy beaches and sheltered waters.

Guy Hamilton handed the telescope back to an attendant seaman and surveyed his ailing ship from the quarterdeck rail, measuring their chances against the worsening state of the vessel and the prevailing weather. Their very survival would depend on his decisions. During the night the water level had crept up as far as the lower deck hatches, the ship was beginning to settle, and time was running out.

In the strengthening light of day, with water visibly rising over the lower deck hatch coamings, the *Sydney Cove* was seen to be listing markedly, her starboard channels constantly awash and waves dashing the length of her oaken gunwales. A little before midnight Hugh Thompson had had the longboat prepared and cleared away, ready for a hasty launching if the need arose, and now his prudence and forethought were being recognised.

The captain turned to the small group on the quarterdeck: 'We dinna ha' much time, wi' the ship settlin' the way she is. If we can keep goin' an' drive her on for half a day longer, we'd mak' yon big island fine, for 'tis there I want tae tak' her. Lookin' at it through the glass I'd say there's shelter ashore an' a fair likelihood o' guid water, more'n on yon rock-gutted beggar,' he added, nodding to the nearer island.

'Check the stores in the longboat, Mr Clarke, if ye please, an' see it's a' ready tae be put over. Ready up the jollyboat too. The carpenter'll gi' ye a hand wi' that. Mak' certain ye've got water, casks, rice, flour, muskets, sailcloth an' plenty o' cordage in the longboat, an' a guid few blankets as well. We'll get the essentials away first if she decides tae go quickly.'

He turned to the chief officer. 'Let's have every stitch o' canvas she can carry, Mister, with a' who're not needed on deck or below workin' aloft. We've had nae ground call yet from the leadsman, so we'll need tae push her in further while she will, an' thank God for a favourable blow!'

Addressing the helmsman, he said, 'As soon as she's answerin', bring her head round more taewards the hills beyont the bows tae starboard.' He pointed towards a low eminence below the main peak of the island. 'Closer in ye'll see wha' looks like a fair bay wi' yon wee scroggie hill behind it. That's where ah want her taken.'

It was not to be, however. Though the crew worked frantically, her beaten, waterlogged hull was so unresponsive, so low in the water that she barely answered the helm. Listing heavily and limping uncertainly, the contrary elements had not yet done with her. Under almost full sail the following winds took her and bore her off in a sluggish drift downwind, away from the chosen refuge so tantalisingly close at hand.

No amount of hauling on the yards could shift her from her final course, caught as she was in the combined pressures of currents, tide and wind. In a ship they knew would soon sink beneath them, reducing sail would only have left them too far out to sea.

The chief officer pounded the rail and swore at their helplessness, while the captain watched their progress towards a small, lowlying rock-fringed island in grim silence. When a call of fifteen fathoms was heard from the bow, he ordered the loaded longboat away, its crew pulling strongly towards the new but unpromising sanctuary.

It lay open to the sea three miles off the larger island, totally exposed, and with no obvious source of water or other sustenance, but they were powerless to go anywhere else. At least they were alive, and at no great distance from either their immediate objective or their ultimate destination.

The bottom shelved sharply as the *Sydney Cove* approached and bore rapidly into a small cove, passing closely between low rock ramparts that skirted another rock-girt island close by to larboard. 'Seven fathoms! *Three fathoms!*'

Men reached out quickly and braced themselves for the anticipated crash, glancing aloft at the heavy spars and topmasts which might easily be dislodged and flung down when bracing stays and other supporting rigging snapped under the strains of impact. Tons of rope, blocks, and splintering timbers could at any second turn the canting deck into a bloody shambles.

But no crash came. Although men staggered under the jolt, and the ship's timbers shuddered and groaned briefly in protest, there was no climactic collision to tear the heart and keel from the ship, no gasping swirling plunge into final oblivion.

For a moment there was silence in the quiet cove, an air of unbelief broken only by the empty, harmless moaning of the wind. Then the sails began to flog noisily as the yards swung briefly free and unattended, before men hurried to hand them in.

Captain Hamilton was the first to speak, his voice betraying the release of tension and the relief they all felt. 'God be thankit, that we've grounded in sand. An open, rocky shore here, an' 'twould have been an entirely different story! Despite everythin' we've been through, we're still alive, aye, an' none of us no more than shaken. For a' its puir appearances an' scant accommodation, 'tis here we're saved, though no' long ago we mightn't 'ae had rights tae expeckit!'

He laughed brokenly, covering his emotions. 'This is our preservation, this wee island an' no mistake, so wi' God's continuing help an' favour, we may get tae Port Jackson yet!'

It was the stillness that woke Will Clarke, as startling in its way as the sharp clamour of a ship's bell. No sound, where sounds should be; silence – unexpected, unaccustomed. For a brief moment he lay confused and disorientated. A faint light from an obscure source; no motion; no sound save a curious muted, indefinable murmur. Above him an inexplicable dark, arching vault.

Then a growing consciousness of the hard surface beneath him and a muscular ache in his upper back and shoulders recalled the crowded events of the previous day, to be reinforced by the first pangs of a gnawing hunger. Sitting up too quickly, he bumped his head against a thwart of the upturned boat and his confusion finally left him as he lay back on one elbow with a groan, rubbing the bruise.

Soon after the longboat had left for the island, the *Sydney Cove* had ground into the sandy shingle to settle immovably. Her decks and masts canted askew towards the large island that lay across the narrow, intervening strait, affording shelter to leeward in an otherwise wave-chopped bay.

Ashore, the longboat had been rapidly unloaded on the nearest stretch of beach and had returned several times for more provisions and supplies, as the castaways worked to secure themselves, nearly fifty men, against any further onslaughts of wind and tide.

The discomfort of his still damp clothing reminded him of his own ride through the waves and breakers, and the scramble ashore with the last of their immediate needs. On that trip the largest surviving item of livestock, a reluctant horse, was pushed overboard and towed ashore. Then followed the toil of securing the ship, of removing the provisions to places well above high water, of collecting firewood – of which there was plenty along the beaches – and of searching the length and breadth of their small island for water, of which there was none.

While temporary sailcloth shelters were being fashioned amongst the rocks, a scratch meal was prepared from such edible provisions as they had been able to salvage, following which men slept as they fell. Will Clarke had finally crawled and slept beneath the longboat which lay propped keel uppermost beyond reach of the tide.

Hearing sounds, and smelling again the half-forgotten aroma of wood-smoke, he scrambled out from beneath his shelter, blinking in the sunlight. The murmuring resolved itself into the gentle sounds of wavelets lapping the indented shore. As he took his bearings, he found himself swaying to the lingering, ethereal motions of the stricken ship. But the ship, as he now saw, was submerged to the taffrail, while the motion was a figment of his imagination.

The wood-smoke emanated from a nearby cooking fire, while several men moved slowly about the island. Their haven was largely rock-strewn, with a thin covering of clumped bushes and spiky tussock grass, its coast an alternating succession of small sandy bays, rocky points and islets. Guy Hamilton and Hugh Thompson sat upon rounded boulders by the water's edge, pipes alight and talking quietly. Both nodded as the young man approached.

'A finer morn this mornin', Mr Clarke, than any we've had for many a day, wuid ye no' agree?' The captain puffed contentedly, tobacco smoke dispersing lightly on the soft breeze. His manner was informal and relaxed after the trials and traumas of their voyage, though his lined face and careworn expression told of their recent ill fortune and its perilous aftermath.

Although he had lost his ship through mishap, his skill and experience had brought his crew through unimaginable conditions and had saved their main cargo. For the moment they were safe, and the new day was blessedly calm. He had earned his moment of relaxation.

The old seafarer squinted from under his tricorne, eyes narrowed against the sand glare. ''Twas a guid day's work ye put in yesterday, Mister,' he said conversationally. 'As fine as any o' the rest o' mah crew. 'Tis guid tae see a man's nae cowed by a wee touch o' that kind of adversity, an' can rise tae gi' the example ye did.'

The captain's tone was light but his words were sincere – he never wasted words on idle sentiment. The chief officer nodded in agreement, and the young Scot felt himself colouring under their gaze. A portion of breakfast given to him by the lascar servant was a welcome diversion.

Confused by Hamilton's unexpected compliment, Will Clarke stammered a reply, his lowlands brogue far less pronounced than that of the older man. 'I – I was only doing what I felt I should, sir,' he said hesitantly, 'I – I couldn't stand by and leave everything tae the men, sir. I wanted tae help – there – there seems tae be so much tae do.'

'Whatever else we are, sir, we – we're all in this together, castaways shipwrecked on a desert island. An' since I don't suppose anyone else can help us, I – well, we'll all need tae help one another, won't we, if we're tae get ourselves back tae Bengal, or tae Port Jackson even? If, as ye say, I did give some kind of example – well, I'm glad tae be able. It's all for a – a common good, I'd be thinking, in – in situations like these.' He shrugged apologetically, partly to cover his rising embarrassment, unsure that he was saying the right thing.

The captain nodded, hiding a smile at the young man's altruism and romantic allusion to desert islands. Both bespoke an innocence and naïveté not yet tarnished by the harshness of life – though that might soon change.

'Aye, well. Ye came on this trip for the experience, laddie, an' that's wha' ye're gettin' – though this sort ye might well do wi'out, desert islands an' a' no'withstandin'. Ah'm thinkin' ye got more'n ye bargained for on this passage! Ah'm on'y sorry it happened aboard one o' my ships but, if it had tae happen at a', then ah'm glad it happened the way it did. 'Tis a pity though, we didna' make yon big island,' he observed, glancing across at the humped shape now bathed in sunlight, silently inviting.

'Still, we cann'ae ask for everythin'. Compared wi' most in these circumstances, the guid Lord's been gentle wi' us. He's gi'en us anither chance in guidin' us here,' he added reflectively, 'so we needs must mak' the most on it.'

They stared at the ship, lying forlornly with her decks awash under the swell of the incoming tide. Her slanted masts tilted their yards towards the rising waters, her rigging taut above and sagging below from the unaccustomed stresses. The remnants of her sails hung lifeless in the calm air, abandoned. It was clear she could not be refloated. She had sailed her last passage, and here would forever remain. No one appeared to notice the tear in the old man's eyes as he quietly spoke an amen.

'She was a fine craft, aye,' he said shortly. 'She was one o' ma' best.'

After a moment's silent tribute to their lost ship, the needs of the day caused the chief officer to break the melancholy. 'You were saying, Captain, before Mr Clarke joined us, there are things to be done. Can I rouse the crew an' make a start on anything, or were you thinking of resting the men today?'

The day was already well advanced, and the sight of idle hands amongst a group of able-bodied seamen ran against Hugh Thompson's principles.

'Aye, Chief, a rest day it is, after lookin' to essentials.' The captain shook himself out of his reverie and returned to the group. 'A day weel-earnt tae recover frae their labours an' a' that they've been through these past few days'll no' be amiss. We've enough frae the ship for our immediate needs, an' 'tis comin' up high tide the noo anyway. For the time bein' she's snug an' secure, though we'll need tae improve on yon lines shortly in the event there's another blow upon us.'

'What we also need, sir, is a well of some sort, or perhaps we'd be better off camped on the beaches or in the woods across the strait,' Thompson persisted. 'There isn't sufficient water on this island. What we've found is no more than a trickle amongst the rocks, and ill-tasting at that.'

The old man considered for a while, drawing slowly on his clay pipe before commenting. 'Ah daresay there'll be water on the big island – that'll be the one Captain Furneaux named Cape Barren – but ah've a mind tae stay here awhile if the weather holds, an' if we can reach guid enough water by diggin'. For one thing, that's a valuable cargo we were carryin' an' it shouldna' be spoiled if we can move it off the ship quickly. For another, there's too much of it tae move across the strait, so some of us will ha' tae stay here a wee while yet.'

'In two or three days,' he went on reflectively, 'when we're fairly settled here, we'll think aboot sendin' off one o' the boats tae try an' reach Port Jackson. Meantime there'll be plenty tae occupy us. Even if we do reach the settlement with our story, there'd no' be sae many ships in Port Jackson as'd come either quickly or readily. We're a lang way frae anywhere in this part o' the world, so those people who don't go off tae get help'd best be prepared for a longish stay.'

Smoke drifted away from his pipe as he considered the prospect. 'That'll mean seeking some other means o' vitt'lin' an' waterin' maybe thirty-odd men for as long as needs be, 'specially since we canna' expeckit such stores as we salvage frae the ship tae last any time. An' especially not when we'll also need tae furnish a boat party. As ye can see frae the state o' the ship, much o' the perishables still aboard are likely tae be spoilt the noo, an' the staples we carried'll no' be feedin' us much.'

He cocked his head and looked at them askance. 'So – the pair o' ye've got some explorin' an' huntin' tae do,' he finished with a grin, 'as well as help seein' tae unloadin' the ship! Ye'd best be takin' your ease while ye may, gentlemen, for come the morn there's work tae be done!'

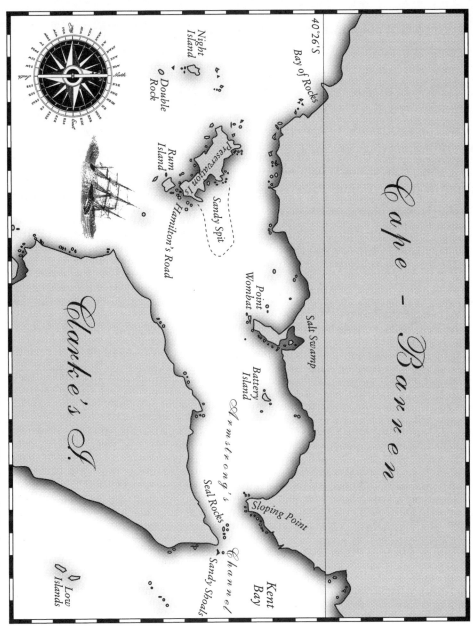

MAP 3. *Furneaux's Islands, Bass Strait, as recorded by Lieutenant Matthew Flinders, 1798, showing Preservation Island, Clarke's Island, and part of Cape Barren Island.*

Night
Island

Double
Rock

Rum
Island

Preservation Is.

Hamilton's Road

Sandy Spit

40°26'S

Bay of Rocks

$\mathcal{C}$ a p e - $\mathcal{B}$ a r r e n

Point
Wombat

Salt Swamp

Battery
Island

A r m s t r o n g ' s

$\mathcal{C}$larke's $\mathcal{I}$.

Seal Rocks

Sloping Point

C h a n n e l

Sandy Shoals

Kent
Bay

Low
Islands

51

The island they had named Preservation was not without immediate resources, despite its tiny size. In shape it resembled a stone-mason's maul, little more than a mile and a half long by a half mile wide at its western end. Although it was one of the smallest in the Furneaux Islands group, it provided a reasonable harvest of crabs and assorted shellfish, as well as a multitude of seabirds and an edible variety of seaweed.

Within a day or two the Indian seamen were making traditional fishtraps, lightly constructed of bamboo from livestock pens broken by the storm, and fishing net from amongst the cargo. These, suitably weighted and baited, they placed amongst the clefts and rock pools, and from time to time were rewarded by catches of fish and spiny lobsters.

The island was periodically visited by a variety of large grey goose which, though wary, promised good eating. Their haven was also the home of a family of small, brown furry animals which the lascars called *kharha*, and which fled away rapidly on two hind legs with audible thumps of an extended tail. These, too, suggested good eating if they could be trapped or shot. The animals' natural curiosity, once they felt themselves out of danger, was something that could be taken advantage of, but for the time being they stayed at the further end of the island.

With good sense and an eye for the future, Captain Hamilton forbade aimless pursuit and excessive killing, preferring to keep the animals alive until their meat was needed. All were constantly reminded of the need to conserve their supplies, and to thank God for His mercy and provenance in sparing them so narrowly from total disaster.

Their early days on the island seemed blessed with a sufficiency of food but there was little water. A thorough search on the first day found only rock pools of rain water, and a discoloured soak beneath a cluster of boulders that proved to be unpalatable. They couldn't discover where the animals slaked their thirsts. A party of men was therefore set to digging a well in the middle of a muddy depression, the most promising spot on the island. At a depth of seven feet or so they found brackish water, with which they had to be satisfied.

Others sought food and water, some used the ship's jollyboat to salvage what useful items they could from the wreck, and the ship's officers, together with a handful of the crew, prepared to recover the most valuable and bulky part of the cargo. In the depths of the ship, still in more than a hundred barrels and all under water, were the 7,000 gallons of fiery spirits they had been carrying.

Unloading such a cargo at a quayside would have posed no difficulties. With the ship on an even keel, each of the heavy barrels would have been levered from its stowage in the lower hold, trundled to the main hatchway for hoisting by block and tackle to the upper deck, and swung outwards on a spar, down to the carts or drays of waiting dock-hands. Unloading at moorings would only have replaced the carts with lighters or longboats, again without real difficulties. However, merely locating the barrels in the flooded depths of the *Sydney Cove* was difficult and dangerous, and their collective ingenuity was sorely taxed.

Will Clarke's head broke the surface of the dark waters of the hold for the fourth time, and he coughed loudly as he clung to the rigged line, his pale chest heaving.

'It's no use,' he said with an exasperated shake of his head, glancing up at the faces above him. 'I can't do it. Even – even taking the deepest breaths I can, there's no' enough time tae swim down into the lower hold, go any distance, find what I'm looking for, and then try tae retrieve it. It's hell-black down there, away from the hatch, and difficult tae – tae distinguish shapes through the water. The effort o' doing much more drives your breath away.'

He shook his head negatively. 'Shifting those casks'll be almost impossible, even with two or three at the task. By my reckoning, sir, no more than a minute's the most any man could safely spend down there doing any kind o' useful work, not counting the swim down an' back. It's – it's no' enough.'

'Aye, laddie, perhaps you're right.' The old Scot sounded resigned to losing the cargo, having already sent a number of men, most of them lascars who were good swimmers, into the flooded interior to try various means of retrieval. Sooner or later, despite their willingness, each had emerged spluttering from the cold, dark waters, including one who had been dragged out almost unconscious.

The captain nodded, and spoke almost to himself. 'Aye, time's a problem. If we could raise some o' the gun-ports we might let in a wee bitty more light, altho' nay where it's most needed. An' cuttin' a hole in the side o' the ship wuid only carry the same problems, or worse. She's a stoutly-built craft, an' yon chippy's nae girt swimmer. Ye have tae work beneath the water, an' haudin' yer breath for any time's the real difficulty, aye, ah see that. Come up oot o' there, laddie, afore ye catch yer death.'

He turned to Hugh Thompson who leaned alongside him on the slanting hatchboards. The rest of the men stood or sat around on the higher side of the deck. 'Well Mister, d'ye have any more ideas? Ye ken ah'd like vera much tae save what we can o' the cargo, if there's the least chance.'

The chief officer frowned in concentration and sucked his teeth reflectively. At length he spoke: 'The only notion I've got, for what it's worth, Captain, is to make some kind o' diving bell. Or a diving barrel maybe, such as Lethbridge invented. I watched one being used once, on a sunken Spaniard in the Indies. That way you'd get air down to whoever's working below, so they needn't come back to the surface so often. It'd be damnably awkward an' cumbersome in the hatch, though. And you'd not get it anywhere 'tween decks, not so's anyone could use it easily. There's scant room for one thing, an' the buoyancy'd be hard to overcome to shift it. But that's where ye'd be wanting it.'

He crinkled his brow, trying to visualise the system but seeing only the problems. 'Ideally you'd need a team o' men below, working together, moving to order. No more than two men could use the bell for breathin' at any one time without getting in each other's way. More than that, they couldn't work together for the time they'd all have breath.' He shook his head and spat down into the water dismissively. 'I don't know if it would work, considering.'

Then Will Clarke, who had just joined them, blanket-wrapped, came up with an unexpected idea: 'Perhaps if each man had a little barrel of air – say, one o' those water kegs there, for instance. By using it tae breathe from it might be possible tae stay under the surface longer? Like the bagpipes turned about, maybe – sucking, instead of blowing?'

Hugh Thompson grinned at the comment. 'An' the best place for 'em too, I'd say – under water!'

'Jist gie the laddie here a chance wi' his ideas, will ye! This is serious business we're aboot, an' no jokin' matter.' The captain's testy words had bite, and the chief officer stifled his amusement. 'Go on wi' what's on yer mind, Mr Clarke. Ye might ha' somethin' worth explorin'.'

The young man flushed despite the chill. 'I was – I was just thinking, sir, that if each man down there could somehow breathe from a separate small cask, one that he could have near him, there'd be no need tae come up for air so often. They could work together more easily since they wouldn't need tae move around so much, and they wouldn't get in each other's way so much.'

'If the – the breather was weighted properly we could take air down with us, an' maybe work down there for as much as ten minutes at a time. That'd be enough, I'd think, tae secure and drag out one of the large barrels, at least. We've got various sorts o' kegs, and plenty of weights an' rope, sir. I'm sure we could work something out, if we think carefully what it is we're about.'

The captain stared at Will Clarke appraisingly, gauging the idea, seeking to grasp his intent. The lad indeed seemed to have something. Was it not said that necessity was the mother of invention? There was nothing to be lost in giving him his head – except the cargo, and that was lost anyway if they failed to find a way of raising it quickly.

'Aye. Aye, ye may jist be right! Ah have tae admit it's as bonny a notion as any ah've heard in a long while.' He could feel his own excitement rising as the possibilities tumbled upon him. 'Aye, if we can mak' up something that ye can take a breath from every noo an' again, an' all o' ye doing it at the same time, why – why, we'd fairly clear the ship i' no time! Let's a' awa' back tae shore for a bite tae eat while we think on't, an' see what we've got tae build it with! It'll keep the carpenter busy too, an' that'll no' be a bad thing, either!'

They assembled the first breathing machine that afternoon. Will Clarke scratched his rough ideas in the sand, some refinements were talked out by the more astute, and the apparatus was finally put together by the carpenter, Will Clarke, and a couple of willing helpers who stood to use it.

It consisted of a nine-gallon firkin, a small hooped cask, around which was fastened a tether above and below the bulge so that it would float upright when held from beneath. A cannonball was trapped beneath the cask by the gathered cords of the tether, to counteract the strong flotation pressure when the cask was full of air. A length of narrow bamboo served as a breathing tube which slanted up into the interior of the air chamber,

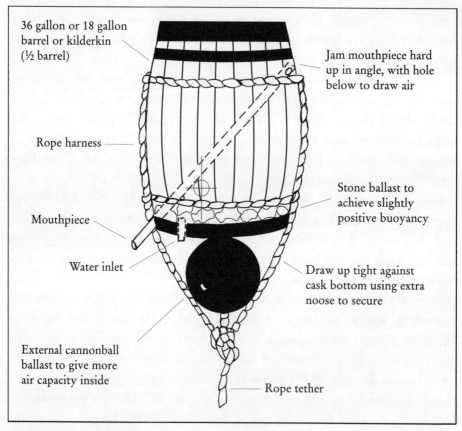

The breathing machine.

while a short length also pierced the bottom to allow water to enter the chamber as air was withdrawn. Any likely leak points were caulked with oakum.

An eager crowd gathered to watch Will Clarke wade out into the horseshoe-shaped cove to test the finished machine. Bubbles regularly broke the surface to tell the watchers all was well, visibly reinforcing the double pull on the lifeline that the captain had insisted on at least once a minute. After ten minutes he re-emerged, shivering but triumphant, to the cheers and excited chatter of the assembled crew.

As helpers rubbed him briskly to bring warmth back to his numb limbs and body, he reported his findings between chattering teeth.

'W-well, sir, it w-works! Much b-better than I'd expected. I-it needs a b-bit more weight on or ins-side it, p-perhaps one or two large p-p-pebbles. I c-could have s-stayed under longer I think, except f-for the c-c-cold, but if – if we get the b-balance right we sh-should know how m-much air there's left, and how l-long we can stay s-submerged, b-by how – how high it f-f-floats in the water. We – we'd need to c-come up with a f-few minutes air left, f-for s-safety, and – an' we'd also n-need to k-keep moving to st-stay warm. But – but it – it'll be good enough, sir, f-for the job we want to d-do.'

Hamilton was elated. 'Well done, laddie,' he exclaimed warmly, 'that was a grand fine job ye did!' The skipper beamed his pleasure and almost boyish enthusiasm. 'Aye, we'll see tae the few extra poun's, and then chippie an' one or twa' o' the others can mak' up a few more. Yon wee machine's a braw touch o' genius if ever there was, an' ah've half a mind tae be strippin' off an' gie it a go masel'! A guid warm day for mah old bones's all ah need. Why, we cuid gang doon an' be catchin' lobsters every day wi' yin o' these! By jings, ah tell ye, if ah was thirty years younger ye wouldn'ae be seein' me stannin' aroon' here the noo!'

The old man was almost beside himself with glee, and Will Clarke bathed briefly in the glory of his own inventiveness and the captain's praise and attention.

'This calls for a wee celebration! Ah'm sure the company wouldn'ae mind us broachin' a sma' cask by way o' marking such an occasion as this,' the captain went on happily, temporarily forgetting his normal Presbyterian abstention. 'We'll draw a wee dram off the first cask that's raised, tae toast the success o' the rest of our venture. All the rest we might put oot on yon wee island, for better safekeeping. One drink's an indulgence, aye, well-earned an' no harm in it – but twa'd be both extravagant an' profitless!'

With Will Clarke's breathing apparatus, two men could work effectively in the dark confines of the hold, but four got in each other's way as expected. It was therefore decided that two should work together until most of their air was gone, hitching each of the valuable kegs with a double noose to be pulled to the surface, whereupon two fresh men would take their places with the second set of recharged air vessels. In this way they would work in relays.

The weather remained fine though cool. The working groups pursued their chores under Captain Hamilton's direction, according to his philosophy that busy men were happy men – but there was indeed a lot to occupy their time.

Each day there was food and firewood to be gathered, and the food surplus dried in readiness for the impending boat journey. The sailcloth shelters which had been set up in the lee of prominent boulders along the spine of the island were strengthened and secured against the inevitable weather deterioration, and salvage work continued on the *Sydney Cove*.

Just as Captain Hamilton had predicted, their menu was frequently improved by the addition of lobsters and a large kind of ormer, a shellfish known to both lascar and European alike, as well as massive limpets. Each of the different kinds of shellfish was available in quantity, and proved quite edible and acceptable – once their natural toughness had been beaten away before cooking.

The unloading progressed well under Will Clarke's eye, and Captain Hamilton soon turned his attention to wider horizons. On a windy day about a week after the *Sydney Cove* had gone aground, a small party led by Hugh Thompson hoisted sail in the jollyboat and angled off the rising sou'easterly towards the nearest point on Cape Barren Island, half a league distant.

'Tak' a wee jaunty oot beyond the beach there, Mister, an' see wha' ye can from atop yon hill,' the captain had instructed, pointing out the landmarks on the opposite shore. ''Twould be canny tae look for more supplies o' fresh water an' other vittles while we've chance. We canna be sure how much time we'll be spendin' here 'afore we're taken off, so off wi' ye an' spy oot the land.' A final thought struck him as the party climbed aboard. 'Aye, should ye come upon eggs frae yon geese we've seen, mind ah'd relish the treat! The few poultry we saved frae the ship seem disinclined tae lay, so be sure ye keep a guid lookout!'

They landed on a small beach close to the rock-rimmed point. Having pulled the boat ashore, half the party explored the heavily bouldered western foreshore and hinterland, while the remainder proceeded east and north, around the beachline towards the beckoning hill. What they saw was not encouraging.

The ground was dry and, apart from a small trickle of water, not much more than they had found on Preservation Island, there was little to refresh them. However, the one tiny source was pleasingly fresh and showed evidence of an augmented flow after rain. They therefore deepened and enlarged a shallow natural pondage to increase the supply. Even this small source helped to wash away the clinging briny aftertaste of the brackish water from their island well.

From the hill they had seen a river valley flowing away westwards from the dark bush-clad mountains, but thick, man-high scrub prevented them from descending. Indeed, much of the island to the west seemed densely clad and impenetrable, whereas eastwards the interior lay more open and inviting. That direction and the bare hills in the far distance seemed to hold the greater promise for later exploration.

The shore party confirmed these first impressions. The bush behind the shore was almost impenetrable. They had made their way carefully across extensive rock outcrops covered with a bright orange, lichen-like growth, finding nothing edible apart from some small limpets and a variety of periwinkle. Where the strand eventually broadened out across tussock-covered slopes, they had discovered an extensive bracken field which, despite its masses of tough fibrous growth, also yielded tender young fiddleheads as their first and only real vegetable find. They found no water along the entire length of their coastal traverse, and finally turned back when the way was barred by a sun-warmed tussock-ground alive with basking snakes.

The wind that blew up later persisted strongly for several days, filling the channel with steep white-capped waves that permitted only one more exploration trip, before confining them to the island. On this second excursion Hugh Thompson took his men north-westwards, seeking to circumvent both the tedious journey through the scrub and the probability of snakes by pushing along the coast by boat, as far as the mouth of the river they had seen from the hilltop the day before. They called a bay which they encountered the Bay of Rocks after the many rounded boulders that broke the waves some way out, deterring any approach to the beaches except through the turbulence thrown up by strongly gusting winds and shallow, rapidly shelving waters.

Turning a point into an adjacent bay they found the river, but its water also proved brackish for as far inland as they could penetrate, having man-hauled the boat across a shallow bar. It was no better than the water on Preservation Island, but the grassy banks of the river supported many of the brown furry *kharha* that leapt away on strong hind limbs, and which might keep them supplied with meat for as long as they remained. They shot five of the animals to take back with them, so helping to conserve the numbers on the island.

The return journey across the narrow, choppy strait was a struggle against a boisterous blustering wind which grew stronger by the hour, and the men were wet and weary when they finally reached the shelter of their cove. As the waves broke over the wreck of their ship and sharp gusts tested the seams of their makeshift shelters, Captain Hamilton forbade any further forays until the wind and seas abated, loath to unnecessarily risk either of the ship's boats.

'There's enough tae be done on the wee island here,' the captain declared, 'wi'oot gallivantin' aroond the bays i' this kind o' weather. It isn'ae necessary, 'specially now we ken what's ower there. Let's be havin' the boats ashore instead, above high water tae keep them frae driftin' awa', an' we can check 'em ower at the same time, especially the longboat, tae see it's fit for its trip tae Port Jackson. It's time we took tae thinkin' aboot plannin' where we gang frae here.'

When both boats had been hauled up, he called Job Duggan and Hugh Thompson, and with them worked out various ways of making the longboat more seaworthy.

'We'll part-deck her fore an' aft tae keep oot the water,' the old man said, 'an' put in stays tae support a canvas spray hood. We've timber enough frae the auld *Sydney Cove* tae do the job well. We've survived this far. What we need now's a guid strong, well-provisioned and well-manned boat that'll stymie Auld Nick, King Neptune an' Davy Jones thegither, an' see us safe the rest o' the way!'

The time passed quickly as they prepared for the departure. Work progressed on the boat, and their stock of food grew. There was an air of excitement and anticipation, tinged with a degree of apprehension.

As yet Captain Hamilton had not chosen the men to make the voyage, though all were aware that the skipper missed little of what was being said or done, as he watched them closely, appraising each man. They knew he was continually but quietly assessing each individual's strengths and capabilities in terms of the potentially hazardous venture.

Men found themselves glancing towards the different horizons more frequently, gauging with seamen's eyes the subtle moods of the elements, and searching for presages of the most suitable conditions in which to set forth. Each build-up of cloud, every change in the wind, the slightest revelation of some feature on Cape Barren Island as its mists shifted and flowed about the higher hills, were all noted for portent or significance.

Though the elements were relatively quiet, they well remembered the lashing fury of the storms that had left them stranded on these islands. Any recurrence of that pattern, or even one of lesser intensity, might bode ill for the voyagers' chances of survival, and would leave scant hope for those left behind on the island they had once called Preservation.

While the winds continued to blow, the old Scotsman also stared out towards the horizon. Several times during the course of the day he could be seen standing alone on a west-facing foreshore apparently deep in thought, or walking towards the higher points of the island, his telescope clasped firmly beneath an arm. So intense was this regular preoccupation that the men began to watch him, just as he watched them, wondering at his new and unexplained behaviour. The puzzle continued until one clear morning Hugh Thompson was offered the solution.

'This'd be a good day, Will, for putting the boats back in the water and doing a little more exploring while we try them out.' The chief officer stretched and yawned widely in the crisp morning air, feeling the rising warmth of the sun over the distant hills. The sky was cloudless and the blue sea sparkled gently.

'Never a better day for it. A bite o' breakfast I'm thinking, if that rapscallion o' mine'll rouse himself, an' then we'll put it to the skipper.' He hurled a sod to wake the cabin-boy, and craned towards the old man's empty bothie. 'Where is he, anyway?'

'I saw him go off earlier, heading along the beach,' Will Clarke replied. 'He had his telescope with him again so I suppose he'll be up amongst the rocks at his usual lookout, searching for whatever it is might be out there.'

'Hmm. Can't imagine what's got into the old fellow, the way he's been lately. It's not as if he's even interested in Cape Barren, where at least there's something to look at. Always out west it is, where there's nothing. Odd.' He shook his head in bewilderment. 'Breakfast first, and then we'll go an' look for him.'

They found him as they had expected, his leather-bound brass telescope balanced across a convenient rock, slowly sweeping the seas to westward. He looked around as they approached.

'Ah, there ye are, Chief. 'Morning, Mr Clarke. Here, Chief, tak' a look through this, an' tell me what ye see.'

Thompson took the captain's place and squinted through the glass, frowning as he swept the horizon slowly back and forth, seeing nothing despite the clear conditions. He finally stepped back, shaking his head. 'I'm sorry, sir, I really can't see anything. The horizon's empty. No ships out there – nothing.'

'Precisely, laddie, precisely. An' I wasn'ae lookin' for ships!' The old man's eyes were eager whilst his manner carried a hint of exasperation. 'If a' that oot there was supposed tae be part o' Van Diemen's Land, as they say, wouldn't ye be expectin' tae see *somethin*'? Land, for instance, or haze or cloud? Eh? Aye, there's nothing there as ye say! So, that ought perhaps tae mean *somethin*' else, am I no' right?'

Hugh Thompson bent to the telescope again, still puzzled as to what the captain was driving at.

'*Nothing*, laddie, d'ye no' see,' the old man continued insistently, 'not even wi' the light behind at sunset, nor again on a morn as clear as this? An' *we* can see a guid ten leagues out frae this height, wouldn't ye say?' His tone was becoming excited. 'No *land* means on'y water, an' on'y water means a *strait*, a *passage*. Och, man, ah'm no' a gambler, but ah'd be prepared to wager ma next ship yon's a wide strip o' seaway stretchin' clear 'atween Van Diemen's Land an' the coast o' New South Wales! An' think o' wha' that would mean!'

Whereupon the captain's point became obvious to both officers together. Away in the distance, south of sou'west, they could see the Van Diemen's Land coast standing pale in the early morning sun, as clearly visible as the cliffs of Dover from the French coast. Then, as it receded westwards, it terminated sharply, leaving nothing but a straight clean horizon, stretching without apparent limit into an empty gulf beyond. 'Aye, I believe you could be right, sir! There's not a cloud anywhere to mark land below the horizon, though it's maybe a bit early yet for that. But then you just said you've seen none … An' there's no smoke, either, such as you can see over there now. Hunters, or cooking fires perhaps.' Thompson glanced up, and they all looked at the handful of smoke plumes rising thinly above the shadow of the distant land.

'Aye, Chief, there's not a thing any of the time. Ah've been comin' up here on an' off ower several days lately, thinkin' aboot the lay o' the wind an' the sea, an' … ' He broke off abruptly, catching a fleeting look of sheepishness in Hugh Thompson's eye. 'An' the pair o' ye thinkin' the auld man's goin' off his chump, ah'll be bound! For shame! Ships indeed!' And the old man chortled at having caught his juniors out, firm in his belief that a sea passage might easily exist where until now there had been thought only for a peninsula, a connection with the mainland to the north.

The captain elaborated as they descended the hill, demonstrating further his extensive knowledge of maritime matters. 'In 1773 or so, when Captain Furneaux reported tae Captain Cook that he *thought* this was a deep bay hereabouts, he hadn'ae really been in tae mak' sure,' he told them. 'Cook was awa' in New Zealand by then, an' he quite understandably believed what Furneaux had said, an' puit it on his charts as such, see?'

'If yon unimaginative, malingerin' duffer had a' done his job in a proper way as befits the seaman he was supposed tae be, we might a' be safe in Sydney the noo wi' a guid sound ship! Hah! Blitherin' English navy actin' like God Almighty again.' He shook his head in disgust.

'Well, anyway,' he went on shortly, 'we ken jist a wee bit more than their Lordships on this occasion, so aye, awa' an' tak' the boats an' mah spy-glass, an' gang across tae yon bay an' up intae the hills there too. Have a guid look whilst ye're there, bearin' in mind wha' ah've jist told ye. It'll be an improvement on Cook an' Furneaux, an' it might jist be a way of makin' sure other people dinna fetch up on these islands the way we did!'

And so they landed on the high domed point which jutted like a thumb into the wide exposed channel, four miles to the north-east of their island. The water they skimmed across was deep, clear and intensely blue, their footing firm as they arrived on a smooth wet beach. From a foreshore of the now familiar granite boulders, grass-grown dunes climbed up a hill from whence they were able to scan the hinterland and plan their venture.

To landward and below them lay a wide rippling lagoon from which the tide was fast receding, beyond which lay more dunes before a belt of thick dark bush. Not far away, where the bush thinned into tussock clumps and grass-like trees, the telescope revealed the edge of what promised to be a shallow lake with banks gleaming white in the sun, giving way to the open scrubland that Hugh Thompson had already noted.

They quickly reached the lake, a broad fresh-water basin surrounded by a springy green sward on which grazed more of the strange, rabbit-like *kharha*. The animals watched them curiously, nibbling and at the same time moving cautiously away from the intruders. They seemed unafraid, unmolested.

The island seemed to be uninhabited, as the castaways had suspected when they had seen neither smoke nor fire anywhere on Cape Barren, and when they had failed to excite any human response. There were also no signs of habitation at the watering place. The only footprints were their own, or those made by animals or birds.

Having drunk their fill of the sweet-tasting water, Hugh Thompson's next decisions were easy ones. He sent the two boats back to Preservation Island to bring as many empty kegs as they could carry. He bade the four remaining crewmen set up camp amongst the trees a little way from the lakeside, clearing scrub, collecting dry timber and setting a cooking fire in preparation for the night. The site was ideal, a sheltered base away from the wreck with the added bonus of abundant waterfowl at the far end of the lake. With these preparations under way, his attention turned to the observations he had been ordered to make.

Together, he and Will Clarke strode inland through the dry, knee-high vegetation. 'Two miles to the nearer hills, Will, or three for the better view. 'Tis no more than a brisk walk if we meet no impediment, an' the exercise will do us good! We can be there and back again by sundown with the job done, whereas tomorrow may not favour us so well!'

The climb up the rock-strewn hills was barely more than a scramble, the bush on the slopes sparse and thin. The only water they found was in a patch of marshy ground near a reed thicket that had burst asunder with the flight of several startled *kharha*. The calm summit seemed clothed in a tangible silence, enhanced by the magnificence of the shimmering vistas.

From the hilltop boulders they looked down onto the arid plain, past the lake and their campsite, now marked by a rising plume of smoke, to the islands beyond the channel. Their own Preservation Island lay thread-like and insignificant against the larger islands, the mountains close to hand, and the blue expanse of the ocean. Van Diemen's Land showed clear to the south-west, deceptively close in the clean, clear air. But to the west and north-west, below the sun, there was nothing. It was a scene that would have been no different a thousand, or even ten thousand years earlier.

Will Clarke found himself caught by such fancies as he looked out from their high vantage, his view a far cry from the thoroughfares of Calcutta or Canton and their teeming humanity. 'It seems strange tae be in a land so wild and empty, so untouched,' he remarked to his companion, in a voice diminished by the magnitude of his musings. 'What we can see out there has probably been this way since God's Creation, an' we must be the first men tae tread this ground. What an awesome thought. It doesn't seem possible. If a small island can be like this, what must there be, unseen and unknown, in as vast and wild a land as New Holland?'

'Wild's right, lad,' Hugh Thompson said, handing the glass to Will Clarke. 'Raw country for as far as you can see, an' then more beyond that. It almost defies imagination. Cap'n Hamilton's right in what he's supposing too, I'd say, an' that means that the rude blackfellows on the mainland can never have reached these parts as they're not sailors like some.'

He paused, a questioning look on his face. 'That doesn't explain how the people on Van Diemen's Land got there, though, unless there is some kind of a land connection.'

For a long moment the only sound was a faint mocking bird-call from the bush below. The truth was far beyond their imagination, but the Englishman's summary response still seemed lamely hollow and inadequate. 'Whatever the way of it, lad, 'tis not for trading men the likes of us to say or try to guess at. More will it likely be known to those with idle time and curious inclinations, or thinking men like the captain, who'll no doubt follow after.'

It was a statement that gave no satisfactory response to the questions remaining in both their minds. Long after dark that night, by the flickering light of the campfire, their philosophical discussions ranged over such matters as well as their plight, their salvation and the fortunes they were party to, the nature of lands in which they now found themselves, and the prospects of the forthcoming boat journey.

Little was concluded with any certainty, however, and their thoughts could only be conjectural, like so much else about this relatively unknown corner of the globe. Men were ranging further afield with each passing year, but for all their probings across the oceans in the name of exploration and commerce, they still only scratched on the surface of the world's deeper, more far-reaching secrets.

As he lay awake later by the dying embers, the stillness pricked by a muted medley of croaking, chirruping night sounds or the whistling wing-beat of unseen swans seeking the lake, Will Clarke stared up at the myriad stars that lit the immensity of the heavens. The familiar shape of Orion shone brilliantly amongst the vast, slow-wheeling constellations, but his attention was held by the cluster they called the Southern Cross. Watching it with a sharp sense of earthly insignificance, he wondered anew at what the future might hold for mankind in these little known lands, and for himself during the days that lay ahead.

4
DEPARTURE OF THE LONGBOAT

27TH FEBRUARY, 1797. *Boat party consisting of Hugh Thompson (First Officer), Willm. Clarke (Asst. supercargo), Job Duggan (carpenter), Francis Gilbaert and Tenby Read (seamen), and twelve lascars, set out today for Port Jackson. Weather settl'd, seas calm, light airs. Given fair sailing good progress shou'd be made, partic. along the coast N. beyond Cape Howe. Port Jackson may therefore be reach'd in c. two weeks, beyond the middle of March, with the prospect of our rescue following sometime near mid-April.*
FROM THE SHIP'S LOG

The entire company gathered on the short curved beach early next morning to farewell the boat party. Every man present was keenly aware of the meaning of the voyage, and of how much their deliverance depended on its ultimate success. The atmosphere was alive with eagerness, apprehension and purpose, becoming almost festive as the crew gathered their scant belongings and made their final preparations.

Seventeen men had been selected to make the journey, more having volunteered than the longboat would comfortably accommodate. Those who were chosen, five European and twelve lascar seamen, combined both skills and fitness to withstand the rigours of a passage in the open boat. Most were already aboard the longboat as it bobbed gently on the tide, securing lines held by willing hands ashore in readiness for departure. The bright sun rising up the cloudless sky above the eastern hills of Cape Barren Island promised another fair day.

From the charts they had saved from the wreck, the captain and his chief officer had calculated a passage of at least 500 sea miles.

'Tae which ye'd need tae be addin' the effects of winds and currents,' the old Scot finally said to Hugh Thompson, as he sat back and filled a pipe. 'An' they might amount tae anither hundred miles or so ower the distance ye'll be coverin' – say, more near 600 sea miles between here an' Port Jackson. It's a fair way, Mister.'

Thompson nodded in agreement. 'Aye, sir, it is. But by your own observations these past three weeks, the winds that prevail from either west or sou'east'll be in our favour, an' so we could reasonably maintain four nautical miles every hour – or more if we're lucky. We rarely seem to be short of a breeze, an' the longboat's never a sluggish craft with a strong wind behind an' a good crew aboard.'

'Continuous sailing at that rate,' he ventured, 'an' especially ahead of any sou'-westerlies early in the passage should mean we could reach Port Jackson in seven days or so, at a minimum, all being well. I suppose, though, with every likelihood of contrary winds an' more bad weather, given what we've already had, an' particularly from the west, realistically there'd be days when it'd be safer in shelter or even ashore.'

'Aye, best not tae push too hard i' the wurst o' the weather,' the old man conceded. 'Yon's still vera much an open boat despite her improvements. Better safe than sorry at any time in waters such as these, dependin' on ye as we shall be. So – since ye'll also be needin' tae collect fresh water alang the coast northwards, we'd best allow seven more days for ye tae complete the journey an' report tae the Governor.'

Thus they anticipated, without further mishap, that news of their plight would be known in Sydney by the middle of March. Thereafter those left on the island could expect to be rescued around the beginning of April – assuming that a ship was immediately available. In the circumstances they could be no more precise, and readily acknowledged the possibility of their rescue taking longer. Captain Hamilton had been right in anticipating a protracted stay on Preservation Island.

Hamilton extended his hand, first to Hugh Thompson, a shipmate whose firm grip he held for a long, emotion-charged moment in silence and understanding, and then to Will Clarke, the youngster whose good sense and willingness had lately earned his respect. As a man so used to command with the minimum of words, the captain was not given to extended speech-making. Nevertheless, he felt a need to acknowledge the nature of the venture they were about to embark on in these unpredictable latitudes, and the risks inherent in an open boat voyage. He held firmly onto the supercargo's hand while he spoke to them both, his words simple and sincere.

'Were I the younger man,' he said, his voice tight with emotion, 'ah'd be makin' this trip mahself. But between me an' you, Chief, one o' the twa' maun stay behind. Ah'm an old man, aye, an' so a potential liability.' He shook his head regretfully. 'Younger men'll stan' more chance o' succeedin', that ah ken, 'specially should things gang agley. So – ah've decided the one's wi' youth an' energy go; the older ones, an' the sick, 'll bide their time here.'

He paused and cleared his throat huskily. 'Ye've a perilous journey ahead o' ye. So may God go wi' ye. Ah'm afeared for all the storms we've had, so best ye go the noo, while all's fair an' well. Providence seems tae have sairved us up a devil o' a spot for sanctuary, though ah shouldn'ae perhaps say it. Hurry on back ye both – ah'd like tae feel there's sunnier isles afore me still, afore ah'm finally through.'

To Will Clarke he said, 'Ah'd no' the right tae expec' ye when ah asked ye tae go along tae support Mr Thompson, in place o' puir Leishman, laddie – though ah'm sair glad ye will.'

'Sir, I-I'd have wanted tae go anyway,' Will Clarke protested, 'and would have asked you tae include me. I was waiting for your choices first, sir. I-I'm happy tae be going, I . . .' He broke off before the captain's steady gaze.

'I'd have sent Mr Leishman in your stead, as a seaman, mind, if we hadn'ae lost him,' the old man repeated. 'But you've got brains where he had experience. May God grant ye'll use one cannily tae get the other afore ye've done wi' a' this. Judgin' on wha' ah've seen sae far, ye've the makin's of a man wi' a guid head.'

He faltered, before concluding, 'It's a rare thing ye're aboot tae tak' on. We – we're a' dependin' on ye, mind. Ah wish ye well. God bless ye, laddie.'

The diminishing figures continued to wave from the beach until an intervening headland shut them from view. As their craft progressed north-westwards under a gentle breeze, angling for the turn of the big island, the longboat crew could see one or two scrambling along the shore to keep the boat in sight, until they too were finally lost in the distance. From his place ahead of the canopy that had been added to the stern-sheets, Will Clarke watched the land slip by to starboard. Under main- and foresail they made good headway, pushed along by a light south-easterly.

Once round Cape Barren Island, the way ahead was clear. Certain island groups were known to exist, their presence noted and approximate positions charted by the earliest navigators. A brief landing late the previous day in a large cove beyond the Bay of Rocks had brought glimpses of the first of these from an adjacent hilltop. It lay off to larboard now, prominently cone-shaped.

All day long they pressed northwards, threading their way carefully amongst the numerous rocks and reefs of Furneaux's Islands, taking their course from the lie of the long mountainous island on the starboard beam. Their passage was heralded by the barking of hundreds of seals, and the wheel and cry of countless seabirds. By late afternoon they were abreast of the northernmost peaks of the large island, and facing the open sea beyond.

As this was likely to be their last landfall for several days, Hugh Thompson decided to pull into a sheltered beach around the westerly cape for the night. The sun setting that evening in a blaze of crimson and gold was a comforting assurance that augured well for the remainder of the voyage.

Despite these auspices, lowering cloud greeted them the following morning as they launched the longboat and prepared to take their places aboard. The gentle breeze of the previous day had shifted sou'westerly, however, suiting them well as it carried them either north from their overnight resting-place to an as yet unknown spot on the mainland coast, or north-east towards Point Hicks, James Cook's first sighting of New Holland.

To see where they would pass, Hugh Thompson scrambled up a rocky gully at daybreak to surmount the nearest hill. Beyond a rock or two in the near distance, the horizon lay empty and hazy, stretching away into the unknown. Though the sea was calm, the wind-shift and the grey clouds carried their own warnings.

'Take the tiller first spell, Will,' Hugh Thompson said as the crew prepared to raise sail. 'We've a long way to go, so it's time we made a real seaman of you!'

The nearest members of the crew grinned broadly, making Will Clarke acutely aware of his shortcomings. During the passage the day before, whilst others took turns at the sheets and tiller or acted lookout in the bows, the young supercargo had felt superfluous, of even less help than Pochari, the youngest of the lascars. He was keen to remedy this, and so took the steersman's place in the sternsheets with alacrity, glad to have a part to play.

Hugh Thompson briefly explained the essence of his task as the others settled down and the sails began to draw them out of the bay. 'For our purposes, Will, we'll bear due north as indicated by the compass here. According to our chart we must touch the coast somewhere ahead since we're on a heading maybe twenty leagues west of Point Hicks.' His finger traced the outline of the known coast from east to west, and then crossed into the speculative unknown area.

'Line the boat up on the compass, pick a cloud or something reasonably fixed above the horizon as a steering mark, an' then keep the boat's head steady by it. Check your bearings every few minutes, an' find a new steering mark if you need to, or shift your last one to a new point on the boat.'

The chief officer and Tenby Read, a young seaman, adjusted the mainsail while two of the lascars reset the foresail against the slanting wind. He took the helm momentarily to gauge the feel of the boat, and glanced over the stern at the rippling wake. He smiled.

'She trims easily, Will, an' could sail herself.' He demonstrated hands-off whilst watching the compass, but the longboat never wavered. 'We're making more than Mr Hamilton asked of us at that,' he went on cheerfully. 'There'll be some drift from this wind, an' maybe the current, depending on how right the Old Man was about a strait out there.'

Will Clarke glanced in the direction indicated, then turned to observe the receding island. It was surprisingly distant. 'If we keep this up we'll be close to the week the captain first calculated,' the young man ventured, 'rather than the fortnight.'

'Aye, Will, we could be. He's a canny old soul, though, an' rarely wrong in this sort o' thing. As a seaman he's more alert and alive than many a younger man I've met. That's why he's lasted as long as he has. He's supposed to be over eighty, though it's hard to credit. So, if the Old Man says fourteen days, that's what it'll be, near enough.'

They spoke for a while about Hugh Thompson's service under Captain Hamilton, and of the parts of the Orient they had visited together. With the island well behind them, smudging against the southern horizon, the chief officer commenced his round of the crew, allocating duties within watches to share the burden of work, and ensuring that those off watch could rest in some degree of comfort amongst the boxes, barrels, spare sails, oars and assorted cordage.

Will Clarke quickly mastered the technique of steering against successive cloud patches. Between observations of the compass, horizon, and full swell of the sails, he looked about the craft and at his companions.

He smiled to himself. William Clarke, 22 years of age. An aspiring merchant still almost raw from the company's cosy offices in Glasgow, shipwrecked by way of experience and now sharing a cockleshell of a boat in one of the world's most remote oceans with a motley crew of sixteen others. His native Scotland was as far away as it could possibly be. They were alone on the sea but, despite their position, the isolation was hard to appreciate. As a group they had been through so much together, and their new craft was sturdily built and durable, giving no feeling of frailty or vulnerability.

No-one appeared concerned at the moment. They had a job to do, and the chief officer emanated so much competence and confidence that there seemed little doubt he would complete this voyage, just as he had so many others.

Without doubt, Hugh Thompson was truly the man for this task, with his quiet assurance, obvious skills, and seaman's agility. As the chief officer did his rounds the young Scot marvelled at the man's unaided balance in the bounding longboat, noting that others moved with equal ease. The ageing captain, for all his wealth of experience, might not have coped so readily. His decision to remain on the island had clearly been the right one.

Most of the lascars he hardly knew as individuals, save two or three like Azim Prakash, who had assisted him during the unloading, or Pochari, the chief officer's boy servant. They were always willing and unfailingly courteous, though they never conversed with the officers. Only Azim, their spokesman, appeared eager to communicate. Perhaps, he mused, this was their way. Even amongst themselves he had heard little sustained or animated conversation.

He knew the other white men a little better, though there was still the inevitable barrier between himself as a known company man, and therefore a ship's officer, and the rest of the European crew. This, he knew, was *their* way. Young Tenby Read, one of the two European seamen, had been allocated by the captain as his own personal servant before their departure, but a slightly vague and hesitant manner made him a doubtful prospect in that capacity.

He checked the compass, and searched for another cloud to steer by. The grey mass was thickening, and the wind across his left shoulder seemed to have strengthened. His glance fell upon the carpenter, Job Duggan, who slept huddled in the bow with his chin on his chest. A difficult character, he was morose, uncooperative and solitary and, like his fo'c'sle mates the cook and the sailmaker, both of whom were left on Preservation Island, was neither officer nor seaman. He kept himself apart, with no time at all for the Bengalis. His presence in the boat was an uncomfortable one, the result of his hostile attitude to the Indian crew and the proximity on the island of so much hard liquor. In the captain's eyes the man was better occupied at sea than left behind with time on his hands.

'That man's trouble, a born miscreant like so many o' his kind. By all accounts, Port Jackson's full of 'em,' the old Scot had said to his second-in-command. 'Tak' him with ye, Mr Thompson, an' see he buckles to.'

Will Clarke had come in at the end of this particular exchange, unaware of the events leading up to it. At the time of the confrontation between the old Scot and the Irishman, he was already at work in the flooded hold of the *Sydney Cove*. He learned from Hugh Thompson later, however, that after broaching the first rum cask they had salvaged for their celebratory toast, more had obviously been taken a couple of evenings later by one or two of the crew, encouraged by the carpenter, who had been unable to work the following morning.

When confronted, Duggan had been openly abusive until felled by a blow from the chief officer. In the circumstances, there was little the captain could have done short of flogging the man, an odious notion at any time, though many another ship's captain would not have hesitated. Since flogging was as much impractical as it was abhorrent, the simpler solution was to place all the liquor on a small island off-shore, which they did as soon as each barrel was raised, and give the carpenter the option of working or starving.

'Nae work, nae rations, it's as simple as that,' the old man had stated flatly. His words rasped uncompromisingly. 'Mak' yer choice quickly, mon – this is no' a situation where ye can bargain! Ye're either wi' us, an' ye pu' your weight wi' the rest, or ye're no' – an' there's no future in that! Ye'll get nothin' from this party, nothin' at a'. Ye're on your own if so ye choose.' He waited for his words to sink in.

'What's it tae be?' He glared at the man lying at his feet, fingering a swollen lip. 'We've problems enough wi'out those ye bring. Let me tel't ye straight – ye're a useful man, but not indispensable. As a younger man I'd ha' half a mind tae knock some sense intae ye ma'sel'! Ye'll find it harder, though, if ye go agang us here. The choice is yours, but ye'll be a lang time hungry, that ah promise!'

The threat was fully intended, and it had the desired effect. While a man might feed himself for a while on shellfish, there was no water to be had, save through meeting the old man's demands.

Duggan had thus worked as ordered, though sullenly and without enthusiasm, and now ...

'Watch the head there, boy!' The sails rattled and strained at their bonds as the chief's harsh warning ripped across Will's inattentive mind. Startled and shamefaced, he dragged the tiller to check the boat's swing while the canvas flogged madly, surprised as he did so that the compass showed only a small deviation from course. Fran Gilbaert took the helm to regain control while the chief officer and two lascars readjusted the sails.

'Sorry about that, Will,' Hugh Thompson said as he crouched down beside the youth. 'I keep forgetting you're no seaman yet. Not entirely your fault – I should have relieved you earlier from your first spell. That was a wind shift, an' they can happen with little warning. Many's the boat that's broached an' filled when caught at the wrong moment by both wind and sea together. Not that the sea's so high yet,' he added, glancing across the darkening waves, 'but there's whitecaps showing out there in places. It'll bear watching.'

For some time the wind continued to swing. The watches were constantly on their toes, trimming the sails through the night and into the next day. The weather deteriorated into hissing rain showers, and while these were no more than a tolerable discomfort as most of the crew were already cold and damp, they meant that the moon and stars were obscured from view. Without these as guides, and unable to see the compass, the helmsman could steer only by the feel of the wind against exposed skin. Before long both their position and direction were uncertain, and only by the early light of dawn could they readjust their heading.

With the wind finally settled to blow briskly from the south-east, a lumpy sea began to rise and soon spray began to break from the crests of the waves. The spray hoods then came into their own as they kept out the worst of the quartering seas, but the boat still lurched sickeningly with every shuddering impact.

By the middle of the third afternoon they could no longer sustain the good progress without risking damage to the sails. For a while, therefore, they ran before the wind on a reduced mainsail and then, when the wind became too boisterous, on the reefed foresail alone. Eyes made raw by stinging salt strained ahead into the evening gloom for any sight of the elusive, unknown coast, or other hazards. To this uncertainty was added anxiety, increasing discomfort, and seasickness.

Men huddled alone in their misery, and little was said except that which was necessary to keep the boat correctly trimmed and moving in the approximate direction of Port Jackson. As their journey continued, time lost its meaning against the greater preoccupation of the irregular and incessant motion, sweeping nausea, physical discomfort and confinement, and lack of sleep. These rigours inevitably had their worst effects on the younger members of the crew whose experiences were still insufficient to inure them against renewed hardships.

The first to go was Hugh Thompson's servant, a small sloe-eyed lad of fourteen. Although most of the men were silent now, he had spoken little since the start of the voyage. He lay miserably against a thwart with his back to the gunwale in a feeble attempt to find relief from the ceaseless pitching until he could resist the nausea no longer. As he lurched to the side with a pitiful moan, it was only the quick hand of his master which prevented a headlong plunge into the sea. Afterwards, huddled in the crook of Thompson's protective arm, he seemed wholly oblivious of his surroundings except when racked by further spasms.

The boy's retchings could not be shut out. Two other youngsters, another lascar and Will Clarke's nineteen-year-old servant, Tenby Read, roused themselves almost simultaneously to vomit over the leeward side. Except for the watch on duty, most of the other crewmen lay or sprawled asleep where they could on thwarts or deckboards, only the occasional groan a telltale sign that the boys were not alone in their distress.

'Sir, how – how much more d'ye think there'll be o' this? Can Mr Thompson tell how f-far we've got to go? This is much worse'n bein' on the *Sydney Cove*, sir. Me belly's achin' somethin' awful, like – like I'm real poorly, an' I don't know how much more I can stand. I don't think w-we're ever goin' to get there in – in a little boat like this! I wish – I wish I'd stayed back on that island!'

The sobbing questions came from an ashen-faced, lank-haired Tenby Read, whose racking seasickness had come in such alarming spasms that he had cried out in agony, and fought to be released from the combined hold of Will Clarke and Fran Gilbaert in an effort to throw himself overboard and thus put an end to his gut-wrenching ordeal. It had taken a couple of hard, open-handed slaps from the older seaman to check his rising hysteria.

Quieter now, but still decidedly wan-looking, he lay shivering between the two men, addressing his questions to Will Clarke, the tremor in his voice betraying the barely suppressed panic. Glancing a warning to Gilbaert, Clarke made his own voice as conversational as he could.

'Just lie still where you are a wee while, and you'll soon feel better,' he replied. 'Mr Thompson's not been able tae take sightings this last day or two, with the cloud cover the way it is. The wind's eased though, and there's no rain around at the moment. I expect soon he'll be able tae work out where it is we are, as soon as he's able tae get another sun sight.'

Despite his matter-of-fact response to the question, the young Scot was aware of the difficulties the chief officer had faced in navigating. Even with an unobscured sun, the motion of such a small craft would have made accurate sextant observations difficult at any time. Given the inaccuracies of their rudimentary charts, and the likelihood of error in the precious timepiece entrusted to them by the captain, plotting a position to within even ten leagues was almost impossible. Nevertheless, he felt the need for a measure of optimism.

'Wherever we are exactly, we're heading in the right direction,' Will Clarke went on with a nod towards the boxed compass, 'and we're managing good sailing, in spite o' the weather. We might well expect tae see the coast of New South Wales almost anytime, wouldn't you agree, sir?' He addressed his question to Hugh Thompson, to draw him into the conversation.

The chief officer had been listening to the exchanges from his place at the helm, and recognised Will Clarke's ploy of making diversionary conversation to help calm and reassure the bedraggled and vomit-stained youth. He stood and stretched, handing the tiller to one of the older Bengalis. A good yarn or two might revitalise more of them, he thought – give them something to think about and take their minds off their doubts, especially with the weather on the mend.

'Aye, that's a fair statement, Mr Clarke. According to my reckoning we've covered more than a hundred miles, though drift would have added something to the real distance we've travelled. I'd need another sight to be absolutely sure, but I'd say we've passed beyond 38 degrees southerly latitude by now, and could we see clearly ahead we'd almost certainly have the coast in view.'

Heads craned at his words and eyes strained to penetrate the grey veil to the north, but their efforts brought no welcome shout. 'We've crossed Captain Furneaux's bight,' he went on, 'though I'm inclined to agree with Captain Hamilton now, after seein' seas like these, that we've more likely crossed some kind of a strait. These are not sheltered waters.'

'So, lad,' he said to Tenby Read, 'we should be over the worst soon, an' it'll improve as we close the shore. In a boat like this, though, you've no real cause for concern anyway. She's a solidly-built craft, an' as worthy a sea-boat as any afloat. Why, 'twas not ten years ago that Cap'n Bligh made his famous passage from the Friendly Islands to Timor in a boat a lot smaller than this, *an'* the same number o' people in it. Three an' a half thousand miles across an open ocean, an' not a man lost! Think of it – and we're to do little more than a tenth of that, an' much of it along a visible coast!'

Bligh! There was hardly a sailor afloat who had not heard the name. Having travelled extensively in these waters with Captain Cook in 1777 as master of the *Resolution*, William Bligh had returned briefly in command of the *Bounty*, before the ill-famed mutiny in mid-Pacific. His subsequent journey in an open, overloaded boat had become renowned throughout the maritime world, as had the later capture and trial of some of the mutineers.

What had become of the *Bounty*, the remaining mutineers, and Fletcher Christian, their ringleader, was still a mystery. Were they still alive on some unknown islands, or had the Pacific claimed them long ago? The crew's interest was caught immediately, in spite of their discomforts, and for some time they talked and speculated, forgetting their own immediate uncertainties. It was an opportunity to lift morale.

When the conversation returned to their own adventures, Fran Gilbaert told of another remarkable voyage amongst the treacherous reefs off the far western coast of New Holland.

'You might not know it,' the Dutchman began, 'but it was my countrymen who were d' first discoverers of d'is land you're now calling *Terra Australis*. Almost two hun'red years ago, long before d' English Cap'n Cook, Willem Jansz found new lands to d' south and east of our possessions in Java. *Duyfken* was d' name of his ship, as I recall.'

'Other discoveries followed in d' next twenty or thirty years, first by Hartog an' others, d'en by Abel Janszoon Tasman. We named New Holland, of course, and later Van Diemen's Land, but no one realised at d' time d'at here was all part of one bigger land. D'at came later. For a long time we had a fast, secret route which our traders used to reach Batavia. Once round d' Cape, d'ey rode d' westerlies eastwards, along d' path of d' Roaring Forties, until d'ey turned northwards up d' coast of Eendracht's Land and Edel Land to d' very west. We would have crossed dat route ourselfs, sometime before d' storms.'

'Some of our ships was wrecked,' he told his enthralled audience, 'very early on. A hun'red an' fifty years ago, at least. 'Twas a bad coast wit' many reefs, a lee shore all along for d'ose unlucky enough to go a little too far to d' east before making off to d' north. Even our own Captain Hamilton would have been uneasy about turning eastwards d'en.' On reflection, Hugh Thompson knew that to be a nice understatement of the Old Man's concern, but said nothing.

'One ship I have in mind was d' *Batavia*, a vessel of d' *Vereenigde Oost-Indische Compagnie*, d' Nederlands East India Company d'at was, commanded by Francois Pelsaert. I don't recall exact numbers, but over three hun'red people was saved at first, and got onto some little islands. D'en Pelsaert, like us, had to go for help. Java was d' nearest place to get it, over a t'ousand miles away. But he got d'ere – with forty or fifty of his people, so dey say, in a boat jus' like d'is one.' He looked significantly at Tenby Read, whose mouth hung open in wonder and disbelief, his illness temporarily forgotten.

'Even so, d' story didn't end d'ere,' he went on. 'No. When Pelsaert got back to d' islands wit' a rescue ship, he found more d'an half d' people he had left behind dead – murdered, no less. He soon discovered d'at a merchant by d' name of Cornelius had made himself up to be king of d' islands, an' his followers had killed over a hun'red of d' survivors, while oders was drownded or died of disease. D'ey had taken d' gold chests from d' *Batavia* an' intended to seize d' rescue ship and turn pirate jus' as soon as Pelsaert returned.'

He had everyone's full attention as each listener pictured the drama. 'However,' he continued, 'after some small fightings d'ey was overcome by Pelsaert and his men, who had been warned by certain of d' other survivors from another island, who joined up wit' 'em. D' ship's officers set up a – a court on d' spot, and tried all of d'ose d'ey said was murderers. Some d'ey hanged straight away, including d' madman Cornelius after d'ey cut off his hands. Oders was taken to Batavia for punishment. Of all d' three hun'red souls saved from d' wreck, only a hun'red or so ever reached Java, including all d' first group with Pelsaert.'

Such absorbing tales as this were meat and drink to the seafarers, and even Azim had seen fit to translate for the benefit of the lascars who could not follow Fran Gilbaert's accented English. They plied him with questions until both his knowledge and imagination were exhausted, but then he had other stories to tell the willing listeners.

'Not long afterwards d'ere was another Dutch shipwreck, of *De Vergulde Draeck*, d' *Golden Dragon*,' he began – but a sharp cry from the lookout in the bows instantly robbed him of his audience.

'*Aranzi! Latmaibahr! Land!* Land ahead an' – an' breakers, sah!' A lascar seaman called excitedly, pointing ahead. Everyone craned to see through the thinning haze, the Dutchman's story forgotten. Not a mile in front could be seen a low-lying coast, impossible to distinguish as either island or reef – a mere smudge of a line with a visible forefront of breaking waves.

Hugh Thompson quickly asserted his authority to quell the rising excitement and to keep the people in their places. Already the proximity of the shore could be felt in the sharper motions of the waves. Any mass movement could further upset the trim. He realised then that these signs had been present for some time. The dying of the wind, the dark persistent haze ahead, and the choppiness of the shallowing sea were normally harbingers of land and should have given warning, but other usual signs – distinct land smells, weed, and increasing numbers of seabirds – were absent.

He stared ahead. The breakers were faintly audible and he could see the narrow strand behind. He had no wish to approach too closely, however, without knowing what else lay in the murk. The coast remained tantalisingly veiled, low and insignificant with nothing visible beyond.

He ordered sail adjustments to turn downwind and pushed the tiller bar across, swinging parallel to the distant breakers, pointing easterly for the first time. Soon they knew they had reached their initial objective, and the first leg was over.

'Break out the rations lads, this is worth a little celebration! The worst's behind us now, an' it'll be plain sailing from here on. As soon as we can find a place to land an' lie up for a day, we'll do that, ready for the last leg. Port Jackson in four or five days, provided the weather holds! If it doesn't, though, we can always shelter close inshore now.'

He awoke suddenly to the rattle and slashing sting of hailstones beating upon them from the night. Lightning briefly split the darkness, its suffused rippling in the low cloud making all the contorted sea visible for an instant. Ranks of cresting whitecaps leapt up beyond the stern, leaving Will Clarke with a fleeting image of Hugh Thompson crouched at the tiller, battling to keep the boat steady, before darkness closed in again. It was bitterly cold.

It had become obvious as darkness fell that the chief officer's earlier optimism had been premature, for the wind had gathered renewed strength, adding a driving rain which quickly obliterated the nearby coast. As the first hail pelted and bounced around the boat and its cowering occupants, the rising wind and a distinctly falling temperature warned them of a difficult night ahead.

'Curse this blasted weather, Will,' Thompson had shouted above the lash of the storm. 'We're like a cork in a maelstrom! If this keeps up we could be in real trouble. Of all the places to encounter this kind o' blow, we're in just about the worst! A lee shore that we can't see,' he yelled, 'no prospect of setting any sail to beat away from the land, an' weather just about as bad as it gets!'

More lightning cracked, and thunder rolled across the leaping seas. The wind caught a breaking comber and swept a cold stinging spray across the boat as she lurched under the impact of a following wave. Hugh Thompson staggered and the boat slewed momentarily, but his skill and seamanship instantly checked the movement as other waves rose and fell threateningly alongside. All was confusion as the seas dashed at them, first one way, then the other, thoroughly soaking everything they encountered in their ceaseless searching swirl.

'There's too much water collecting under the bottom boards, Will! Kick some o' these laggards into life an' get them baling! I've a feeling we'll be spending most o' tonight just keeping ourselves afloat an' alive. It's getting worse by the minute!'

To add weight to his words another massive wave crashed over them and brought a frenzy of movement to those so abruptly awakened. They needed no encouragement to shift the cascading waters back over the side. Most had been at sea long enough to recognise the dangerous situation they were in, after the earlier excitement and welcome reassurances of the day. The chief officer's cries gave an extra edge of urgency.

'Look lively there, an' bale fast! Use whatever you can! We haven't come this far tae sink in this God-forsaken backwater, damn ye! Put your backs into it!' He flung out words in both English and Bengali, though they made little difference to the crew's already frantic efforts as wave after wave burst across them. The weather cloths with which they had raised the height of the gunwales turned much of the green water that tried to climb aboard unbroken, whilst the carpenter's improvised canopies fore and aft saved them more than once as the longboat plunged and rolled, reared ponderously and then plunged anew with each successive wave.

More than two hours passed, with the crew visibly weakening under the constant need to bale and the untiring onslaughts of the elements, before Hugh Thompson was forced to make the only possible decision. To ride out the storm so close to land was virtually suicidal, and yet they were powerless to run away from the coast without risking their precious sails or broaching in a beam sea. The wind blew a strong sou'westerly, threatening to drive them ashore if they raised so much as a rag. In such a precarious position, however difficult it might prove to be, they had to remain as close as possible to where they were.

The chief officer beckoned. 'Will! Go for'rard an' have the carpenter prepare the bow anchors for letting go when I give the signal,' he called out. 'Then come back here. We'll have to lie bows-to in this sea. We'll put one over first an' drift off it, then drop the second an' adjust the warps to lie evenly to the two. Tell him to allow plenty of scope for riding this lot out – he'll know what to do!' The supercargo nodded vigorously and turned to pick his way through the scooping throng, while Thompson addressed the lascar foreman.

'Azim, have six of your people set up an oar each while we secure ourselves on the anchors! Make sure the rest keep themselves an' the water down while we swing beam on. It'll be rough!' In almost continuous lightning flashes, white teeth showed briefly in the man's dark streaming face, acknowledging the officer's needs before a broken stream of Bengali had the half-dozen fittest lascars retrieving the oars and fitting them between the pins.

One anchor was dropped, then the other as the first caught and turned the bow. As the anchors seized and held, the seamen manoeuvred against the drift with difficulty while the necessary adjustments were made to the cables for safely riding out the storm. Thus secured, they began the battle for survival in a titanic struggle against the raging, merciless sea.

For most of the people in the longboat, that night was the longest of their entire lives. While the seas crashed in weltering foam, and the winds battered and roared with rising intensity, every man knew raw fear in those grim dark hours, a yawning terror born of their frenzied efforts to stave off any final cataclysmic plunge. Each felt the close proximity of death, alone in the open ocean as the waves clawed and surged and broke upon them, threatening almost every moment to swamp their frail craft.

Times without number enormous crests poised darkly above them, awesome in their proximity, whilst the boat pitched and slanted amongst the piling, lightning-lit masses, every hour a lifetime, every minute an urgent battle to free themselves of their swirling burden before the next could plunge the entire complement into watery oblivion. It was a gruelling night of nonstop, seemingly unendurable labouring, of endless backbreaking toil, borne only in order to preserve their very lives.

So much depended on the anchor's grip in the sands beneath, and on their slender, jarring lines. In a boat often half-filled with water they each faced fear and anxiety at every turn as the night wore on, drawing on incredible reserves of strength and fortitude.

By early morning, as a grey day dawned, they knew they were close to total exhaustion, their courage and endurance spent. The shore was not too distant, but a violent surf showed whitely through the rising salt spray, driving inland across low-lying dunes ahead of the blustering wind. It was a coast devoid of features, without help or haven, but they had to move on.

'Ready-up the fores'l for hoisting, lads, an' let's have some oars outboard.' Hugh Thompson croaked and gestured wearily, his mouth and throat salt burned. They were all in the same sorry state. Shelter would have to be found soon if they were to recover enough for the remainder of their journey. 'We'll need to cut the anchor cables to free ourselves here. We'll never raise them otherwise after a night like the last, with us worn out an' the flukes dug hard in. Sever the bights,' he indicated to Azim and the carpenter, 'an' make sail as soon as we're free. Ready there with oars, an' watch her as she swings!'

As the lines parted and the sail began to fill, there was no way that anyone could have predicted what happened next. Hugh Thompson had intended to free the craft, then move aslant of downwind parallel to the shoreline until they could find a suitable cove, bay or estuary in which to lie up or land, to somehow start a fire and regain their strength before venturing on. In the leaping seas and deep troughs, however, partially blanketed from the wind, the narrow foresail was not fully effective, nor had the boat gathered sufficient steering way to respond quickly enough to the mischievous waves, or to prevent the disaster which followed.

A large quartering sea rose alongside to tilt the craft landward, robbing her sail of what little pull and windage had been gained. The tiller was useless in Hugh Thompson's fist as the boat lost way and slewed sideways, still tilting beam on. The pitching of the longboat smashed oars from the hands of the helpless sailors, turning them into water-borne projectiles.

The angle of the boat dumped a handful of men sideways to the lower gunwale at the same time as another rising sea punched upwards against her clinkered flanks. That instant was enough to badly upset her already precarious trim as the lee side dipped further and swirled beneath the foam.

Cries of alarm sounded as the head swept round and men flung themselves upwards in a desperate attempt to throw their weight back into and against the stricken longboat, to steady and right her in an automatic response to deadly peril. Stern on to the shore-bearing seas, her bows pitched heavily under the sluggish deadweight of water and the tangle of men who floundered within, but at least her rudder gained some slight purchase. However, nothing remained of the sail and the carpenter's spray-hoods.

'*Hang on lads, we're going ashore!*' Hugh Thompson roared his warning as a huge, surfing roller hurled their craft bodily towards the beckoning strand. For the unfortunate men already in the sea they could do nothing.

Because of the excess weight of water inboard, the longboat did not ride well, though their angle to the oncoming waves saved them from any imme-diate broaching. The massive wave surged ahead whilst their craft was momentarily becalmed, helpless and half-filled, in an intervening trough.

'*Bale, for Christ's sake,*' bellowed the chief officer urgently, his voice hoarse with strain, 'don't sit there like a line o' bleedin' bollards! Bale before we're swamped!'

To add weight to his words, he lashed out with a length of anchor cable, his words lost in the next mighty surge that gathered them up and swept them towards the beach at terrifying speed.

'*We're going in! Hang on tight before she hits!*' Powerless to determine where they went, from the top of the high comber they saw the conflicting turmoil of receding waves pouring back down a steep beach into the seething maelstrom that lay ahead, and then the boat twisted, slewing upwards an instant before the tumbling break.

The boat canted and rolled, flinging men helplessly into the boiling surf, rising briefly before canting steeply again into the foaming torrent.

Will Clarke felt himself lifted in a blur of darkening green and swirling grey, the breath smashed from his body as he was plunged deep beneath the scouring rollers. He felt the powerful backwash draw him down, his hair and ears filled with rolling sand, cold salt water stinging his eyes, filling mouth and lungs as he choked, gasped and fought his way back to the broken surface around him. Once more he was lifted bodily and flung shoreward like limp flotsam, though he still clung to enough of his senses to reach out for a dark, sodden mass that surged lifelessly against him, and to race towards the tortured beach with it clutched in his grasp as the next wave caught and swept him forward.

Hugh Thompson quickly lost track of the bewildering events in the paling dawn. As the bows dipped he clung hard to the tiller and braced himself against the sternsheets, feeling the boat falling away beneath him. For a weightless instant he hung out of the craft as it turned over, tossing most of those still aboard into the welter of foam. Almost in slow motion the lee gunwale dipped further and further beneath the crests, all their bundles and carefully stowed packages bursting forth in abandon, oars and thwarts and other loose timbers flinging asunder as if blasted by cannon shot.

He saw the carpenter standing waist deep and horror-stricken for a second before the sinking bow plunged him fully under, then a moment later clinging like a rag doll to the stump of the broken mast, together with two of the lascar crewmen.

A snatch of grey sky and windswept beach, a swirl of mounting foam to lift them high and fling them forward, sensations of strength in his right arm still gripped hard to the helm and of a soft body held against his own by his left arm before a tumbling, raging roar burst over and around, chest-high as he struggled to stay upright. The chief officer's fleeting impressions were interrupted by a sickening lurch that cast him headlong into the icy swell, battering him cruelly against the crippled craft.

At that moment Fran Gilbaert let himself go and allowed the surge that had dumped the longboat hard against a submerged bar to carry him out and forward as it swept towards the sloping sands. Though his lungs threatened to burst as he struggled towards the foaming surface, he swam powerfully to keep some kind of station, letting the currents carry him where they would.

In the water near to hand, he counted half a dozen heads, European and lascar. The longboat still plunged ahead of him, rolling violently until lost from view beyond an intervening crest. As the waters again gathered beneath him, he struck out shorewards, glimpsing the longboat wallowing beam on, seemingly empty, the waters around littered with spreading flotsam. With an effort he flung himself onto the next boiling surge that bore swiftly towards the shelving beach, noting that several of the lascars did likewise, Azim close by with another at his shoulder.

Shifting sand moved around his feet for a brief second and he let himself be thrown forward as the wave broke, saving his own energy until that of the wave was spent, whereupon he struck out valiantly against the suck of the undertow. After what seemed an eternity he felt firmer sand and shingle beneath his feet, and the dragging weight of his sodden clothing as he stumbled forward to collapse at the water's edge.

'*The boat! We must hold the boat!*' The sharp cry from Azim pierced his brain. Unthinking, he pulled himself to his feet to help, staggering under the unaccustomed weight of his clothing and the unyielding *terra firma*.

'The longboat, Mr Clarke, sah! We must bring in the boat!' The repeated cry, this time from Azim to the supercargo who was struggling ashore with the limp body of an Indian seaman. Another lay at Azim's feet, prone beneath the foreman's outflung arm. The boat was slowly being drawn out to sea again. Their sole means of survival was slipping away while they lay defeated on the sea-beaten sands.

Three men plunged heedlessly back into the cascading surf, but the upended longboat was already purposefully rolling in again towards the shore.

'Don't get too close to d' boat if she comes in fast, sir,' Fran Gilbaert called to Will Clarke. 'She's a heavily built craft an' could easily break d' legs of anyone she's flung against near d' beach! We'd best wait wit' ropes near d' shore to hold her when she grounds, oderwise she's like to break up quickly if she's dump too offen!'

Weak with exhaustion, Will Clarke numbly concurred, for it was all he could do to stay afloat. They struck out together, using flotsam to carry them in. Fran Gilbaert angled off and collected the inert body of Tenby Read, which he dragged to the beach before collapsing again at the waterline.

For the longboat, though, there was little they could do. As others struggled ashore through the surf, the upturned craft seemed to hover indecisively between sea and strand, wallowing sluggishly. Then, broached once more, a chance wave cast her upright and bore her rapidly towards them. A second breaker following through with much greater power took over the boat's momentum, and, though the bewildered men prepared to seize the rampant craft, there was nothing they could do to halt the wave's headlong rush as it hurled the huge boat bodily onto the steeply shelving sands with an ominous, rending crack.

The stoutly timbered vessel weighed many hundreds of pounds and was deadweight on the sloping foreshore as the tumbling waves momentarily receded. Before the confused and weakened seamen could act to secure the craft, the next surging wave had seized it greedily, and borne it away from their feeble grasp.

The forceful cycle was repeated yet again whilst the onlookers stood by helplessly, or were brushed aside in dangerous attempts to restrain the boat, as each surging rush was accompanied by the sound of breaking timbers. Through the thundering roar of the pounding waves, each shattering impact sounded like the knell of doom.

By the time they had retrieved enough rope from the drifting tangle of flotsam, it was too late. The longboat had been their one real prospect for survival and rescue, the sole means of journeying safely to Port Jackson with news of the shipwreck, and the only likely hope for Captain Hamilton's party still stranded on Preservation Island. Now she lay splintered on the beach as a forlorn and battered wreck, her bows badly smashed in a welter of tumbling foam, her clinkered sides broken and scattered by the attacking sea.

5

MISFORTUNES UNKNOWN
AND UNPITIED ...

12TH MARCH, 1797. *The severe weather of the past few days has eas'd, together with the trials of the people. The shelters we have, tho' cleverly made, have proved no more than makeshift defences against the inclement wind and rain of our expos'd situation. It is to be hoped that the longboat party made progress enough to escape the worst of the squalls and now stand fair towards Port Jackson. At times such as these are we remind'd of our own fragile dependence upon them, and how tenuous is their venture. Two men, one the cook, have become ill from consuming taint'd water.*

FROM THE SHIP'S LOG

A few hours later, the wreckage of the stricken longboat and its contents lay strewn along the high water mark for some distance up and down the beach. The scattered relics of their late craft were punctuated by thick rolls of kelp, swollen stubs of native vegetation, heaps of broken shell, and the odd half-rotted carcass of some unfortunate sea creature.

Though the storm was past its peak, the tumbling waves still drove threateningly ashore, breaking and spreading whitely in the irregular sunshine. The receding tide and the raggedly stepped beach front meant that the recumbent bodies of the survivors higher up the sands were safe in their exhausted rest. During the hour after their stranding they had succeeded in wrestling the cumbersome longboat ashore and hastily snatching objects from the waves, though few in their advanced state of fatigue were fully aware of what they were doing, or why. Their ordeals had left them stunned, wearied, and overwhelmed. Responses and movements had been automatic and unthinking, until one by one they had collapsed to sleep where they fell.

In the early afternoon Hugh Thompson stirred from his resting place, as sure as he could be that they had saved all they were able to. Whatever the days ahead might bring, they at least had some material resources. Also Will Clarke had told him that everyone in the party was safe and accounted for, which in itself was a miracle, and almost unbelievable.

Will Clarke mumbled and moved uneasily in sleep, but the chief officer forbore to speak and so fully wake him, instead soaking up the warming sun in his aching bones a while longer as he turned their plight over in his mind. Despite the privations of the past few days, he suspected the real ordeal was only just beginning.

Unless they could make the boat seaworthy – and that seemed distinctly unlikely – they were faced with the forbidding prospect of a long arduous trek through totally unknown country, with only scant resources and their fortitude to see them through. It was a forbidding prospect.

He shook his head. His mouth was dry and the taste of salt was strong on his lips and whiskers. His eyes felt raw and red-rimmed as he stared around the beach, and his clothes hung damply, adding to his discomfort. Upending a keg they had broached earlier, he drank deeply of its cool contents, forgetting the need to conserve water, and in doing so felt better.

Hearing dull footsteps and movement on the sand, Will Clarke rolled over and sat up, staring uncomprehendingly for a moment before reality once more asserted itself.

Seeing the movement, Thompson spoke. 'Aye, Will, a pretty pass you'd be thinking, an' rightly so. We are at least four hundred miles from Port Jackson, on a deserted shore an' barely two sticks of our boat holding together. With the grumbling bellies of seventeen starving men, an' the fact that no-one knows we're here, I'd wager it'll take some beating as a second disaster!'

He embraced the scene with the sweep of an arm. 'Welcome to *Terra Australis Incognita*,' he added wryly. 'As you can see, there's a lot of it,

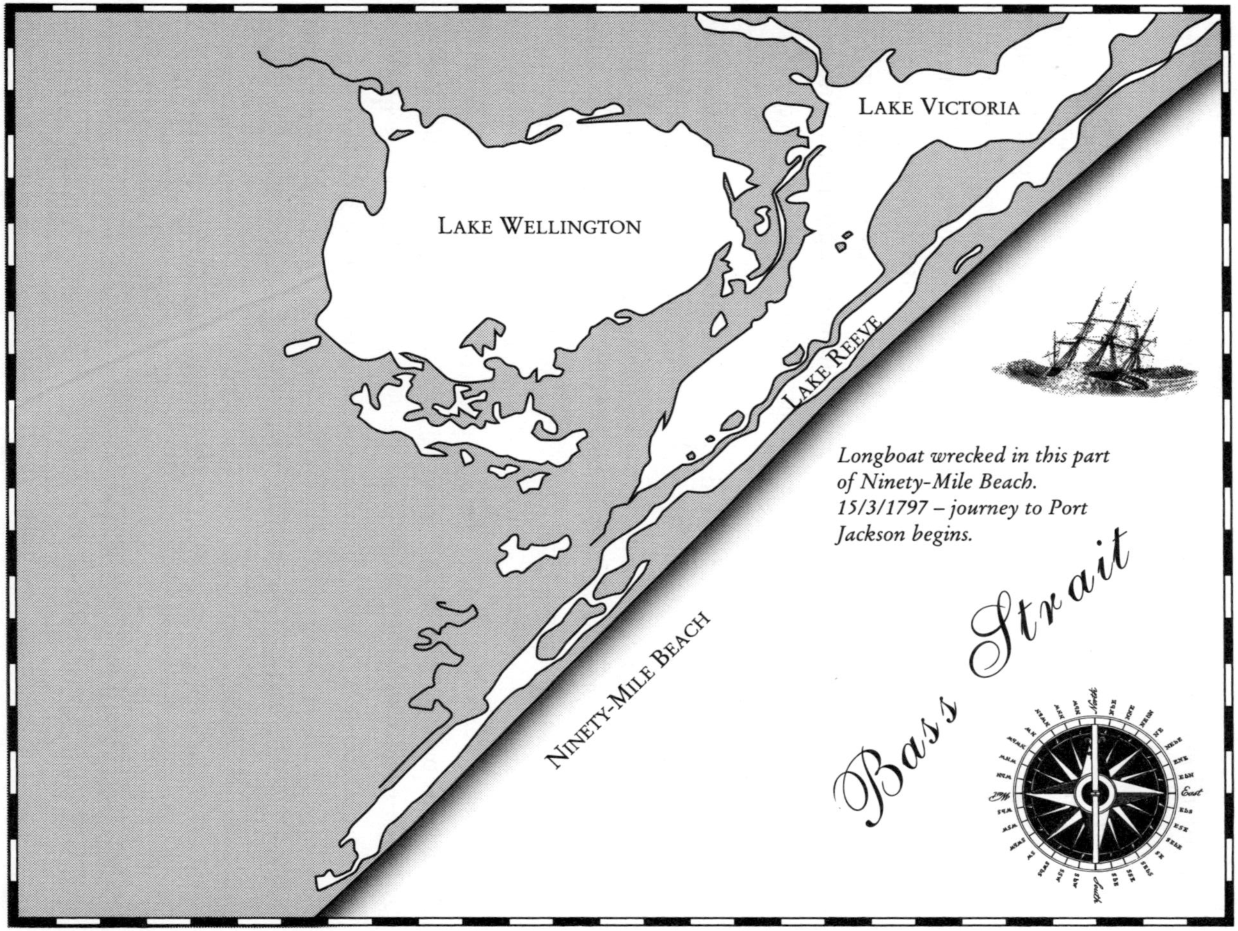
LAKE WELLINGTON
LAKE VICTORIA
LAKE REEVE
NINETY-MILE BEACH
Longboat wrecked in this part of Ninety-Mile Beach. 15/3/1797 – journey to Port Jackson begins.
Bass Strait
North
East
South

MAP 4. *Present-day western area of the Gippsland Lakes, Victoria, and the vicinity of the longboat wreck site. Journey to Port Jackson begins 15 March 1797.*

though it's not overly inviting or encouraging. Maybe it'll improve, as we get to know it better over the next few weeks. Judging from the look of the wreck, I'd say we've got a lot more walking to do yet, my friend.' He pushed the keg across.

Will glanced about thoughtfully, drying his mouth on the back of a hand. The remains of the longboat lay at the water's edge, a contorted mass of sprung planks and smashed thwarts, the bones of the craft already embedded in the shifting sands.

In several parts and showing a splintered keel, it was beyond repair. Though stern and midships appeared reasonably sound, the bows had been badly stove in by the passage through the surf. Whole sections of the starboard strakes had loosened or broken free, to become almost half-buried in the storm-piled sand.

All around them he saw nothing but scrub-covered dunes backed by dark bush, an arid grey-green carpet which spread out and merged eventually into the distant, shadowed hills. With the sun temporarily behind a leadenly persistent cover of cloud, the country had a gloomy, unappealing aspect, without colour or warmth. The young supercargo shivered.

'Do you – do you really think we can make it?' he asked diffidently, his voice still hoarse from the salt-dryness. He gave a nervous laugh and gestured towards the woods. 'I mean tae say, four or five hundred miles o' that, our food stocks very likely spoiled an' seventeen of us for a journey of . . . I couldn't guess how long. Do you really believe it possible?'

The chief officer sucked his teeth reflectively. 'It'll be no mean walk, I'm prepared to admit. I'm sure you'd be the first to agree though, we don't really have much choice. We've got to make at least some kind of attempt, or sit here an' rot. Put bluntly, it's march or die! We have to face that. Captain Hamilton an' the others on Preservation Island are relying on us for their salvation, so we have to get through to Port Jackson somehow for their sakes, as soon as we can, if we can, an' God willing!'

He paused in thought. 'Even so, if I'm absolutely honest, one or two of us mightn't make it all the way. It'll be a fair test, I'm thinking, but one we should all be capable of. Our servants, as two of the youngest among us, might give us problems – but we're supposed to be the best an' fittest of the crew, lad, didn't the Old Man tell us so himself? An' you should be the fittest of us all, I'd say, what with all the tramping you've already done round Cape Barren Island. Maybe I should send you on ahead, eh!'

The Englishman's attempt at levity and encouragement failed to penetrate Will Clarke's doubt and apprehension.

'Is there water here?' the latter persisted earnestly, emphasising his concern. Food, water, clothing and adequate footwear, arms and equipment – all matters usually needing a supercargo's attention. There was much to be attended to.

With a flush of guilt, Thompson remembered his earlier extravagance at the water cask. 'We've only got what we've salvaged. If there *is* a shortage of water, we're in trouble.'

'More trouble' he added reflectively. 'We'll send out parties as soon as we can get the people organised. Meanwhile, let's rouse 'em an' shift that boat further up the beach out the way o' the tide, even if it is useless.'

He grinned and clapped his companion on the shoulder as they rose together. 'We have to look on the bright side, Will, even if things do seem bad, as they no doubt will from time to time. To have survived one shipwreck an' escaped as lightly as we did is good fortune indeed, an' right lucky we were. To have survived two, though, is nothing less than divine intervention! The gods are smiling, so they're surely on our side! What's a few hundred miles, then?'

Job Duggan confirmed the chief officer's pessimism about the broken longboat. As they examined the wreckage, the carpenter's words put an end to any hope there might have been of either salvaging the vessel or building another from her remains.

'Sure, Chief, an' if I had a full set o' tools, an' time enough for the work t' be done the way it deserves, I daresay I could've fashioned a stout little craft from most o' this.' The carpenter kicked dolefully at the splintered woodwork, part of which broke away in spongy flakes. He stooped and crumbled a piece between thick fingers, shaking his head.

'Ye can see why she broke up so easily, as unseaworthy as she was, an' all. Well past her best, an' rotten in places. Firewood it is, no better,' he went on bitterly, 'an' all we had t' save ourselves. 'Tis a blessing that we're not all drowned, days ago!' His tone held a hint of righteous hurt and reproval.

'I might likely have been able t' patch one or two o' the sounder timbers t'gether on the best parts, well-caulked mind, with mebbe just a saw an' brace. But with only the axe ...'

He let the sentence hang. 'There's not even a single stone around, t' help keep it sharp. Sure, an' it's no use. It's the walkin' it'll have t' be, if we're t' leave this cursed place!'

Hugh Thompson's lips tightened beneath his beard. There was nothing he could add or suggest, and for the first time in many years he felt inadequate and helpless. Whether the carpenter could indeed have constructed a small boat, using materials from the larger one was moot, and beside the point anyway. They had lost the most useful items aboard the longboat during the spills in the rampaging surf. An ill-made or crudely repaired vessel would expose them to too high a risk should they ever be rash enough to commit their trust to it.

As the sinking of the *Sydney Cove* not so long ago had already shown them, a single sprung plank could quickly threaten them all. Hugh Thompson therefore accepted the Irishman's authoritative verdict, if for no other reason than that the man would not welcome the prospect of a four or five hundred mile walk if it could be avoided, any more than he did himself.

The fortunes of the group were thus irrevocably cast. Over the next two days each man came to terms with the prospect of a taxing, arduous journey through unexplored land. The European sailors each wondered privately how he himself might fare, and what they might together encounter in their daunting undertaking. Despite all the unknowns, however, they accepted the reality of their fate, knowing there were no options and hoping for the best. The alternative to pushing through to Port Jackson was to perish in the unfriendly bush, though this realisation struck some less forcefully than others.

Azim Prakash and his men, on the other hand, accepted their lot with an almost cheerful resignation. Their Hindu beliefs had long conditioned them to accepting circumstances more readily and with less trepidation than their European shipmates. For the lascar seamen this adventure was unavoidably part of each man's destiny, and the outcome lay in the hands of their collective gods, unknown but unquestioningly accepted.

The first and second days of their stranding were spent in collecting any further articles that washed ashore, in sorting and preparing the meagre resources left at their disposal, and in arranging their plans. Hugh Thompson wished to ensure that all was completely ready before setting out, and that the men were fully recovered and rested from their ordeal and subsequent exertions a whole day before the final commitment to the march. The two youngest, the lascar Pochari and Tenby Read, having been dragged ashore comatose by Fran Gilbaert and the chief officer, himself barely conscious, had lain mutely ill, and it was essential that they be restored to health before the move.

But there was much to be done while they regained their strength. A scouting party sent out that afternoon returned quickly through the overgrown dunes, eagerly reporting the discovery of tolerably potable water in a long, narrow lake beyond the thick tangle of coastal scrub. The news was heartening and gladly received, for all knew that they would never progress far without this vital refreshment. It was to be a nagging concern, nevertheless, all the way along this unknown, mostly unbountiful coast.

Immediately after being cast ashore, the crew had managed to rescue four nine-gallon water casks from the longboat, all full and intact. A fifth was split and contained only seawater, another had been crushed by the madly plunging vessel as it smashed through the surf, and the other two had been lost entirely. With an alternative water supply assured for the time being, the four precious casks were slung on poles fashioned from cut-down oars for carrying with them on their journey. Wherever possible, other water would be collected during the march in order to sustain their reserves against uncertainty.

But although they had this reassuring means of replenishing and transporting enough water for seventeen men, the quantity of food they had been able to save was by no means so encouraging, nor so readily replaceable. The supplies of rice and dhal from the ship and dried meat from the islands had been sufficient only for the expected duration of the boat trip, to be supplemented by any game, fish or greenstuffs they could secure wherever they might subsequently land. However, it would now take much longer than planned to reach their destination.

The overall duration of the journey was no longer estimable with any degree of certainty. They had no real idea of where they were, and their rescued sea-charts, no more than a little damp in their hollow bamboo stowage, told them nothing of the way ahead except for direction and a dozen or so notable landmarks. The distance they would have travelled by sea had been a best-estimate, drawn from a series of straight-line projections along the crudely mapped shores. That would have been arduous enough, but now they faced a journey far different, of many hundreds of miles on foot along a tortuous coastline.

Because of the coast's unknown nature, the charts had taken scant account of the multitudes of lesser bays, headlands and river mouths that were to add an untold number of miles to their wanderings, and of the mountains, swamp and scrub that would inhibit their progress. These would inevitably add to their fatigue, and might eventually stretch their resources – physical, mental and material – to breaking-point. It was a discouraging prospect.

Where previously their provisions had seemed adequate, the reserves from the longboat shrank alarmingly on closer examination. Some of the rice had been spoiled despite the double bags in which it had been carried, and was thus eaten quickly to avoid its total waste. Great efforts were made to dry the rest in the heat of the sun, whilst part of the meat hoard had to be re-sorted and dried again.

Much to their dismay, they discovered that their entire reserve of dried shellfish had not travelled well. Having developed an unpleasant smell, even without the slime from prolonged wetness in the boat, it was too dangerous to either keep or consume. Sickness from bad food was something they dared not risk, and so the whole unsavoury mass was discarded – on Thompson's instructions.

As for the prospect of hunting, the one musket retrieved from the wreckage had quickly rusted and refused to discharge, although the powder had been carefully dried and the rust scraped away. Neither were their two remaining pistols in any better state. They were left with only their dirks and a brace of cutlasses, neither an effective means of hunting. It soon became obvious, from their reduced means of self help and from what remained of the shipboard provisions, that their stock of foodstuffs would have to be severely rationed to last the journey unless, like water, other sources could be found along the way.

The adequate feeding of seventeen men each day loomed as a spectre that was rarely to be banished. The prospect of malnourishment during the walk, with an accompanying likelihood of scurvy, did not augur well for its success. With the possibility of needing to rely eventually on friendly natives for food, they decided to take with them such pieces of cloth, metal and other trinkets as they could muster, in order to obtain by barter what they could not secure for themselves.

Having stripped out any usable sailcloth and cordage, they burned the boat to recover its nails and fittings, as well as for warmth. To one or two who looked upon the flames, this destruction seemed a portent, a final severing of links with the outside world. Whatever else might befall, there could be no going back.

On the morning their journey was to begin Hugh Thompson called his men together in readiness for departure. On a stretch of smoothed sand he traced the known coast as shown on their copy of the chart originally drawn by Captain Cook. With Azim translating his words so that each lascar would fully understand his intent within the uncertainties of their position, he began to outline the plan of their march, as far as he was able.

'Here we've got Botany Bay, Cape Dromedary, Cape Howe an' Point Hicks,' he stated, pointing at each. 'Just north o' Botany Bay we've got Port Jackson, while southward here is Van Diemen's Land. We ran the *Sydney Cove* ashore here, on Furneaux's Islands. The gap you see there, which Captain Furneaux believed to be a deep bay, is what Captain Hamilton believes is a strait – which would make Van Diemen's Land an island. Here's where we sailed in the longboat.' The longboat's track became another groove in the sand.

'Well now,' he continued, warming to his subject, 'as I see it, we're on a long coast running almost due east-west, as we can judge from the rising and setting of the sun. The chart shows no such coast. If Captain Cook's chart's right, an' I'm in no position to disagree with him, this'd tell me three things. Firstly, I'd say no European ship has ever been along this way to offer corrections to the charts of these waters. The French or the Spaniards might have,' he added, 'but they wouldn't tell us, of course.'

'Secondly, Captain Hamilton's probably right about a strait, in which case it would run back west here into the Southern Ocean. There it is behind us now, an' it's not looking much like a bay to me. Thirdly, we must be somewhere west of Point Hicks, in the blank area there, on the coast o' the strait.'

He looked at Will Clarke, who nodded in silent agreement. 'It makes sense, especially after the rough passage we had. Those waves didn't build up in enclosed waters. I don't rightly know where we are, though, as we got no sights before landing and the sextant's out there on the seabed.' He nodded seawards, to where the longboat had capsized.

'No matter. My guess is we're about here,' he went on, making a cross on the etched sand. 'And that would mean we're a good four hundred miles or more from Port Jackson, maybe even five hundred if we count in all the curly bits. Coves an' forelands,' he added, in response to Azim's puzzled glance. 'They'll very likely add a lot to the distance.' The Indian flashed his white-toothed grin and translated into rapid Bengali, but there were no smiles from the lascars.

'So, by my reckoning, if we can cover fifteen miles each day we ought to reach Port Jackson in thirty days, or a bit longer if we're held up. Mr Clarke can note how long it takes, an' will keep a log.' He pointed to the northward-reaching coastline on the sand-map. 'At least those who've seen the shore here recorded it as fairly straight, with no big bays or estuaries to confound us. Let's hope so, for the going'll be a lot easier then.'

He scanned the faces around him, awaiting comment or reaction. It came in tones of veiled truculence and doubt from Job Duggan.

'Ye've just said ye don't know where it is we are, an' now ye're saying we've got all this way t' walk, an' then mebbe more! Are ye sure ye know we'll be goin' in the right direction when we start? I mean, we wouldn't want t'be travellin' all these hundreds o' miles, on'y t' find we haven't arrived when we get there. An' how'll we know where it is we are when we do get there, if ye don't even know where we are now?'

He looked at the other crewmen for support, but Azim had ceased his translation. The carpenter's feelings were nevertheless evident in his rebellious tones. 'Seems t'me we might well go the other way to Port Jackson,' he concluded with a scowl, 'partic'larly if we sailed past it in the storm. It wouldn't be so far t' walk then.'

The chief officer looked steadily at his challenger, sensing the carpenter's distrust of his plan, and possibly his leadership. This was discord they could not afford. The man's objection made no sense, and he was obviously incapable of reading the simplest indicators of their position.

'Navigation's my department, Mister,' Hugh Thompson retorted bluntly, 'same as working wood's yours. We've both been doing it for years, so I won't tell you how to do your job, an' you don't try to tell me mine.

We didn't pass Port Jackson in the storm,' he went on pointedly, 'because we haven't been out long or far enough, an' the winds were more likely blowing us west.'

'Because of the contrary winds,' he explained patiently, 'we're close to where I said, but we won't be more sure until we've seen Point Hicks in relation to Cape Howe – the coast turns sharp north there. As for the right way, we've only got two choices – east along this beach, or west to God knows where, an' I'm pretty sure I can tell t'other from which! You had your decision on the state o' the longboat. This un's mine an' ye'd better believe it!'

The carpenter dropped his gaze, but his scowl deepened. 'That's a chart drawn by real seamen ye have there,' he persisted, 'real explorers from the King's own navy who were sent out special like t' make it, an' yet you'd be tellin' us it's no good! An' why, I'm askin'? Why, Captain Cook would've used it t' come here two, three times, but ye're still believin' old Captain Hamilton when he says it's all wrong.'

He glared at Thompson defiantly. 'What does that old man know about it, when it was good enough for a man like James Cook? He got us wrecked, an' dam' near drowned in the first place. Why, sure, an' if it hadn't been ...'

'Belay that, blast ye! I've heard enough!' Hugh Thompson roared angrily, knowing that no amount of reasoning would mollify the man. He cut swiftly across the spate, stepping forward sharply and brandishing the switch in an unmistakable threat. The carpenter backed away smartly.

'One more word against the captain, or any more o' that mutinous talk,' he snapped harshly, 'an' I'll give ye the thrashin' he only promised! Ye know nothing about this, an' ye never will, so you're best leavin' it to those who do! If you're so keen to try your luck the other way, off ye go, but I'll wager you'll be on your own! If ye choose to stay, keep your mouth shut. I don't especially care which ye do, but I'd sooner not have unwilling burdens! If you're with me, you'll hold your tongue unless you've something worthwhile to say!'

He glanced grimly around the gathering, and even Will Clarke shifted uncomfortably under his wrathful eye.

'All right,' Thompson declared at length, 'we've no more doubts on what we're about!' In quieter tones he continued, 'We'll need to keep together, an' I'll call a halt from time to time for any stragglers, but we must keep pushing on. If you fall behind at any time, just remember that some of the native blackfellows are said to be cannibals!'

He had no idea if this were true, but had no compunction about lying if it spurred the group on. A brief exchange of startled glances showed that the point had been taken. 'Remember also your shipmates, waiting for rescue back on Preservation Island.'

He covered the remaining points succinctly, for it was time to leave. 'We'll need to go easy on food and water. You've all seen how little there is. We'll catch or collect anything worth eating on the way. We want greens whenever we can find them. Drink as much as you can wherever we find reasonable water. We'll eventually have to live like the natives, so best get used to travelling barefoot. This'll avoid rubbing up blisters, an 'll be a lot easier on your feet than damp boots half full o' sand. Your boots won't last long anyway, so get your feet hardened on the beach as ye go. The first part of the walk'll be fairly easy. We'll stop somewhere near that far point tonight, to rest up an' see how we've all fared.' The indicated headland lay some fifteen miles away, just visible in the haze, with a more prominent hill close behind.

He paused and looked around the group, his angry outburst apparently forgotten, then nodded along the line of creaming surf. 'Well, lads – Port Jackson's about five weeks an' a few hundred miles along that way. We'll get moving as soon as the tide ebbs an' gives us firm sand. Good luck, an' may God speed us on our journey.'

Apart from necessary breaks, the men of the *Sydney Cove* walked steadily for two whole days along a broad, straight, almost featureless beach, the sands warm beneath their feet, a constant breeze on their shoulders. Their footsteps trod a pitted frieze along the edge of the lapping waves, the line of trampled sand a temporary testament to their passing.

They marched in a ragged line, sometimes two or three abreast, mostly led by Hugh Thompson or Will Clarke, though occasionally by one or two of the others. The chief officer recognised the tedium and looked for change and relief where it was offered.

The communal burden was evenly shared, the loads secured in roped canvas rolls or knapsacks, cut and sewn from the sails of the longboat. The four water casks were each transported by two lascars, the containers lashed to shoulder poles whose bearers were changed regularly so that no man's burden became unduly onerous.

The still inoperable pistols were given to Will Clarke and Tenby Read, the cutlasses were worn by Hugh Thompson and Fran Gilbaert, while the single musket was sometimes carried by the chief officer, and at other times by the young lascar servant.

Thompson and Clarkes' servants were jointly responsible for the fire lighters and cooking utensils, while the main supplies of rice, dhal, dried meat, tea and flour were severally shared. The precious chart in its bamboo tube, and the compass they had found and repaired only a few hours before their departure never left Hugh Thompson, whilst the axe similarly remained with the carpenter.

As they were without tents or other shelter, they slept as best they could each night, with sand or dune grass for a bed and their individual bundles as pillows, seeking natural shelter only when necessitated by the weather. They rose early and recommenced their journey after breakfast, always alert to other edible pickings along the way.

Thus they progressed at a purposeful fifteen miles a day. None of them were overburdened as their supplies were so scant, and none were taxed by the soft footing and even terrain. Their first two days of travel were easy and heartening, and promised well for the rest of the journey, provided they could somehow obtain the extra food they would inevitably require.

They met their first major obstacle on the third day. It was a river which they were quite unable to ford even at low water. The earlier obstacles had either been slight or shallow, or they had offered a barred mouth to ease their passage. However, this one flowed swift and deep, too wide to cast a line over and too fast to swim, and it offered no shallower crossing, even a mile or so upstream where it gathered in a lake basin.

'Well, it's my guess this won't be the only one like this,' Hugh Thompson observed to the others, 'so we'd best start learning to build a raft of some sort.'

The others gathered about as he explained their needs, and soon a number of stout driftwood logs were being dragged to where the carpenter trimmed them to approximate size. Bundles of rope were used as lashings, and before long a platform capable of transporting two or three men was under construction amidst a babble of mixed voices and expansive gestures.

'Nothing fancy now,' Thompson instructed. 'We're only going to use it once, so it'll be enough if it floats without upsetting.'

As the raft neared completion he again strolled towards the river mouth, the young Scot beside him, both men gauging the set and speed of the currents as the tide began to turn and stream in once more. 'When the tide's up a bit further an' flowing well in, there'll be a point where the race starts to slacken as the two flows of water, salt an' fresh, are near equal. We should then be able to get a strong swimmer across. That's no mean river, though,' he went on, 'and I was never much of a one for the water myself.' He laughed shortly.

He declined his companion's offer to swim the river, as he sensed it would be too much for Will. Such risks were unnecessary. 'No lad, there are others who'd do it more easily than you. You'll be more useful in other ways before long, I'm thinking, whereas some of the Bengalis are naturals at this. Let's spread the work around on this trip,' he grinned. 'There are plenty of us, so each to his own.'

He called to the Indian foreman who was tensioning the last of the lashings. 'Azim, are any of your people capable of taking a line across

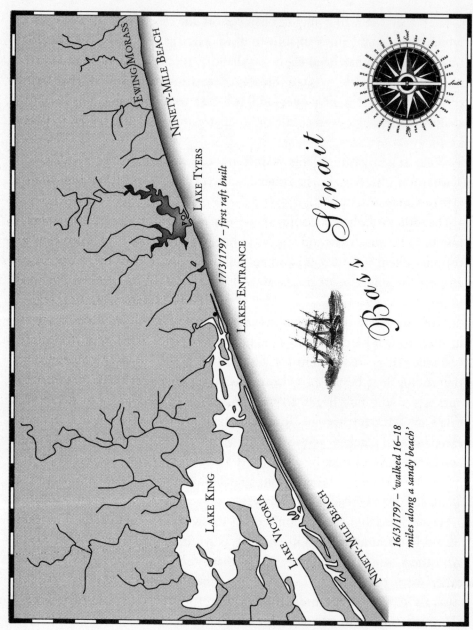

MAP 5. Present-day Ninety-Mile Beach, Lakes Entrance and Ewing Morass, Victoria. Approximates journey of 16–18 March 1797.

here?' He waved an arm over the stream which was flowing inland under the pressure of the rising tide, its surface boiling slowly where hidden currents rolled in conflict.

The lascar eyed the moving surface dubiously, noting the signs of the undertow as an indicator of its depth. 'Oh sah, this is not a safe river,' he said gravely, 'and not one easy to be swimming over. But, if anyone can do it, Showa Devi can, but it would still be with uttermost difficulties. Also, he is an only son. Perhaps we should be trying instead to row across when the tide is once more full?'

Showa Devi cast an impassive eye on the waters, but was clearly no more enthused by the task than his leader.

'I could swim across, Chief, if you'll let me.' The quiet statement came from Fran Gilbaert, who had wandered over to the river bank during the exchange between the chief officer and the Indian foreman. 'As Azim said jus' now, it might be difficult wit' d' currents d'ere are, but a strong an' not heavy line would be most easy to get across, tied to one more stronger for pulling d' raft forwards and back.'

'Good man, you've got the right idea,' said Hugh Thompson with feeling. 'Go to it quickly, if you think you can do it, before the flood turns again and becomes too strong. Give a shout if you're not going to manage it, an' we'll haul ye back!'

But he made it. He had the best physique for the test, being well-muscled without being bulky, strong without being broad. After tentatively feeling the waters, he struck out vigorously, drifting to the left with the attached line as he fought his way across the swelling flow. A thin cheer greeted his success as he waded ashore on the farther bank, and just over an hour later they had all been ferried over in groups of two or three, ready once more to continue on their way.

Late the following afternoon, soon after rafting the last big river they began to notice that the interminable line of dunes lying parallel to their route was increasingly backed by low-lying swampy ground, from which issued the multitudinous sounds of amphibian swamp-dwellers and the screech and caw of intensified bird life. It was as though the dunes themselves stopped any water from escaping to the sea, and so it lay entrapped, together with all the creatures that throve there, a larder for the plundering by anyone skilled in the ways of the native inhabitants.

Increasingly too, they became aware of burned areas of dune scrub and occasional seared trees, with a scattering in such places of old footprints partially filled with sand-drift. In the distance eastwards, a pall of thinning smoke marked the place where yet more fires burned, and the likelihood, therefore, of a continuing native presence.

Then, from among the dunes some way ahead there emerged a small group of dark-skinned figures, who stood silently, staring at the approaching travellers. As the castaways drew closer, the natives were joined by several other hunters, all of them males of varying ages.

It was clear that their approach had been known to the natives for some time, for they were all armed with spears and short curved swords. Their silent immobile stance carried no threat, however, and Hugh Thompson sensed curiosity rather than menace when he realised they could have attacked with much less warning had that been their design. Three more figures crossed the dunes to join the original group, bringing their numbers to fourteen. All were stark naked.

'Easy lads, don't be alarmed,' said the chief officer quietly. 'Just remember we're probably a good deal stranger to them than they are to us. We're used to seeing different kinds of people, where they never have. Move slowly an' talk softly, an' let them see we mean no mischief.' To prove his point, he gave his musket to Pochari, raising both hands in a clear and unmistakable gesture of greeting and goodwill. 'Ho, there,' he called as the two groups closed. 'We are friends, an' wish you no harm. We are travellers,' he added, pointing eastward.

A faint murmur stirred the huntsmen, but drew no other response. He repeated his call, gesturing with all the meaning he could that they intended to move on. One or two of the blackfellows began to edge cautiously towards the cover of the dunes, but the main body of them sought out one of the older men and pushed him forward to answer the chief officer. With his bundle of spears before him he padded slowly to within a few yards of the big man. He stopped and regarded them warily, eyeing first one, then another.

He was tall, thin, and quite unconcerned about his nakedness. Animal teeth and small pieces of bone adorned his forehead and temples, but his black face was dominated by a broad flat nose pierced by either bone or reed above thick lips, the whole topped by long, lank hair that was as unkempt and dirty as the rest of his body. When he spoke he revealed irregular gaps among his teeth, thus offering a most unwholesome spectacle.

They understood nothing of his rapid, irregular babble, though his own gestures towards the east conveyed some measure of mutual understanding, without knowing the full meaning behind them. Hugh Thompson nodded and smiled, urging his men to do the same whilst still addressing his remarks to the uncomprehending native.

Sufficiently sure of their good intentions, the man stepped forward to tentatively touch Hugh Thompson's sleeve, and then that of Will Clarke. Both men smiled and held out their arms encouragingly, inviting the man to investigate further that which had held his attention since his first approach. Their clothing was obviously both puzzling and fascinating. He beamed a hesitant broken-toothed grin into the faces of the pair, then turned to his fellows. In the irregular babble of their language, he apparently urged them to come and see for themselves.

The chief officer glanced at the carpenter, who had watched the natives' approach with nervous apprehension, licking his lips in fearful anticipation, his axe faced in readiness.

'Are you preparing to sell your life dearly, Job Duggan?' he asked. 'I've been watching you, an' I can smell your fear from here. So too might the blackfellows. Put that axe up, take it easy, an' let them come up an' satisfy their curiosity. They're like children, an' you can see they're friendly at the moment, so don't you go thinking of doing anything we might regret.' His words carried a stern warning, though the smile never left his face.

'Don't trust the buggers,' the carpenter exclaimed with a discernible catch in his voice. 'Savages, that's what they are. Just – jus' look at 'em, an' – an' all those spears! It's cannibals they must be too, did'n' ye say so ye'self only a day or two ago? Just look at them awful bones through their noses, will ye! Jus' look! Holy Mother o' God, if these creatures aren't cannibals, then I don't know what are! Well I'm tellin' ye, Mister, they'll not be gettin' Job Duggan if they start on anythin' here, oh no.'

'Stand fast now, blast ye,' the chief officer smiled through clenched teeth, his grip strong on the other man's arm, 'or I'll fetch ye a hard one beneath the ear myself! Then they can do as they please with ye! An' smile, dammit!'

The grim menace in his voice wholly belied the beaming pleasure that wreathed his face, and altogether was a far greater threat than the amicable chatter and laughter of the blackfellows. The carpenter was silenced, but he maintained a firm grip on the axe.

Close up, the natives were even more unwholesome than their ambassador had been. Though they were strongly built and lean-muscled, their bodies gave off a rancid penetrating smell that caught at the mariners' throats and nostrils, their hair especially being heavily greased with some kind of fish oil which added its own rankness.

Will Clarke caught Hugh Thompson's grimace of distaste and his summary comment. 'Phew, Will – the last time I smelled anything as bad as this was during a couple of seasons, years ago, as ship's boy on a rotten whaler!'

With nothing to fear, the natives closely scrutinised their visitors' bodies, clothing, the weapons upon which the castaways kept a close hold, and all the bags and bundles. They shouted and laughed loudly with every new discovery or realisation. It was easy to see that they believed the clothing and bodies of these strangers to be as one. Jackets and shirts were opened, trousers tugged, while the fair hair of Fran Gilbaert and Tenby Read was examined minutely, much to the latter's discomfiture, and they were astonished by the demonstrated sharpness of axe and sword.

For a while the men were encouraged to indulge the natives' curiosity and put up with the occasional indignity in the interests of goodwill. However, there was a need to keep moving.

EWING MORASS

NINETY-MILE BEACH

18/3/1797 – *first friendly native encounter*

Bass Strait

19/3/1797 – *'pretty large river'*

SNOWY RIVER

ORBOST

20/3/1797 – *'high bluffs and sharp rocks'*

CAPE CONRAN

SYDENHAM INLET

MAP 6. *Present-day Ewing Morass, Snowy River and Sydenham Inlet, Victoria. Approximates journey of 19–21 March 1797.*

'Keep a hold on whatever you've got, lads, an' we'll break off in a minute or two. We'll give 'em some strips of the calico, and then break away when I give the word. We don't want 'em with us, so don't forget to wave as you leave, makin' it clear we're going. An' *smile!*'

The woven material was well-received by the natives who chattered delightedly as it was tied around spears and willingly extended arms, or used to decorate hair. Hugh Thompson's pleasure had become entirely genuine by the time he had tied his last knot, and stood back with a wide grin to examine his handiwork.

The dark waving figures receded and then disappeared as the seamen resumed their march. Will Clarke fell into step beside the chief officer as they walked once more along the firm sand.

'Another couple of hours or so, Will, an' we'll call it a day.' Hugh Thompson looked back, but saw nothing save their trodden path. Of the hunters there was no sign. 'We need to be a few miles yet from that lot before we settle for the night.'

His companion nodded, but nevertheless asked, 'Did you consider staying with them a while, Hugh? They might have been able tae catch more than their daily needs, and pass the rest on tae us. Better tae make exchanges where we can, I'm thinking, rather than giving away what we might otherwise trade.' He looked questioningly at the big Englishman as they trudged the beach together.

Hugh Thompson smiled. 'Ah, there's the supercargo an' upcoming merchant talking. Never miss a chance, eh?' His response held no rancour. 'Aye, lad, I did think on it. But at this stage we don't need extra food, especially when we'd have it to carry an' maybe not know whether it was good for us. Sickness we don't need, either. This was only the first group, an' we don't know their measure yet. There'll be others. We had no idea how many more might have been out in the woods, or hiding in the swamps, nor how far we could trust them.'

'This is their land,' he went on, 'and I'm not sure how welcome we are. Me an' the captain knew well enough that there've been tales of trouble now and again from the Port Jackson settlement an' one or two places round about, involving natives an' farmers, and sometimes even the soldiery. Who knows what they've heard hereabouts? For a while we'll need to tread warily. Crude as their weapons may be, we both saw that they were armed to the teeth, an' neither did they let go of anything.'

'We're on our own out here, an' we know just how pitiful our defences really are. It's a troubling thought I'd tell no-one else, but with our few weapons the way they are, the blackfellows could take us at little cost to themselves. I fancy they're all pretty handy with a spear, same as I'd handle a cutlass. 'Cept *they* don't need to get to close quarters,' he added soberly.

'We need to avoid conflict, an' we shouldn't take anything for granted, so I want a fair distance between us an' them until we're more sure of 'em. I'd prefer not to have 'em around at night, if only because we can't afford to lose anything, except in exchange.'

The young Scot nodded enthusiastically. 'Aye, that's right enough. They must be among the most wretched people on earth! After having seen such hideous fellows, I can think o' far more welcome neighbours tae have around at night! I can't imagine a more miserable way o' living – you'd have tae say they hadn't grown any since the days of the Creation. Not a stitch were they wearing, an' no women either, I noticed.'

'Och, they heard you were a'coming laddie, an' locked them away!' Both men laughed. 'Lord, if they were the menfolk, even though we did make 'em prettier, can you imagine their women? Perhaps ye understand now why I wasn't keen to start trading with 'em, an' maybe staying around. We have to get on while we can, but more than that,' he concluded, 'for myself I'm not yet ready to accept their hospitality, an' begin feasting on frogs, snakes or whatever else it is they exist on!'

They crossed another large river at low tide next day, there being no suitable timber with which to make a raft. Fortunately, the mouth was all but blocked by the heaped beach sands upon which they walked, and which added further weight to their speculations as to whether the sea on their right was indeed a strait, and on the strength of the tides and currents which could build up such quantities of sand.

They speculated, too, on the interior beyond the ranges of hills. Some undeniably awesome amounts of water were clearly needed to create a river of this size, which even now stretched deep, still and lake-like between widely separated banks. Yet the water was obviously so irregular and infrequent that its flow to the sea could be cut off by the workings of the restless tides, while no great pondages had built up behind the barriers.

'There are things here I can't understand, Will,' Hugh Thompson declared as he looked at the huge dunes they occasionally came across, some of which were the size of steep hills, far higher than the masts of the tallest ships they knew, and which filled adjacent streams with their sand. 'I've never seen a coast like this before, not in all my days of sailing. I've seen shifting shoals an' sandbanks that change their position even between the start an' finish of a single voyage, but always under water. But this ...'

An adequate explanation defied him. 'In a land as big as this is supposed to be, you'd surely expect rivers as big as those in Europe, the Americas, India or China, more than a few of which you can safely take a ship well up. Why, you can do that in England an' Scotland in a dozen places!'

There was no answer to his puzzlement, but he quickly recognised the ease of their progress if all such impediments were to be as useful. On most of those early days they maintained the planned distances, and so they travelled on, the miles slipping steadily by.

When the hills at last came down to the sea they began to traverse a number of rocky points and small headlands that yielded shellfish, limpets and greeny black periwinkles, together with occasional small crabs that were a welcome if meagre addition to their daily fare. So far the greenstuffs they had tried had been largely dry and unpalatable, though they had found certain seaweeds to be edible, but only available in limited quantities. They collected mangrove beans in quantity when they occurred, for boiling in two or three changes of water, but they could not effectively remove their underlying bitterness, nor the consequences for unaccustomed stomachs.

After their first friendly encounter with the natives, the few they saw later were nervous of their approach, and fled quickly into the woods whenever they attempted to establish any form of acquaintance. Their camps, when discovered, were seen to be poor affairs which yielded little, and it soon became apparent that the natives, like themselves, lived at a level of bare subsistence. This was clearly not a land of plenty.

While the rocky shores provided them with food supplies, they also impeded their travel. The broad beaches they had traversed at the start of their journey frequently gave way to narrowed shores with high bluffs or steeply sloping cliffs, some only passable at low tide. The sharp rock slowed the party as they picked their way along the most accessible paths.

From one high bluff they were able to see the distant aspect of a substantial inlet or lagoon across acres of burned scrub, which enabled them to circumvent it by an inland route some three or four miles from the sea. In so doing they found themselves in an extensive forest of tall, stately trees and verdured clearings, and saw for the first time a land of picturesque beauty with sharp-scented valleys, quiet streams, and lofty blue hills in the distance. Though the countryside still offered few rations, their senses were fulfilled by the richness of their surroundings, the sights and sounds of an exuberant and colourful birdlife, and the clarity and tranquillity of the very air they breathed.

They only experienced bad weather on one day during the first part of their journey, when heavy rain ceaselessly beat upon them to the point where they withdrew inland to seek shelter in the denser timber, so chill was the downpour and the wind which scoured the beaches in bleak abandon.

It was on this day, before making camp, that they passed a rocky landmark so sharp and prominent, despite the shrouding elements, that they wondered if this was the point named for Zachary Hicks, the man

WINGAN POINT

Camp within view of Point Hicks

POINT HICKS

22/3/17974 – 'constant heavy rain'

TAMBOON INLET

21/3/1797 – second raft built

Bass Strait

MAP 7. *Present-day Sydenham Inlet to Wingan Point, Victoria. Approximates journey of 22–23 March 1797.*

who had first sighted this part of the continent from the quarterdeck of Captain Cook's *Endeavour*.

They had thought the same thing when passing a similar point two days earlier. They still yearned for some kind of certainty as to their position, but the charts told them little, except that somewhere ahead lay Cape Howe, and the coast's marked turn northwards. By Hugh Thompson's reckoning this still lay two or three days' march away – provided now they were indeed camped in their huddle of feeble, rain-lashed shelters within view of the great explorer's most celebrated landfall.

6
ULTIMATE STRENGTH ...

24TH MARCH, 1797. *Today buried the sailmaker, who died in the night. Cold winds and rain continue to assail our small island, with no sort of substantial shelter at a gale's height. The men bear their unease well, nevertheless, hearten'd by the warmth of fires which a plenitude of firewood mercifully allows. Salvage work proceeds where weather and our more pressing needs for survival permit. We can expect Mr Thompson's report of our plight to have set arrangements for our rescue in train, which may not be long hereafter.*
FROM THE SHIP'S LOG

The sound of a distant axe and movement amongst the trees revealed where the carpenter and his lascar assistants were gathering material for the party's third raft. The day had become warm and airless, and flies buzzed and bit persistently. The woods were alive with activity. Every now and again the intrusive noises were augmented by the creak and crash of another falling tree.

Efforts were being made to find enough accessible timber to make a raft of some substance, such was their need. Whereas before they had made shift with a rough-hewn driftwood float capable of carrying one or two men, now they faced a far more formidable barrier in the shape of a deep, crooked embayment, the passage of which would clearly require a transport sturdy enough to safely carry several members of the group across the wide, rippling waters.

As a compound of impediments, a challenge to their ingenuity and slender resources, the estuary lay broad before them as a series of finger-like river inlets, gnarled and twisted like those of an aged crone, each one

118

heavily-bushed to the fringes, an obstacle in itself. Although they had ventured a little way upstream along the nearest branch, they had soon found the scrub so heavy and impenetrable as to force them to retreat and cross the open waters, necessitating yet another raft.

Just as the countryside denied them food, so it failed to readily supply the materials for a conveyance of the desired size – though it seemed to give ample support to myriads of voracious winged insects. The common scrub which grew locally was totally unsuited for their needs. On the one hand it consisted of dense thickets of a papery-barked sapling no wider than a man's wrist, whilst on the other it comprised the many contorted straggling trunks of a saw-leafed, heavy-coned tree which yielded nothing. Only by pushing deeper into the bush towards isolated specimens could they find what they were looking for.

All the sounds and associated activity were noted by the *Sydney Cove's* chief officer from where he and Will Clarke stood, on a knoll overlooking the bay. In addition to the carpenter's people he had sent others in various directions, seeking food, water, and the remote possibility of a land passage around the latest obstruction. A party walked the beach below him searching for shellfish, while another, some way off, was clearly contemplating how to entice a bevy of wary black and white pelicans to come closer to the shore.

His main preoccupation, however, was with their immediate whereabouts, and a fresh uncertainty concerning their distance from Port Jackson. The presence of so large a bay as lay before them, and its absence from the chart puzzled him.

Neither it nor the distant island they had first seen from further down the coast were included on Captain Cook's original plots and observations, though both appeared to be worthy landmarks that might help guide the mariner on a coast devoid of features. His frown deepened.

'That's a biggish island, Will, and yet it isn't shown,' he remarked to his companion. 'And the bay here's broad and deep enough to shelter a whole fleet, but it's not shown either.' He gazed across the blue expanse of water to the island beyond. High sand hills bathed in sunlight beckoned invitingly in the far distance, but this unexpected hindrance had checked their progress, stretching their patience, adding to their frustration and concern.

'I had a feeling we might have been close to Cape Howe by now from the distances an' directions we've travelled. Having come upon this though, with not a single reference on the chart, I can't be so sure any more. If that island an' this bay are anywhere near the Cape, Cook would surely have noted them. And yet there's nothing like them shown anywhere between Point Hicks an' Cape Howe.'

His fingers traced the lines on the curling chart. 'If these are landmarks no-one's seen before, we're probably much further west than we'd imagined, with a lot further to go than I calculated. An' if all *that's* true, we still have to be some way to the west of Point Hicks – an' maybe as much as a week or more out in my original reckoning.' His lips tightened with the realisation, and he swore quietly, without vehemence.

Will Clarke sensed and shared something of his friend's emergent despondency. Another week perhaps, dwindling food supplies, and all those extra burdensome miles. 'Well, I'm no navigator, Hugh, but I'd have tae agree wi' ye,' he nodded in reply. 'I don't see any other explanation. Yon island's certainly no' something you'd be expecting a man like James Cook tae miss. Unless they passed it at night,' he pondered dubiously, 'or perhaps just before dawn? We'll no' be knowing, though, until we get beyond both bay and island here.'

Hugh Thompson glanced across in appreciation. He seized on the observation with a glow of renewed hope. 'Will, lad, you're a cheer,' he said, 'an' that's a fact! For all his skill an' reputation as seaman and navigator, Captain Cook could still make mistakes, or omissions at least, as we already suspect from Captain Hamilton's notion of a passage between Van Diemen's Land an' where we are now. Remember what the Old Man said about Furneaux not doing his job thoroughly?'

The chief officer visibly brightened. 'Aye, why didn't I think of it before? There *were* times on Cook's first voyage when he stayed away from the lee coast hereabouts because of storms, so he might easily have missed the bay, an' even the island, in poor light or bad visibility. More than that, though, after he left Botany Bay he actually missed Port Jackson as a far better haven, just a little way further along the coast!'

With his enthusiasm mounting and faith restored, Thompson rolled the chart and stowed it carefully in its bamboo tube. 'Anything's possible where so much is still unknown, so keep your fingers crossed, Will, me lad, an' let's get that raft moving! We might still be right where we thought we were, an' if that's so, the cape we're seeking could be just beyond those hills!'

Raised voices and angry shouting carried from the direction of the wood-cutting party as the two men made their way towards the foreshore.

'That sod of a carpenter again,' Hugh Thompson growled as they hurried towards the source of the disturbance. 'I'll wager a guinea to a groat this is more of Job Duggan's doing!'

The sounds erupted anew as they neared the spot, angrier and more abusive. They discovered a scene of confrontation between the Irish carpenter, scowling and red-faced, and a group of the Indian crewmen. One of the latter held the frayed end of a broken rope, attached to a weighty log, whilst two other lascars, one still lying on the trampled ground, fingered the raw abrasions of recent heavy blows. Azim and another stood warily with knives ominously drawn, facing the carpenter who stood straddle-legged against a tree, his axe held defensively before him.

'What in hell's going on here?' The chief officer's voice snapped forcefully across the dramatic tableau as he thrust through the last of the resisting scrub. The knives disappeared in an instant and the group stood cast in frozen immobility. Hugh Thompson's tones were sharp as he repeated his demand.

'Weaklin's! Idle buggers an' malingerers, that's what we've got with us here! I'd take a whip t' them, I would, if they won't shift this lot!' The

Irishman's flushed countenance scowled ferociously, and his accent was thick with fury. 'We'll niver get away from this place if it's left t' these pagan divils, an' that's the truth on it, so help me. Just you leave 'em t' me, Chief, an' I'll see they work their passage, or I'll flay 'em all alive otherwise ...'

'Hold your rantings man, an' put that bloody axe down! There'll be no whippings or flayings while I'm around, so stop your blather. Azim! What's going on? What's all this about?'

The Indian foreman grinned in relief, glad to be out of a precarious situation. 'The chippie has been chopping trees for the raft, sah, and we are telling him these are too big for our needs.' He indicated the log lying at their feet. 'They seem very heavy, even for small size, and are so difficult to pull through the woods, even when, except the carpenter, we all pull. As you will see, sah, the rope we have is broken from pulling so hard, and yet the carpenter is calling us lazy black bastards and knocks these men around. He is not right to do this!'

Hugh Thompson turned a glowering eye on the Irishman, who continued to scowl heavily. Azim went on to deliver his condemnation with an air of ruffled dignity. 'What does this carpenter man intend to do with such logs of – of this size, we are asking ourselves? Is he about to rebuild the *Sydney Cove* perhaps? We say, they are too big for making rafts, but he says to – to mind our – our own bloody businesses, an' just to pull!'

'These are not the words or manners of a European gentleman, sah, oh no, an' – and we should not have to work in these circumstances with one of such – such rudeness and brutality. I know my people work as best they are able, yet this man uses – uses evil words towards them. Perhaps you will advise him to mend his intolerable ways, sah, for us all to work together! And only to chop the timbers which is best for our needs.'

Job Duggan broke in to forestall any reprimand. 'These timbers are fine for what I've a mind t' be makin',' he growled, 'an' pulling out one or two big logs for the splitting saves these idle swine pulling out more o' the smaller ones, if on'y they'd see it! Sure, an' have I got to explain meself t' those who don't need t' know now? An' won't we be needin' next to ask 'em nicely if they'd t'ink o' givin' us a hand in the work, bejasus! Why, even the old captain was never so soft as . . .'

The carpenter faltered and broke off his tirade, having caught the beginnings of a murderous glint in the chief officer's eye.

'Just remember, Mister, that what we want is nothing grand, an' nothing fancy,' Thompson said tightly.

'Just build us something that'll do the job the once, since we're not well off for lashings, and cannot afford to waste any. Got me? It's a once-only raft we're after, not the *Great Harry*, so I'd go along with Azim an' say these timbers are too big, and any others'll need to be smaller.'

The Irishman's expression changed from defensive anger to heavy indignation. 'Well now,' he challenged huffily, 'that's the way of it, is it? An' you'd be for telling me me business as well, is that it? An' didn't you yourself not long ago say skipperin' was your work, an' the fashionin' o' wood mine? Well jus' remember, Mister Mate, that this here's part o' that work, which aren't I tryin' my best t' do – an' so be good enough would ye please t' leave me to it!'

With a flush of renewed anger the chief officer rounded sharply on Job Duggan, his face close to the Irishman's. 'You'll remember what I've just said, an' have a care for your tongue before it gets you into real trouble! You're sailing mighty close to the wind on this trip, an' by God, I'll be down on ye smartly if you overstep your mark again so much as an inch! We've got a job to do, unless ye've a mind to spend the rest o' your days here, so get back to work, an' less o' your cuffin' an' yelling! You'll treat these people as shipmates an' work together, or I'll know the reason why!'

'Reasons, is it? Reasons! I'll give ye reasons!' The man's control flared and snapped. He backed away and shook his axe at his tormentor, glaring from livid features, his voice the snarl of a trapped animal.

'Well, the Black Hole o' Calcutta it was, that's the reason! Aye, I expec' someone o' your – your fancy ways an' learnin'll have heard of it! Close on a hundred an' fifty souls died in that hell-hole, an' all because o' these murthering bastards an' their motherless, God-forsaken heathen princes or whatever!'

'So many people crying an' a-dying they were, abandoned by the cursed English high an' mighty who ran off t' save their own skins – an' not one miserable scrap o' feeling amongst any o' this lot, not even t' give 'em room t' breathe, nor a drop t' drink! Locked 'em all away they did, an' left 'em t' die, an' you – you expec' me t' call 'em shipmates?'

Hugh Thompson stood aghast at the intensity of the man's outburst, not believing what he heard. 'But – but dammit, what's this got to do with us? The Black Hole was more than forty years ago, man! How in God's name can ye blame these people for what happened so long ago? Some weren't even born then, let alone involved! Have you gone off your head?'

'Over forty years, ye say! Aye, 'twas all o' that – June o' the Lord's Year 1756, t' be exact, an' why should I care, eh? Well I'll tell ye why, Mister, an' then mebbe you'll understand! Me own father was one o' those who perished in that vile, unholy dungeon o' theirs, I'd have ye know! An' wouldn't that just send a man's son off his head, knowing the way his dada suffered an' died, murdered by this offal? Sergeant Patrick Duggan of the Calcutta garrison, I'm tellin' ye – an' no finer soldier ye never could meet!' Emotion thickened the man's voice, and Thompson glanced at Will Clarke, who caught his eye in equal disbelief. The carpenter raged on, unheeding.

'It broke our poor mother's heart, when she finally got word. Dead within a month she was, an' not a penny from nobody! Six kids, with me as the littlest, fending for ourselves in a part o' the country where most folks was already starvin'. The English landlords an' their lackeys, an' the soldiers – there wasn't nothing for motherless waifs like us! An' as the runt o' the pack, more often I got nothin' even when there was a few crumbs around!'

'Forty years, ye say! Aye, it may be now, but for a young 'un with not a morsel in his belly day after day, an' no-one left t' feed him, 'twas always jus' yesterday. Of all the hungry bellies in Ireland, sure an' didn't

I feel mine was always the worst, when I couldn't fight for any o' the few scraps we did get!'

'Misery, that's what it was! A hell-sent misery on six starveling bairns, on'y a pair o' which'd come through. I'm tellin' ye, Mister, I've known hunger an' misery such as you two in yer comfortable lives wouldn't have dreamed of, not in the worst o' yer night horrors – though mebbe ye might on this trip! An' Job Duggan'll be there t' see ye suffer!'

His voice rose again as he glared at the lascars, who had backed quietly away. 'T'ings might ha' been a lot diff'rent for me an' mine, if it hadn't been for these bastard heathens an' their misbegotten ways! I'll not be forgettin' what they did to our dad, nor will ye make me! Work together an' treat 'em like shipmates, ye say! *Hah!*'

'Never, mister, d'ye hear me, *never!*' There was froth on the man's lips, and a hoarseness which told he was near breaking. 'Shipmates? These? Sure, an' isn't it bad enough havin' t' be near the buggers all me time, let alone be callin' 'em mates! By God an' all the saints, I'd sooner work with a pack o' their stinkin' pariah dogs, an' ye'll not be changing that neither, no matter what ye say or do!' He flung the axe to the ground at Hugh Thompson's feet, but the Englishman never flinched.

'If you're not satisfied with how I get things done with these murtherin' curs, go an' do the bloody work yerself! I want nothin' of it, or them.' Hurling a stone and wedges down alongside the axe, he turned on his heel and stumbled into the bush, his emotions spent.

For a moment there was silence, broken only by the sounds of the carpenter's departure. With an effort Hugh Thompson swallowed his anger and exasperation, kicking at the heavy log with the heel of a bare foot. Thickly he said to the lascars, 'Get what ye can of this lot to the beach. See to it, Azim, then join us as soon as ye can.'

He glanced at Will Clarke as they turned to walk down to the shore. 'As if our problems aren't trial enough, we end up with one like Job Duggan. The skipper was right. A born troublemaker, an' now half-mad to boot! Just can't help himself, it comes right easily. I reckon before this jaunt's over we're going to be sorry we brought him along.'

'Did we have tae? You'd have been right for thinking him a madman as he was back there,' Will Clarke said. 'An' the Irish do have prodigious long memories!'

The chief officer shook his head regretfully. 'We could do nothing short o' leaving him ashore on the big island, an' he'd not earned it then, so much. No, the Old Man couldn't have handled him on Preservation Island, 'specially not with all that strong drink. Can you imagine him with time on his hands an' only Captain Hamilton between him, the grog, an' the Indians? Jesus, it doesn't bear thinking about!'

'It would have been like returning to the *Batavia*, all over again,' Hugh Thompson went on, 'or some other kind of mayhem. Remember Fran Gilbaert's story in the longboat? God's truth, an' I'd right gladly be shot of him, because now we're carrying the bastard. But better he's here, for the captain's sake, I suppose, than there. He'll always be a bad lot, ill-disposed an' evil-tempered, who'll pick an easy fight so long as he's fairly sure o' the outcome. You'll have seen he never troubles Fran Gilbaert? Now, there you've got a good man,' he added with emphasis.

They broke out from the trees and crossed the sands, the exposure fresh and cleansing. 'I've seen Duggan's type many a time before,' Thompson continued as they reached the water's edge. 'They're the worst sort to have in any crew, an' they're always down quickest on the blackfellows. They're an easy touch generally, just so long as they're not Arabs with knives. Not that *he'd* know so much – Azim an' his lads'd be no easy pushover if they put their minds to it.'

'No, tho' he's got all the Irishman's blather, Job's none too bright, but he carries the white man's righteousness an' arrogance at their very worst. Add his kind of ignorance, an' it's a bad blend. Unless we curb that mouth of his, hard an' soon, there'll be real trouble before we reach Port Jackson.'

'Could there be any use in trying tae talk him round?' his companion enquired. 'Would you like me tae have a go with him?' The youngster sounded none too confident, despite his offer.

The chief officer pondered Will Clarke's question, but shook his head.

'Nay, Will. No disrespect to you, but I'm sure he'd see you either as my lackey, or as a pure company man – which might be worse in his eyes. You'd get nowhere. Besides which, it's my job. Sure, you should be able to win a reasonable man over with the right kind o' talking, or reward if need be, but words'd be lost on that one, who hasn't got overmuch in his skull, an' he's certainly due no more reward than any of the Indian crew. Less, in fact.'

'Maybe you're right, though,' he acknowledged at length as they turned back towards the camp, 'since the shipboard hard line doesn't seem to make a deal of impression shoreside, as we are now. 'Twould be different were we still aboard the *Sydney Cove*, I can tell 'ee! My real inclination'd be to lay about him severely with a rope's end or belaying pin, an' no mistake, then throw him in the brig for a week.' He referred heatedly to the traditional way of stirring laggards and recalcitrants along a desired path of action, or of suffering the consequences.

'Soft words don't come easy at the best o' times in my trade, an' 'specially not with his sort, but – well, I'll think o' giving it a try, after I've asked Azim to keep his lads sweet.'

With all their requirements gathered, they assembled the large raft on the foreshore next day, its heavy timbers split, lashed and cross-braced to support a sapling platform capable of bearing six of the group.

According to the chief officer's plan, they were to land in fours on the far side of the bay, the remaining two returning with the raft by way of each point of land on the indirect journey, four trips being required to ferry the entire party. Each trip on the cumbersome float might take four or five hours, so vast was the estuary complex. But the doubts of the previous day as to the quality of the local timber were soon shown to be valid.

With much heaving and pushing, the massive structure was coaxed into the water. But the materials chosen by the carpenter were so dense, green and heavy that it scarcely stood above the surface, without its complement. With only two men aboard it was already beginning to founder, and it was quickly realised that it would never carry six, while even two might be taking a risk. But two, at least, were needed to bring the raft back ...

They were hungry and subdued that night when they went cheerless to their beds at the end of a wearying, wasted day. Even without the chief officer's acid comments about Job Duggan, the castaways knew they would have to repeat their labours, scouring the thick undergrowth for more buoyant materials. They faced the prospect of another day of windless heat, persistent flies and shortened tempers, for which they blamed but one man. An unspoken hostility hung heavily upon the already chagrined carpenter, causing him to once again withdraw from the group. The silence of the men was condemning, but their near empty bellies were a greater, more personal concern.

On the chief officer's orders the food reserves from the longboat were being strictly rationed. They had seen no natives recently from whom other food might have been bartered, nor had they caught much of their own. Along with a number of large white birds with markedly curved bills, the pelicans they had seen on the first morning had cautiously taken themselves off to the other side of the placid blue waters, where they continued to paddle and fish undisturbed, mockingly at ease.

What meagre edibles had been available from the land and the shore had already been consumed. Every day they spent on the western edge of the bay moved them a step closer to the beginnings of starvation, and they began to fear bad weather or storms that might prevent the bay crossings.

One or two of the slightly built lascars were already displaying early signs of lethargy and unwillingness to move, and were frequent stragglers on the march. They would need to be watched if they were not to be the first to fall by the wayside. Tenby Read was another whose march was occasionally irregular.

The crew's mistrust of the carpenter after his resentful outburst, as well as their thinly veiled contempt of his incompetence as an artisan, marked him as a man reviled by his fellows in circumstances where fellowship, trust and mutuality counted above all else. He was becoming isolated. He was avoided by almost all the crew, and the awkwardness of his actions and manner became those of an outcast.

For a while Will Clarke watched him from where he undertook his own task, then decided he would try to talk the man back into some sense of belonging, if at all possible. The carpenter had swung his axe halfheartedly at a pile of the lighter papery-barked saplings for the past hour, but wasn't getting very far in trimming them to size across a log.

'Good day tae ye, Mr Duggan,' the young Scot ventured. 'Do ye think I might give ye a hand in what you're doing?' The carpenter pretended not to see or hear him for a few moments, but glanced up from beneath beetling brows, frowning, when the question was repeated.

'I've never handled an axe as big as that one,' Will Clarke persisted, 'but if you could spare the time tae show me how, maybe we could finish the job sooner an' be on our way again.'

The carpenter appeared to consider his point, but then shook his head and turned away with a heavy growl. ''Tis not a plaything, an' I'd be trustin' no-one but meself with it. Away wi' ye, boy, an' don't you be troublin' me. Can't ye see this is a man's work?'

The reply was blunt and uncompromising, but not unexpected. Having made up his mind, the supercargo had come prepared to stand his ground, in order to try to win the man over and re-establish some of their group unity. 'It's not hard work I'm afraid of. What I've done this morning hasn't been much, and I'd gladly give you a break here, if you'll let me.'

The Irishman's axe cleaved viciously through the air with such force that the chopping block split violently asunder, its flying pieces causing Will to jump aside, his face pale beneath the colour from the sun.

'Blast yer mischief an' impertinence, boy!' the man roared, a blazing anger contorting and suffusing his features. 'Ye're niver doing much, 'cept talking t' that bastard of a chief officer! Can't ye see I don't need the help o' babbies? Clear off wi' ye! When I want the company o' snivellin', snotty-nosed landsmen the likes o' you, I'll seek it ...'

'*Duggan!*' Hugh Thompson's harsh shout was like a pistol-shot as he hurried towards the new uproar. 'By Christ, man, ye're going too far with yer insolence! Ye'll alter your tone an' show a measure o' respect for Mr Clarke as your superior, or it'll be the worse for you!'

'Respect? Respect is it now, then? No, Mister, I'm tellin' 'ee I'll not be having respect for him, for you, nor for any other man here! We're away from the ship, an' in this as equals now, I say – no rank, no privileges nor favours, an' on'y the best among us get home. There's none better than Job Duggan right now, for you're not on yer quarterdeck any more, Chief, an' yon company whippersnapper counts for nothin' neither. We're equals, see, all of us the same! "Respect Mr Clarke as your superior", is it? Well, I'm onto your game Mister! 'Tis after yer own ship ye'd be, I'm thinking, wi' talk like that, toadying t' the company's boy ...'

The chief officer stepped forward and punched the carpenter hard in the mouth, stopping his rebellious tirade in full flow. The stocky Irishman saw the threat looming, but moved too slowly to absorb the blow, staggering though he did not fall. Mouthing curses and spitting from bloodied lips, he recovered with a roar like an enraged bull.

Without a second's hesitation he threw aside the axe and rushed forward, his fists bunched and swinging dangerously, furiously intent on ridding himself of a persecutor. For a wild moment both men traded punches without real effect, the carpenter bellowing obscenely, until Hugh Thompson suddenly ducked under one rushing assault and drove hard and low beneath the man's ribs as he lumbered past.

Such a punch would have stopped a lesser man, especially if followed swiftly with another of equal force, but a flailing fist caught Thompson a backward glancing blow to the side of the head as the Irishman turned back sharply on his attacker, finding him unexpectedly dazed and unbalanced, and close enough for a crippling kick.

Too late he realised he was no longer wearing boots to do any real damage, and as Hugh Thompson twisted aside he rammed a fist deep into the carpenter's unguarded midriff, driving the breath from his antagonist. This was succeeded immediately with a hard hooking right as the man doubled forward and crumpled at the feet of the chief officer, who then delivered a fierce swinging kick low in the belly, underlining the lesson he knew was now long overdue.

In seeing Will Clarke set out on his self-appointed task of winning the carpenter over, Hugh Thompson had guessed the likely outcome. Young Will had to learn, he thought, knowing that he himself had been equally unsuccessful with the man the day before. Since further conflict seemed inevitable, it was simply a matter of allowing the Irishman enough rope in the explosion that his friend had unwittingly primed, then choosing the most opportune instance to intervene.

Having beaten the carpenter soundly in a way he would understand, respect and remember, he delivered another savage kick as the man struggled to his feet, still glaring and growling murderously, finally laying him on his back.

While his outmatched opponent lay writhing and gasping, Hugh Thompson stood over him, staring into the other's agonised face, his own chest still heaving from the intensity of the struggle, a stinging sweat in his eyes. The noise of the conflict and the sight of the finally humbled carpenter brought crewmen hurrying from the scrub, as the chief officer reached for his dropped cutlass.

Unsheathing the blade slowly, he held the point of the weapon against the man's throat, deliberately indenting the flesh, waiting for the man to recover his senses, whilst the crew warily gathered round. There was the sweat of fear upon the fallen man's brow as he tried to wriggle out from beneath the threatening steel, but Thompson followed, leaning more heavily on the point to keep his trembling victim still.

The ship's cutlass was essentially a heavy-bladed slashing weapon for use in mass action and so was broad-pointed, unlike the lighter rapier or duelling sword designed for thrusting in individual, face-to-face combat. The carpenter was therefore in no real danger from the poised weapon as long as Hugh Thompson held off pressure, and so long as he lay still. Nevertheless, a small trickle of blood oozed brightly from a nick in the skin depression.

'One more display like that, Job Duggan, just one more'll be your last, I promise,' the chief officer said evenly and deliberately, speaking into the man's sweating face. 'We've trials enough, an' more to come shortly, without you an' your warped notions. As like as not, your mouth'll be the death of you, one day. You're a bad 'un, Job Duggan, an' one we don't need – an' that's the way I'm beginning to think.'

He raised the fingers of his left hand one by one as he continued. 'Insolence, insubordination, mutiny, rebellion, assault – at sea I'd have you flogged for any one, or worse. The old-timers had fewer scruples than I or Cap'n Hamilton about marooning, keel-hauling or hanging a man, but anywhere else, Mister, an' I'd hang you now for what you are. You're a troublemaker of the worst kind, who's too thick-headed to learn. Here, you're nothing but a bane to us all.'

'So – what to do with you?' he went on, ready to answer his own question. 'As we're all half-starved here, there'd be no hardship in cutting your rations, an' we've lost all the niceties o' keepin' shipboard discipline, more's the pity. So instead I've a mind to leave ye trussed out in the scrub, abandoned as ye might cast a man adrift at sea. While we might not spare the time to hang you, we'd easily spare a yard or two o' rope to leave you tied to a tree. It's the nearest thing I can think of to putting you ashore from a ship.'

'If ye got free, ye'd need to save y'self as best ye may, in company with the blackfellows you despise so much. I'm thinking they'd take to you an' your ways no more readily than we do, so you'd be on your own.'

He looked around the assembled group who had listened to his words in awe, certain he meant what he said. 'Ye've all heard me,' he declared. 'Would any of you have it otherwise? Speak up, if there's anything in this man's favour which says we should treat him differently.' He paused, but the silence was condemning in its enormity.

'So be it, then.' He glanced down once more, seeing terror and disbelief on the bruised countenance.

'This is the last warning,' he said, shifting the sword to jerk the Irishman to full alertness. The man's eyes widened in response, and a fresh sweat erupted on his brow. 'From here on, you're on your bond. Our lives, an' those of Captain Hamilton and the rest o' the crew on the island, depend on us reaching Port Jackson safely. The skipper charged me with taking this group to Sydney Town – *all* the group. I'll do it if I can, but if I have to leave you behind for the good o' the rest o' the party, mark my word I'll do that, too. As the captain once said, "Ye're either with us, or agin us." So which is it to be? I'll not see any man's safety or welfare jeopardised by your mad talk or attitudes. You came to us as a stranger. You'll likely leave that way unless you're prepared to mend your ways.'

'There'll be no more o' this,' he concluded, nodding towards the bush. 'It'll be simpler just to leave you out there in future. Think well on it, Job Duggan, for it's your last chance.' Raising the reddened blade to the level of the man's brow, he asked, 'Have I made myself perfectly clear?'

'Sure, Chief, y-yes, anything you say, Chief, on'y – on'y, please don't leave me out there! Please!' He shifted his face away from the glistening point, babbling, and Hugh Thompson knew he had won. Any further problems with the carpenter would be trifles.

To be sure, he gave the axe to Fran Gilbaert for safety, not fully trusting the chastened Irishman, then drove home the man's expendability by completing a serviceable raft without him.

Early next day, by Will Clarke's diary the 27th of March, they began the bay crossing. The extra time on the western shore had allowed Hugh Thompson to re-assess the problem, and instead of making long single passages with extensive waits for those not on the raft, he had decided on a series of shorter stages, using the raft as a shuttle between three headlands within the bay.

With short crossings across the narrowest waterways, he reasoned, the men could walk along the intervening beaches gathering food on the way. It also meant that help would be so much nearer should anything go

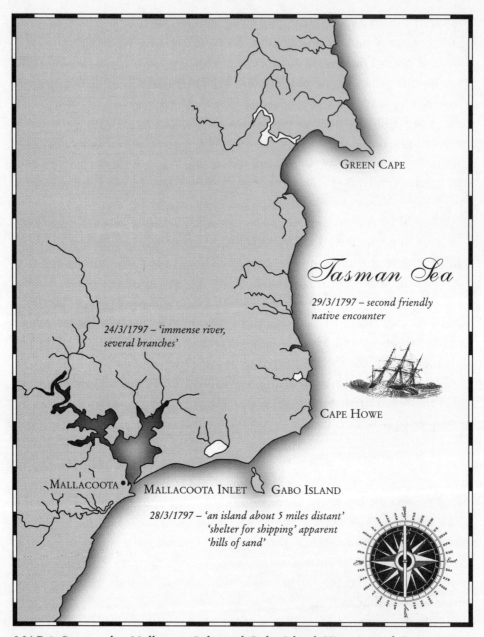

MAP 8. *Present-day Mallacoota Inlet and Gabo Island, Victoria, and Green Cape, NSW. 24–30 March 1797, including three days raft building.*

wrong. The last raft trip of each stage was to overtake the last of the walking parties in moving on to the next departure point ahead.

It was with a sense of achievement that the group leaders landed the first party on the eastern side of the estuary. They had been fortunate in the weather, for even a recurrence of the earlier swell might have rendered the exercise perilous. While the two officers returned with the raft to pick up another four of their number, Azim and his trio strode confidently ahead, to find within a short distance a watered campsite in full view of the island which now loomed so much closer.

On the second trip from the last departure point they noticed a covey of pelicans cruising close by the shore. It was a sight which reminded them of their earliest fruitless attempts to catch the birds. Seeing them again so close to hand led to the tantalising thought of roasting one of them on open coals.

Amongst the passengers on the raft was Showa Devi, earlier singled out by Azim Prakash as the strongest swimmer amongst the lascars. In some excitement and a barely comprehensible mix of Bengali and broken English, the Indian outlined a plan to capture one of the birds.

'No wind, no wind today,' he explained, with gestures. 'Bird, him *hawasil*, is – is heavy. We see, can not today fly easily.' He mimicked the awkward flapping of the pelican's efforts to take to the wing on windless days like theirs. 'I go into water, quiet now, so. And I am swimming then, also quiet – down below.' Here he demonstrated the sinuous motion of a fish. 'Close by him, I take hold him feet. He not very pleased, oh no. You come – most quick to help. Yes?'

The chief officer's response was an enthusiastic affirmative, and immediately the atmosphere became charged with eager anticipation. Slowly they manoeuvred the raft as close as they dared, then backed away as the birds began to move. With a reed through which to breathe, the Indian slipped quietly beneath the surface from the back of the raft, then swam off towards the birds, his dark body invisible in the water.

Not a swirl marked his progress. Only by searching hard for the slim reed showing here and there, each time a few yards nearer the quarry, could they know his exact whereabouts. They waited for what seemed an eternity, hardly daring to whisper. They became anxious when the birds began to show signs of nervousness, some odd sense having warned them of a lurking menace.

A sharp splash, and cries of alarm from the water mingled with a concerted flurry of black and white plumage suddenly galvanised the raft party into action. 'Paddle, for Christ's sake,' roared the chief officer, 'that's our dinner he's holding!'

There was panic amongst the birds as they broke formation in the face of this new threat. The sea surface erupted, beaten into a foam by the frenzy of wings and feet as they tried to escape the trap. Two other Indians dived overboard as Showa Devi's head emerged alongside the bird he had seized, desperately trying to keep hold of his captive and avoid being drowned whilst warding off the thrashing blows that rained about him violently.

For a moment all was uproar. The big bird struggled valiantly and regurgitated part of its last meal in a futile attempt to take off. Hugh Thompson made a mental note to collect it afterwards, expecting to find undigested fish in its belly. The creature began to weaken as the other swimmers closed in, and between them they subdued it by holding it beneath the surface until it finally drowned. For his pains, its captor streamed blood from a ragged cut at the hairline, the result of a blow from the massive beak, nevertheless he grinned in triumph, particularly when promised a double share of the catch.

Though its fish taint was strong and the cooking imperfect, they ate well of the large bird that night, by the dancing flames of a driftwood fire. There was ample for all, with nothing wasted, and their bonhomie touched even the carpenter, whom Hugh Thompson had not the heart to exclude.

The following afternoon the castaways stood together around the summit of a bare-domed sand dune, looking back westwards to the island they had passed earlier, south towards an empty unbroken horizon and then northwards at last, along a new coast that must eventually lead them to the safety of the settlement at Port Jackson. They were exhausted from the day's exertions, plodding stolidly up and down an extended series of high sandhills, but had been greatly cheered after Will Clarke's call and excited waving from some way ahead. They had hurried forward to join him on his vantage point, there to look upon what they soon realised was Cape Howe – the end of another stage of their journey.

Hugh Thompson withdrew the chart from its holder while the others drew closer to seek confirmation. 'Well, we'd be a lot more certain if that island back there was marked as we can see it,' he said after checking what they saw against the detail depicted, 'but there's probably good reason why it's not. Captain Cook wasn't blind, an' he fairly knew what he was about. I have to say, though, that I'm pretty sure this is his Cape Howe, the point ye see here,' he continued, running a finger along the line of the known coast to an elbow-like prominence. The shoreline they were looking down on seemed to correspond.

'It wouldn't be d' headland out d'ere instead, would it, Chief?' asked Fran Gilbaert, pointing to a dimly-defined tongue of land perhaps five leagues away on the northern horizon, blue in the hazy distance. 'It looks as if d'at could be quite a lan'mark.'

Hugh Thompson glanced at the seaman, then in the direction he was pointing. 'Aye, I'd wondered that myself,' he acknowledged, turning to the chart again, 'though I reckon that's more likely to be this point here, a bit to the north o' the main cape, with no name on it. It all fits, see.'

His forefinger retraced their route with mounting certainty. 'That being the way of it, where we camped in the rain about a week ago really would have been Point Hicks as we thought. The distance from where we are now'd be about right for that, an' since the coast here takes a sharp northward turn as well, I'm saying this is Cape Howe, an' just about where I expected it.'

He grinned across at Will Clarke. 'Seems we were on target after all,

Will – not that it's so heartening, though, knowing how far we've still to go!'

But better than not knowing, he thought, as he re-rolled the chart and stowed it away. He handed it to his servant, Pochari, with a familiar wink. The lad smiled pleasurably in response, and Thompson laid a fatherly arm across his narrow shoulders as they moved off down the sand slope together.

'All we need is more vittles o' the sort we had yesterday, matey, an' some sweet, fresh water now an' again, an' this walk'd be a real pleasure. Aye, we could walk all the way to India if need be, on fare like that!'

They walked only a little further that afternoon, despite the chief officer's whimsical indulgence for the benefit of his servant boy. A small lake with tolerably fresh water flowing in from the hills offered them good shelter amongst the dune vegetation along its shores, and there they stopped, some twelve miles from their start that morning.

By Hugh Thompson's estimate, they had travelled about 110 miles so far. Over a hundred gone, leaving three hundred or more to go – it seemed a daunting prospect still, and one that the men shouldn't be continually reminded of. The spectre of finding sufficient food to feed seventeen hungry men each day raised itself again. Although they had remained reasonably fit and healthy, and still covered the ground without any appreciable difficulties, equally they had to go on hoping for regular sustenance as they moved northwards, if they were to maintain their pace and cohesion.

As each day passed, the rations they had salvaged from the longboat dwindled further, no matter how they tried to eke them out. At best, it was clear they would last only another week at their current rate of consumption, unless more could somehow be coaxed from the land. This meant they would either have to be more fortunate in finding their own sources of food, or try to win the friendship of any native bands they might chance upon.

Of the latter they had seen none for several days, which was not surprising considering the apparent poverty of the countryside. Pretty and appealing though it might be, it offered little with which to even temporarily assuage their grumbling bellies. A stark question loomed. If the natives found this area non-propitious, how could they expect to wrest provisions from it?

These were disturbing, uneasy thoughts. The raucous cackling from the bush at dusk most evenings seemed to mock their fortunes, and their intrusion into this barren land. In low tones by the firelight, Hugh Thompson and Will Clarke talked until well into the night about the numerous possibilities and various means of reaching their goal unscathed.

Was there any real alternative to them staying together, and making the best pace possible in the circumstances? For the time being, at least, they decided not. If the countryside had offered more, the prospect of sending a fast-moving party of five on ahead would have had real appeal, that number of men making fewer demands on the country's immediate reserves, including those of any natives they might encounter. But the remaining twelve might fare less well.

Their collective security was also a major consideration. Together they formed a formidable body, apparently well-armed, and had so far outnumbered and overawed the few small native bands they had met. To reduce their numbers by splitting the party might render both groups vulnerable, and neither of them forgot the disturbing reports of conflict with natives further north. Division would pose the kind of risk that their meagre supply of arms could never offset. The thought of Captain Hamilton's dependence on them finally banished all talk of separation, and they resolved to go on as they were doing for as long as they could, trusting in God that their way and their worries would shortly be eased.

They renewed acquaintance with the local natives whilst crossing a deep, narrow river the next day. At first they had been challenged angrily by a single individual, but they were not deterred even when more appeared from the bush. They still outnumbered the blackfellows, who quickly changed their demeanour when presented with a few strips of cloth as a gesture of goodwill. The weapons of the castaways, well displayed but

They renewed acquaintance with the local natives ...

passively handled, also had a sobering effect as was obvious from the frequent covert glances they attracted. But they were offered little in return.

Within minutes the men were surrounded once more by a crowd of laughing, gleeful natives, including on this occasion the women and children, who had been called from the nearby scrub. All were as unashamedly naked as the first group they had met. The newcomers, the first of their kind these people had seen, were regarded with both astonishment and amusement, such was the volume of the accompanying chatter.

For their part the sailors regarded the tribal womenfolk with parallel amazement. As the first of the native ladies they had set eyes on, they were seen to be just as dirty and uncomely as their warriors. Coarse features and raw mannerisms showed that they were not far removed from the most primitive of savages.

Closer proximity and their unbridled curiosity in tugging and touching raised feelings of repugnance and disgust that were difficult to conceal. Within a very short while it became quite obvious that they were not a people who had anything to share, nor was their acquaintance otherwise welcome. As soon as they could, therefore, the travellers broke away to continue their journey.

The aspect of the countryside gradually but perceptibly changed as they progressed. Instead of the dry, sandy ground they had traversed before Cape Howe, they were now crossing a spacious, grassier terrain featuring less of the thick, encumbering scrub, and more of an agreeable open heath and mature forest.

The vegetation had distinctly changed. One dominant variety amongst the taller trees was outstandingly dappled and spotted along the length of its towering shaft, its presence adding to an already pleasing landscape. In the undergrowth, the hardy bracken seemed to be giving way to groves of an elegant, spike-fronded palm which brought a further touch of the exotic as each fresh panorama unfolded before them.

There was extensive evidence of burning along their coastwise path, the boles of many trees being charred and blackened near the ground, even though their crowns were still healthy and burgeoning in full leaf. And in the space of only a few miles the country began to give rise to a succession of fresher, faster streams while the coast itself grew rockier, the beaches less extensive. It was, indeed, a wild and curious place.

As an unwanted product of their changed direction, yet another river barred their way the day after their native encounter, one that was too deep and wide to ford. Hardly had they begun to prepare a raft, however, when three of the natives they had met the previous morning reappeared. Before long it transpired from their babbling cries and expressive gestures that they had purposely followed the castaways, appreciating the difficulties they might have in crossing unfamiliar waterways that were so well-known to the local people.

Such spontaneous help was as unexpected as it was well-meaning, and the assistance they were so generously offered saved both time and effort.

They were to meet them again and receive similar assistance, two days later.

To the men of the *Sydney Cove* it seemed that their concern had been recognised and their prayers heeded, for the verdant, flower-strewn land they subsequently travelled allowed them three days of easy passage, including one spent walking the shores of a deep divided bay, and an accompanying awareness of greater distances covered than at any time since the start of their venture.

Even after a day when they were beset by a harrowing sequence of high bluffs, sharp reddish-coloured rocks, and thick brushwood entanglements which left them much bruised and footsore, there was still relief to be had in the welcome form of a broad, shallow river where, for most of a day, they rested to regain a little of their strength and at the same time catch some of the abundant fish. By chance, one of these was a young shark, almost four feet in length, which had become stranded by the receding tide amongst the channels. A single blow from the carpenter's axe had it promptly dispatched, whereupon, with improvised gaffs and a noose around its tail, it was quickly hauled ashore and butchered.

They thanked Providence that night for such bounty. Since the capture of the pelican they had been reduced to a daily staple of a quarter-pint of rice per man, and another temporary respite from ever-threatening starvation seemed like a godsend. But they were also beginning to experience the first signs of creeping exhaustion.

That day they had spent most of an anxious morning waiting for sight or sound of two of their comrades who had become separated from the group the previous day. One they knew was troubled by a persistent, hacking cough and given to halting frequently. The other was the oldest of the Indian seamen. While they had passed the time in adding to their diminished food reserves, they had also used the opportunity to nurse their own sufferings, a number having been quite lamed through what had been the severest test so far. When at last the stragglers made their appearance, much to the relief and joy of their companions, they showed such signs of acute fatigue and distress that Hugh Thompson decided on

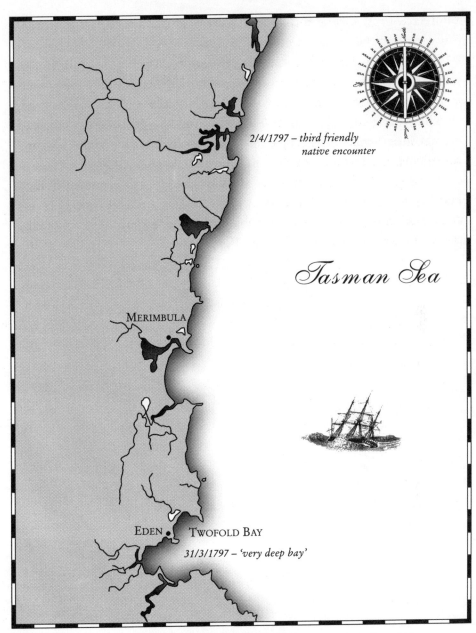

MAP 9. *Present-day Twofold Bay to Mimosa Rocks National Park, NSW. Approximates journey of 31 March to 2 April 1797.*

a full day of rest for the entire party before any more became lost through privation and the demands of their journey.

Like the extra fish provisions, the gesture was well-received and they spent the next day at leisure. Fully recovered, he thought, the men would make better progress than in trudging dispiritedly without a break, day after day. The weather was holding fair, and the group was still intact despite their diverse mix. They were a hardy bunch, he readily acknowledged, and had suffered much with little complaint. Visiting them around the campfires later that evening he again felt that they had justified Captain Hamilton's faith – but he felt equally as sure that no matter what his own care or concern for the men might be, there were already several amongst their number who would not reach Port Jackson.

7

A VERY
PLEASANT COUNTRY ...

6TH APRIL, 1797. *For almost a week now have we realistically
expect'd our rescue. Each day we are occupied in seeking sight of a
sail, and praying for deliv'rance. While it may be too early for
concern, we are naturally wond'ring how Mr Thompson's party has
far'd. Aside from some water sickness, the people here are tolerably
well on a sufficiency of food and good water for the fetching,
when the seas allow it, altho' Nature continues to treat us unkindly
much of the time.*
FROM THE SHIP'S LOG

'*A horse! A horse! My kingdom for a horse!*' The words of the
Bard fell easily from Hugh Thompson's lips as he stood
atop the steep hill they had just climbed, spread wide his arms,
and looked across the softly-muted colours of the undulating countryside
below and to the north of them.

'Aye, it'd be grand riding country all through there, Hugh,' Will Clarke
panted, clambering up beside him, 'and a bonnie pleasure it'd be too, as
a welcome change from walking! Are you perhaps thinking of cantering
into Sydney Town in style?'

'Who, me? Riding?' The response was a fair imitation of old Captain
Hamilton. 'Och, laddie, ah'm a seaman, no' a horseman! The way mah
belly feels the noo, ah'd more a mind tae eatin' the beastie, than tae puttin'
a saddle on him!' He grinned across at Will Clarke, who shook with
laughter at the unexpected retort, adding in his normal voice, 'Come to

145

think of it, Will, the way I feel now, a juicy well-oiled saddle'd go down nicely, as afters!'

The young Scot wiped the sweat from his brow. The path from the coast to their lookout had been rugged, and the day was warm. 'Well, since you've no horse nor saddle to dine on, you'll need tae make do by taking up another notch in your belt like the rest of us.'

Hugh Thompson's grin broadened. 'Ah, but you're a bit late even with advice like that, boy. It might just have been the saving of me early this morning, only – I ate it at breakfast time, along with all that remained of me last boot.' Though his words were belied by the broad leather band still holding the cutlass to his waist, Will Clarke recognised his friend's sentiments, and appreciated his undiminished wit. The shark they had caught, for all its size, had not been in any way filling.

Together they gazed out from their high vantage point, a hill on a spur of the mountain which bulked large immediately to the west, blocking much of the view of the interior. The way to the summit was inviting, even though the slopes appeared to be thickly wooded. Time would not allow any dalliance, however, since they knew they had to catch up with the shore party, now some way ahead.

There was no doubt now as to their whereabouts. They were obviously standing on the highest prominence on the coast, with nothing else approaching it in size for as far as they could see.

'It's easy to see why Captain Cook called it Mount Dromedary,' Will Clarke said, referring to the double-humped shape by which they had identified it. 'But the cape of that name's nothing like the one on his chart. You'd hardly think a man such as he would make another mistake so obvious.' The cape he referred to was depicted on the chart as triangular and standing some distance into the blue ocean, whereas the view to seaward held no more than an insignificant rocky point, and an island four or five miles offshore.

'It's easy enough to say, as ye see it today, Will,' Hugh Thompson countered, shielding his eyes from the sun, 'but who knows what the weather was doing here at the time? Imagine all this from the sea, maybe out as far again as that island. Mount Dromedary would be visible for miles, but a blanket of sea mist low down, and an unwillingness to approach too close to a lee shore with islands like that nearby – which might have looked like a headland at the time – and it would be quite a pardonable error. Strange though it might seem, we're the first white men ever to have seen it from this viewpoint. Others would have stayed well clear.'

'And maybe it's not such an error,' he went on after a pause. 'If you're not sure, an' don't want to mark a passage you haven't sounded for yourself, be cautious an' mark it as land. That way it'll be given a wide berth, rather than inviting a ship into what might be a spit, or shoal waters. Though the skipper charged Captain Furneaux with neglect in not confirming what he took to be a deep bight between Van Diemen's Land an' New South Wales, imagine the results of marking what he *thought* might have been a passage if it had, in fact, only been a bight.'

'The early voyagers did a fair job then, you'd say, leaving it tae others to fill in the details?' Will Clarke queried.

'Right,' the chief officer nodded. 'That's the way it's always been, little by little. They did the best they could, without getting too close in completely unknown waters. They were the first, with nothing at all to guide them save their eyes, the leadsman, an' a fair measure o' caution. A single unseen rock or reef could have done for them.'

'We're here now because Cook discovered the entire eastern seaboard of this continent, then came home an' told us where it was. That wasn't even thirty years ago, but he only came the once. Obviously he couldn't chart every last island, bay an' headland, so navigating these shores'll need care for a long time yet if sailors are to avoid running into them! You're a long way from home if that happens and o' course no-one knows that better than us.'

They started through the open scrub, northeastwards behind the lake beneath them. It was an easy traverse and their route was clear, the terrain a rich coastal grassland plain interspersed here and there with a few trees.

'Just imagine, Hugh! All this empty land tae roam in! What wouldn't you do here with time and a couple of good horses?' he asked.

'Less than you might with seventeen,' began the sober response, although humour immediately welled again to the surface. 'Give 'em to that bunch o' bastards as they are now though, an' they surely would eat 'em!'

By rejoining and following the trail of footprints along the beach, they caught up with the other members of their expedition resting by the narrow neck of a lake in an open forest of stately trees. In a shady glade nearby, a group of seamen stood around a fire upon which bubbled a kettleful of shellfish, mussels, winkles and small crabs collected from rocks along the way. Such was their hunger they were not inclined to wait long before dining on whatever gritty morsels they could find.

While they ate their meagre handfuls, prying carefully at the shrunken contents of the shells, Hugh Thompson sketched a picture of the route before them.

'From what we could see from the hill, there looks to be a number of lagoons ahead of us, an' certainly one large area – maybe another estuary like the one that delayed us before Cape Howe – we'll need to skirt if we can. I couldn't be sure because we couldn't get high enough, but there are some obvious clearings in the bush which are either lakes, lagoons or swamps, so we'll go in behind them to save time an' avoid having to backtrack. That'll be tomorrow, I'd say. If we come across any blackfellows, maybe they'll lead us through, but if we go a mile or two inland to cross the rivers, we might save time in not having to build rafts or backtrack.'

A deep, grumbling roar suddenly sounded from the tree-tops above them. Instantly heads craned to see the source of the noise, which was repeated in grumpy fashion as if their presence was disturbing whatever the creature above might be.

A mixed jabber of English and Bengali greeted the excited discovery of a furry grey animal lodged high in the fork of a tall trunk, almost invisible against the mottled bark. 'There! There it is! *Janwar! Bhalu! Khaanaa!* Can we knock it down? Can we eat it?'

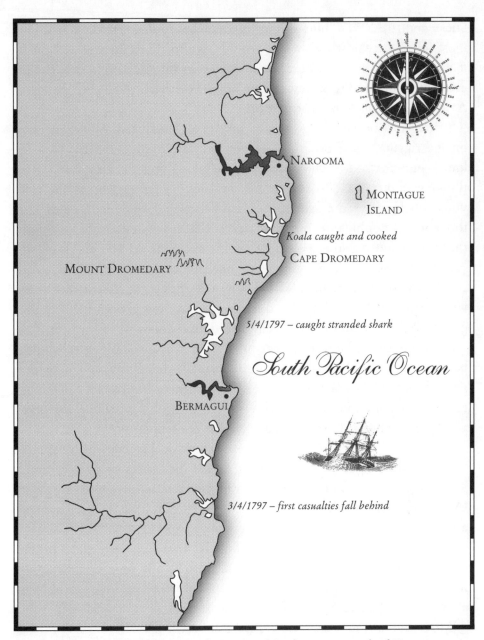

NAROOMA

𝕴 MONTAGUE
ISLAND

Koala caught and cooked

CAPE DROMEDARY

MOUNT DROMEDARY

5/4/1797 – caught stranded shark

South Pacific Ocean

BERMAGUI

3/4/1797 – first casualties fall behind

MAP 10. *Present-day Mimosa Rocks National Park to area north of Narooma, NSW. Approximates journey of 3–7 April 1797.*

Sticks and rocks were hurled into the branches to dislodge the beast, but most fell short. Clearly someone would have to climb the tree and catch it if it were to be their next meal. It was an unmistakeable thought in everyone's mind. From amongst another concerted gabble of Bengali, Azim Prakash made his voice heard.

'Cuttagee! You should go up for him! You have been the fastest man on the rigging, most often, so up you go with a stick and try to – to knock him down. Mr Thompson will be giving you an extra share I am thinking, if you can do it quickly, and not be falling out of the tree yourself!' He flashed a grin at the chief officer, who nodded assent. The thought of a double portion of whatever meat it might provide was more than a spur. With a stout pole between his teeth, the man began his climb.

The tree, however, was a secure haven for the furry animal, who continued to voice his displeasure. The tall shaft rose almost forty feet without so much as a knob, and before the lascar was even halfway up, gravity and the smooth thick trunk had defeated him.

A second, then a third unsuccessful attempt was made by other would-be climbers – until Hugh Thompson forbade any more, much to the anguish and protests of the rest. But a broken arm or leg was not something they could risk, and so they gave way reluctantly, unwilling to forgo anything so obviously edible and there for the taking.

To solve the problem, Job Duggan leaned with uncharacteristic diffidence towards Hugh Thompson, muttering words the others could not catch. The chief officer nodded towards Fran Gilbaert in an approving way. 'Aye, it's certainly worth a try,' he said, 'so let him have the axe back for a while.'

With it once more in his possession, the Irishman seemed to regain something of his former stature, and he wasted little time in voicing his intent of redeeming something of his former standing in what he was about to do. He spat upon his hands in readiness.

'Move out o' the way, will ye, lads, an' let a man have a go! I'll be showin' ye how it's done. Just give me room t' move an' we'll soon be havin' that little fellow in the pot! Aye, move back now, move away, an' don't you forget t' keep an eye on where he falls! Watch out now!'

He spat again. With a vigour he had not displayed for many a day, the carpenter swung his axe mightily at the base of the towering stem, each ringing blow shivering the branches to the crown, each flying chip accompanied by a sprinkling of narrow, spice-scented leaves that tumbled from above. The animal they were after peered down anxiously, shifting its position amidst renewed growling, but its fate was already cast.

With a sharp crack and a splintering groan, the stately tree began to sway, to lean, and then to topple with rapidly increasing momentum.

'Watch out! Stand clear!' The tree crashed to the ground with a rush above the screech and flap of birds, and the earth shook as the bole rebounded, filling the air with leaves.

'Catch it! Don't let it get away!' Excited shouts and hands casting away broken branches filled the woods with the sounds of mass pursuit, but the animal was too badly shaken to hobble more than a few yards. A swishing club finally put an end to it.

It was a heavily built creature, grey-white in colour and shaped like a small bear. By the weight and feel of the body it promised a rewarding feast, and for the rest of the march that day its dangling bounce at the end of the carpenter's shouldered axe kept them all reminded of their hunger, and the meal that lay ahead.

Round the cooking fire near the beach that evening they cut up eighteen equal portions of bear meat, keeping what was left for the following day. They cooked their latest catch carefully, in its skin over the glowing coals, heaping the fire and turning the carcass until it was thoroughly done. The extra care prolonged their eager anticipation. Nothing like this had been contemplated since Preservation Island, where the flesh of the brown-furred *kharha* had always provided a succulent treat.

Silence descended on the group as all began to eat. Hugh Thompson seated himself on a driftwood log, his handful of meat nestled in a clutch of leaves to keep it off the sand. It was much tougher than he had expected. And the taste was – different, if not unique. Strong, definitely, though not exactly rank. Certainly gamy, he decided, as he chewed with determination. He glanced around the others munching in the firelight.

He could see that Will Clarke wasn't happy. No longer was he showing the gusto of five minutes before. He grinned encouragingly. 'Eat up, Will, that's the way! You never know where your next meal's coming from. I've been looking forward to this all afternoon.'

The young supercargo stopped chewing and looked back at Thompson, then at the bear meat in his lap. His expression conveyed a measure of perplexity. 'Is this meat all right, Hugh?' he asked uncertainly, the strong flavour catching at his throat. 'I mean, it wouldn't be off, or – or poisonous or anything, would it?'

The chief officer shook his head emphatically. 'Meat doesn't come much fresher than this. You heard him groaning in the branches just a few hours back. Definitely not off – just a bit different.'

One or two others nearby had stopped eating to listen to their conversation. There was a distinct air of doubt and hesitancy.

'Maybe he was groaning because he was ill,' the youngster ventured. 'He wasn'ae moving very quickly when we caught him. He looked sick tae me.'

'So would you lad, if you'd just travelled a hundred feet on the end of a falling tree.' Hugh Thompson fought to keep his face straight, thankful for the flickering darkness. Will was more than a little unhappy, he knew. 'No, in my experience you can eat most of these things, especially when you're hungry. I've been served worse at sea. If there's a beast alive anywhere, there's usually another close by that'll feed on it.'

The youth picked at his share without enthusiasm. 'I'm sorry, but I don't think I can eat any more,' he said apologetically, recognising the waste.

The more Hugh Thompson chewed on his, the more he agreed with his friend, ravenous as he was. The waiting had sharpened his appetite and his stomach had rolled noisily in anticipation but, yes, the after-taste was definitely something new, and not particularly pleasant. A kind of bitter, oily . . .?

Could Will Clarke have been right in his doubts about its edibility? He caught the lascar leader's eye. 'What do you think, Azim? Have you tasted anything like this before?'

The Indian's face was a picture, even in the fading firelight. He shook his head emphatically. 'Most certainly not, Chief. It has the kind of taste for – for which you wish you did not have. Like the *chiriya* – the pelican of before, it seems to be the way these animals are, from what it is they are eating. I think perhaps, it would be better curried.'

'And I think, perhaps it would be better buried!' The chief officer's throat closed and refused to swallow. He spat into the bushes. 'That's about the nearest thing to a length o' tarred foot rope I've ever tackled,' he said, rinsing his mouth. His glance fell on the carpenter, who had obviously reached the same conclusion.

His smile broadened, and he felt laughter rising. 'An' poor old chippie there's got himself a double portion!' His mirth exploded at the man's discomfiture, and he was joined immediately by most of the others in unsympathetic glee, their own disappointment forgotten.

'Oh Lord, oh dear,' Thompson gasped between breaths. 'All afternoon, *two* helpings, an' a taste like that! This really must be, it just has to be, the luck o' the Irish!'

At a pace which kept the group together, their detour inland into the face of the northern sun took them around a wide and complex network of braided creeks, deep lakes, twisting channels and reedy lagoons. On every hand the system was surrounded by extensive swamps, whose fringes were alive with the sounds of countless unseen marsh dwellers.

There were numerous birds, darting in solitary flight and hovering on a blur of gossamer wings, or swooping and screeching in colourful flocks, though never within reach or stone's throw.

In contrast with the watery expanses, firm islands were seen here and there, including one standing high and large back on the coast itself, all of which supported a vegetation of low trees and thick bushes. Even the broad-lobed sandbanks they frequently crossed were solid enough to give hold to a cover of man-high scrub resembling willow. That this was the haunt of animals and their hunters was obvious from the well-worn meandering pathways they occasionally came across and gladly followed, certain they would lead towards or along dry ground, wherever it existed.

Much of the land they trod was soft and unstable, so wet as to be barely worthy of the name. Between the drier levels the earth was a quaking morass, a maze of shifting runnels and crumbling sandbars, within which oozed treacherously deceptive quicksands.

The group stopped to drink and bathe at a creek that ran fresher than most, relishing the rare luxury of untainted water. Though their hunger was unassuaged, they nevertheless appreciated the simple lift in washing their bodies and salty, mud-stained clothing, both of which dried readily in the sun.

Occupied in their own ablutions, Hugh Thompson and Will Clarke each heard the sudden cry and shrill scream, though neither could immediately see the cause nor sense the direction because of the screening bushes. The chief officer stood, quickly donning his shirt, a half-frown of alertness awaiting the next sounds.

Someone shouting and running through the scrub brought them both to their feet, the urgency of the pace indicating a mishap. A lascar seaman burst through the underwood, his expression alone confirming their fears, his breathless words stinging them into action.

'Chief! Oh, Chief, Mr Thompson, sah! Please to come quickly! Your boy, he has fallen into – , into – *chorbalu*, sahib, oh – into sand, water, up to here! Come now, come most quickly sah!' The man's face was anguished, but his chest-high gesture and urgent pointing towards the nearby estuary left no doubt of his meaning.

'Quicksands, for God's sake! Hurry man, show us where to go!' With barely a pause to seize up a rope, Hugh Thompson pushed the seaman through the scrub, breaking into a run behind him.

One or two others had been drawn by the shouts and commotion. They found the boy struggling ineffectually in a chest-deep mire of liquid mud and sand, out of reach of the longest branches available. Footprints and a crumbling of the far bank showed where he had gone in, while making his way back to the group. The lad's light build and lack of weight prevented his sinking very fast, though sink he did. Even with help close to hand, his mud-streaked face held a terror-stricken expression, and he moaned as he attempted to claw towards them.

'Lie still there! Don't struggle, now. You'll only go down faster. Take hold of the rope and we'll soon pull you out!' The rope plopped down and was quickly grabbed with both hands by Pochari, but as his rescuers drew it taut his muddy grasp failed. His distressed wail sounded pitifully over the frustrated watchers.

'Keep your hands high, Pochari, out of the mud. Keep them high an' we'll have another go. Stay as still as you can,' Thompson called urgently. The boy was now deep to the armpits, and beginning to struggle desperately as fear took a firm hold, despite his master's instructions and encouragement.

Once more the rope splashed alongside him and was frantically clutched. 'Wrap the rope around your wrists, 'Chari! Round your arms to stop it slipping!' Hugh Thompson's tones were becoming more urgent as his servant sank deeper while he sought to show him what was meant. 'That's it! Hold on tight now, an' we'll have you out in a jiffy!'

The lad gritted his teeth against panic, pain, and the resisting pull of the quicksand, feeling himself drawn forward as the rope bit roughly into the skin of his bare arms, chafing abrasively against the harsh sand grains. The strain on his shoulders grew until it seemed his arms must be torn from their roots. An agonised cry escaped with the breath he had been holding as the rope slipped again, leaving him flailing weakly, still in the deadly grasp of the bottomless bog.

'I'm going in after him,' Hugh Thompson snapped, throwing off his shirt. He could see that the youngster was tiring rapidly and would soon give in, unable to do more to save himself. Even though he swam but poorly, he knew there was no other way. Even a strong swimmer would have little advantage here.

Deftly twisting a bowline into the end of the wet rope, he made a noose and quickly slipped it over his shoulders, adjusting it for security and comfort. 'Three of you take a good hold,' he said, flinging the loose end towards Fran Gilbaert and Will Clarke. Azim Prakash and another lascar joined them. 'Take up the slack as soon as I reach him, an' make sure you waste no time in pulling us out!'

He plunged into the mire as far as he could, instantly sinking hip-deep, floundering forward as long as his momentum lasted. He came to rest within arm's reach of the young Indian, who struggled anew towards the familiar figure upon whom he had depended for so long. Their hands met across the quivering surface.

'That's fine now, matey, you're almost safe,' Hugh Thompson gasped, feeling the insidious suction and a weird sense of creeping horror as he sank chest-deep, each movement seeming to draw him irresistibly downwards, swallowing him alive. 'Easy now, take a good breath an' let me pull you in,' he said reassuringly. 'Aye, that's the way, slowly now. I've got you. Easy does it.'

Slowly the pair came together as Thompson drew on the lad's wrists, then his arms, and finally had him by the shoulders in a firm grip. Pochari himself grasped wildly at the man's neck, enfolding him gratefully and clinging as though he would never let go.

'Pull now, get us out of this! Heave, and an even draw, not a jerk!'

As the rope tightened and dug into his chest and armpits, he let himself relax into the morass, moving his legs to break the resistance, the tense body of his servant-boy held trembling against his own.

They were hauled onto the dry bank with a cheer and a babble of excited chatter. The chief officer shrugged off the chafing rope, still holding the boy who shook visibly. Both were plastered in clinging mud, the youngster's slim frame as sharply outlined as a clay figure. Hugh Thompson quickly slipped his shirt around the lad's trembling shoulders.

'Come on, matey, let's go an' get rid of this muck,' he said to the barely sensible boy. To the others he called, 'The rest of you get everything together, ready to move off smartly when we get back. We've been too long in this place. We'll need a good camp an' a fire somewhere back towards the shore before sundown, so half a dozen could press on now. Let's see to it!'

From the camp site within sound of the surf, they walked a distance of some nine miles or so along the beach next day before being stopped again by a broad river. There was material enough in driftwood heaps to build any number of rafts, but an inspection towards the mouth of the flow showed the usual inroad of sand which marked the might of the rising tides over the fluctuating strength of the intermittent river. The ever-shifting balance between the countervailing forces of nature had resulted in a series of encroaching sandbanks just beneath the conflicting waters, which they could clearly see from the rocky promontory overlooking the heads. At low tide, the river would be shallow enough to cross.

The delay in waiting for the waters to ebb gave the stragglers a chance to catch up. For over a week now, Hugh Thompson had noticed that a number of his men, particularly amongst the lascars, were struggling on the walk, making painful progress where once they had stepped lightly across the strand. The entire party had been chosen as the fittest of the *Sydney Cove* crew, but hunger and privation were beginning to take a toll, making their mark daily.

In worst condition were the pair for whom they had waited a whole morning several days earlier. The cough of one was no better, irritated by the rigours and pace of the march. The older man was nearing the end of his natural years and was close to exhaustion. Three of the other lascars showed bleeding feet and varying degrees of lameness from sharp rocks, the dirt, sand and salt water causing them to limp painfully on their raw, unhealing sores. Tenby Read showed no visible hurt, but wandered vaguely along with the group, sometimes ahead, sometimes behind, but always a little remote from the rest.

Remote for other reasons, Job Duggan kept a similar pattern of movement, sometimes leading the group, straggling at other times as the mood took him, but apparently fitter and leaner for his efforts. Pochari plodded doggedly along at the heels of the chief officer as always, despite his recent ordeal. Of the remainder, a handful displayed signs of reluctance and lassitude at the beginning of each day's march, but no more than the growing debility felt by all of them, Hugh Thompson included.

Hunger and restless sleep inevitably took a toll of all of them. Each one had covered good distances in the last two days, sixteen or so miles yesterday, near eighteen the day before. But for all that, the persistent stragglers would still need watching . . .

While they waited for the tide to recede, their presence on the river bank had been noted. Several spear-bearing natives challenged them from the dunes on the other side. It seemed from their shouts and gestures that any crossing might be contested, but the seventeen castaways were the larger group and therefore unconcerned. Despite the hostile attitude on the far bank, they had every intention of going on since they had no other options.

As soon as they were able, they began their crossing in single file, stepping carefully across in the thigh-deep water, Pochari hanging grimly on his master's belt. The natives had disappeared, apparently having made themselves understood, or tiring of their token defiance. The only signs of their presence were a scattering of trampled footprints leading into the dunes, and a single spear planted upright in the sand.

Whatever the latter's meaning, for it did appear to have one, they assembled on the far bank, preparing to move on. Hardly had they done so, however, when their way was barred by the largest and most threatening native group yet, between forty and fifty adult males, all forbiddingly armed, some with spears held poised for throwing.

Hugh Thompson took in the scene at a glance. The natives seemed to already know of the seamen, or at least of other white men. There was not a spark of interest in them as visitors, travellers, or even curios. The group that had emerged from the dunes was clearly hostile, or at least not friendly. The chief officer felt as though he and his party were trespassers, and not particularly welcome.

'Come up together, lads,' he said quietly to those behind him. 'Keep the weapons shown, but not over-ready. Just hold your ground, quietly like. We don't want to start anything with this lot if we can avoid it, but we don't want to seem ready to run for it, either.'

He looked amongst the tribesmen for signs of an obvious leader, but saw none. It was as if the natives were unsure what to do next. 'Just give 'em a chance to say what they've got to say, even though it won't be meaning much. Give your boys the message, Azim.'

There was a muttering amongst the group opposite and some broken shouts from the rear, but no one appeared willing to step forward to parley. To break the stalemate, Hugh Thompson proceeded to address them as he had the earlier bands.

'Friends,' he began, signing elaborately and raising his hands in weaponless greeting. 'We are friends. We have travelled from places beyond the big mountain,' he said, pointing behind them, knowing what he said would doubtless be unintelligible. But some initiative was needed to reduce the atmosphere of confrontation.

His aim was to talk, to make gestures of friendliness, to get some kind of communication going and break down the tension. 'We come from across the oceans, going far, to the town of Port Jackson.' He emphasised his northward gestures, wondering if by chance the settlement was known to these people.

To his surprise, one of the men close to the front took up his gestures, first south, then north, apparently explaining their purpose in his own language. Then he stopped, and waited.

'So what now?' the chief officer muttered to Will Clarke beside him. 'How do you explain India or England to this lot when they know no more than their backyard? Or a shipwreck when they've probably never seen a ship? Van Diemen's Land could be up on the moon for what they might know of it!'

To gain time, he nodded vigorously and repeated his gestures, then went on to mime hunger and the need for food. Whether his audience understood or not, there was no response.

Since there had been no attempt to molest them, and they were clearly making no real progress in a livelier or more amicable communication, the sailors prepared to continue on their way.

This brought an immediate reaction, albeit a further threatening one, from the natives. The group became more agitated and vocal, more spears were hoisted, and one or two moved across their path. Another spear was jabbed upright in the sand. There was a concerted gabbling amongst some of them, accompanied by repeated pointing at the castaways, and gestures northwards. The exchange carried the sounds of an argument, but Hugh Thompson was able to detect no single sense of purpose amongst them.

'They don't seem to know how to handle us, Will, an' there seems to be no chief who might decide. Obviously we're not going to get past 'em yet, though they seem to know we want to go on.'

'Maybe we should try them with some nails or such,' Will Clarke ventured, 'or some strips of cloth. I get the feeling they own this stretch o' turnpike, and maybe the river back there was some kind of boundary. The spears they keep sticking everywhere seem tae be warnings against passage. If we have invaded their bailiwick, perhaps we should be thinking of paying our way past them with a few trinkets – like a turnpike toll, do you think?'

Hugh Thompson grinned. 'Will, you'll live to make a fair merchant yet! You're probably right. They're obviously not going to eat us or they'd have started by now,' he said, 'but we'll have to offer something soon if we're not to stand about here for the next week. Try them with a few strips of the calico. We'll keep the Crown Jewels for later.'

With beckoning signs of encouragement and other elaborate gestures, the two officers took a small bolt of Indian cotton from amongst their several assorted bundles and began to tear off strips, offering them to the still hesitant blackfellows. Their interest was immediate, and tension quickly evaporated as the natives came slowly forward to inspect the gifts.

It soon became clear, though, that they would not be bought off with small strips, having seen so much of the material in the hands of Will Clarke. One individual, bigger, perhaps older, and certainly more calculating than the others, elected himself as spokesman, and clearly demanded much more than was being proffered, scowling, stamping noisily and pounding the ground with the butt of his spear as he berated both the seamen and his fellows. Whatever his arguments, they won over the rest, and before long the spear points were once again levelled menacingly.

The chief officer smiled pleasantly into the faces of the demanding mob, nodding placatingly. 'Well, gentlemen,' he said to the glowering assembly, 'a more unholy bunch o' pirates we've yet to meet, an' it's plain to see you're out to get the better of any bargains. Anywhere else mind, an' ye'd surely swing from a gibbet for highway robbery!'

The adopted smile never left his face as he continued, 'In the name o' God, Will, tear off as much as they want an' hang the expense! I'm sure the company would be glad to have you back whole! What's a few yards o' plain cotton, faced with these ugly buggers! If it pleases them, let 'em have it. Then let's try an' get out of here while they're arguing over it, an' while we've still got clothes on our backs!'

Satisfied that they had been well paid, the tribesmen took themselves off into the bush, while the seamen moved on down the beach to keep themselves sufficiently apart as evening approached, much relieved to be rid of such a distrustful and unpredictable body.

Early next morning, however, they were dismayed to see the same group once more approaching them, even more belligerent. They came across the dunes and foreshore with clear intent, shouting and rattling their weapons as they advanced, but their noise gave the castaways enough warning to prepare for an attack.

The natives had appeared so untrustworthy at their first meeting that Hugh Thompson had decided that some kind of plan was necessary in case of full attack. They thus faced the threat resolutely, their own weapons fully displayed, including an array of clubs and improvised pikestaffs they had wisely put together the previous evening.

Their unwavering stance puzzled the natives, who had intended that their demonstration should put the seamen to flight, so that they could be run down like prey. The show of strong resistance caused the tribesmen to falter, still shouting, stamping and clashing their weapons, but Hugh Thompson's party's own shouts and their solid front in the face of superior numbers had stalled their enemy's schemes.

In a developing lull, Hugh Thompson took a chance and stepped forward to turn the attack, verbally assailing the natives in rich and colourful naval invective, robbed of its offence in being totally incomprehensible, but tempering his tone shortly to normal though still assertive speech. The natives didn't know what to make of it and stopped, seemingly bemused.

He saw that tone, stance and actions would probably be important at this level of communications. And gifts, for which he was prepared. With just a hint of ceremony, Thompson summoned Will Clarke to give him a handful of nails from the longboat and then offered them selectively, gesturing to the older men of the tribe, whom he assumed to be their elders, if not chiefs.

Whether his assumptions were right or not, the ploy worked, and the gifts were accepted. Although spears were still held in place on throwing sticks, ready for instant discharge, after a few more words and scowled nods and signs, the natives began to move away. It was impossible to gauge their thinking, to know if they had finally departed, or whether they planned greater treachery in the hours ahead. For now, though, the men of the *Sydney Cove* were left alone.

As the last one slipped into the bush, Hugh Thompson breathed an audible sigh of relief. 'I don't know what you think, Will,' he said, 'but I'm beginning to feel that meeting up with these people is like smoking your pipe on a powder keg. You're never really sure what's going to happen next! After an encounter like that, you have to wonder what might have happened if we'd tried to run for it, or not stuck together, or if we hadn't had those nails, eh?'

It was a point they cared not to ponder. Without appearing to be in too much of a hurry in case the natives were still watching, they left the spot as quickly as they could.

They were not to be fully rid of their disagreeable company until later the following day, when they once again found themselves pursued by a small band from the larger group. The blackfellows were clearly opportunists, but fewer in number on this occasion than the seamen. Feeling that a greater show of offence would not be amiss, the sailors faced about with an obvious display of all their weapons, the naked blades of the cutlasses glinting warningly in the sun.

Though the natives came forward with their own weapons prudently lowered, their attempts to parley brought them no reward. While the two parties were talking together, however, Will Clarke's eye was caught by what appeared to be the tail of a large animal being carried by one of the tribesmen.

'*Kanguru, kanguru*,' the natives explained in answer to the supercargo's questioning glance and emphatic hand signals. The animal, it seemed, had been a *kanguru*, a creature that appeared from the size of the tail to be a bigger version of the *kharha* they had known on Preservation Island, a belief which the hunter shortly confirmed by leaping around in imitative demonstration. An exchange was therefore quickly struck, a strip of cloth to the owner in return for the fleshy tail, the bargain this time going to the sailors.

'What do you think they'd use the cloth and nails for, Hugh?' Will Clarke asked his companion when they were once more on the move. 'Both items are so foreign tae them, with neither clothing nor metal weapons about anyone we've come across so far. How do you suppose they value them, other than as curios? After all, they willingly gave away a big meal for them.'

These were the type of questions the young man was given to asking in response to unfamiliar experiences in a new, wild country whose inhabitants were such savage and outlandish people. Hugh Thompson's mind was on other matters, however, and would not be diverted.

'Who knows, Will? The calico'll not be going into kerchiefs, napkins nor tablecloths for these people, that I'll wager! It's all a matter of what they want an' value most, according to what it is they have or haven't got. They've got some nails now, an' can stick 'em through their noses for all I care! More importantly, we've just got ourselves a fat, juicy *kanguru* tail – and I can tell you precisely what we'll be doing with that, and the sooner the better!'

In the course of the next few days they were to meet other bands of natives, though always of more equable demeanour and in marked contrast to their hostile neighbours further south. All were friendly and disposed to help within the limits of their means, willingly sharing what meagre fare they had with the travellers where they were seen to be in need, which was most of the time.

Only once was their generosity marred, by a persistent notion of Job Duggan's that it was the white man's right to take anything that the blackfellows possessed in order to meet their own needs, in yet another exchange in which he was swiftly disabused by the chief officer and forcefully reminded that their welfare, if not their very lives, depended on native goodwill.

Their relief in seeing smiles and laughter amongst the first group they came upon, foraging on the shore, was such that the castaways soon allowed themselves to be led through the woods to the native camp. By the side of a large lagoon they found a cluster of rude shelters fashioned from bark and branches, where they were noisily presented to the women, children and other kinsfolk of the tribe.

Here the native hospitality was so unexpected, with an invitation to partake of a meal of plump mussels, that their guests felt warmly inclined to reward them with gifts of cloth strips, nails, and some other metal fittings from the longboat. Whereupon they were prevailed on to spend the night at the camp in relative security, an invitation which was gladly accepted after their two previous nights of sleepless unease.

As they sat together at the campfires through the evening, by means of signs, gestures and what seemed to be universally understood facial expressions, Hugh Thompson attempted to convey something of the unfriendly treatment they had received from the last tribe they had met. In reply, it emerged that the group to the south were at war with their hosts, a statement which caused some excitement amongst the young warriors, who wanted to assuage any ill treatment suffered by their guests at the hands of their enemies. The leg-weary seamen were further prevailed upon to stay longer, but the knowledge that their shipmates still marooned on Preservation Island must be growing anxious as the weeks passed, without sight of a rescuing sail, acted as a spur to their protesting minds and bodies, and sent them on their way.

To help them, other natives who at first appeared timorous were soon reassured and won over to act as both guides and provisors to the wanderers who, having finally consumed what remained of their staples, were reduced to foraging for themselves. The greatest measure of assistance came from one group, who were on hand to ferry the weary band across impeding rivers on no less than three occasions over the space of many miles. They were thus saved many hours, if not days, of effort which would otherwise have been spent in trying to assemble heavy, cumbersome rafts from the dense timber which seemed to grow most prevalently in the bush.

They soon saw that the natives in this area had overcome that particular transport problem by constructing rough canoes of bark, the first they had seen. They were crudely contrived vessels measuring some eight to ten feet in length by two in breadth, tied at each end with vines, in which the natives somehow managed to carry themselves across and along the rivers, despite their obvious flimsiness and inherent instability.

The blackfellows, it seemed, were blessed with a sense of balance wholly lacking in the men of the *Sydney Cove*, as evidenced by their numerous duckings. The local people handled their simple boats adroitly, often carrying three or four men aboard with ease, two of whom stood to pole the canoes along, whilst the seamen stumbled and splashed into and out of the primitive craft, much to the occasional amusement of both parties.

While they were in company with the natives, Will Clarke discovered his capacity to communicate with them, and to understand their responses by means of gestures and mime. It was a discovery he first realised in trading for the *kanguru* tail from their unfriendly pursuers of some days earlier, recognising that not only were they hostile, but also that their acceptance of his bargaining had deprived them of more than one substantial meal. Hugh Thompson had obviously not been wrong about relative values, even though at the time he had not treated it seriously. Either that, or the young Scot could be especially persuasive ...

Equipped with this small ability, the supercargo went about satisfying his curiosity as far as he was able, on their food, their simple way of life, some of the words they used for everyday objects, and their weapons, all of which they willingly demonstrated. Of the last, the one that most caught his appeal, since he could not understand its principles, was what they had taken earlier to be a curved wooden sword. In use, however, it was seen to be thrown by the user, out in a wide circle through the air, returning to and often being caught in flight by the thrower.

At once intrigued, he signed to be allowed to try the object himself, but he failed in his purpose, as did Hugh Thompson and a number of others who had looked on in wonder. It was not obvious why it should work the way it did except for the curve. Though discussion on it was voluble, he regretfully knew he could not understand their explanations, even supposing that was what they were attempting. It was, the natives said, a *wo-mur-rang*, and mostly used against flocks of birds, small animals, and their troublesome southern neighbours.

'How far do you reckon we've come, Will? How many days have we been walking?'

Hugh Thompson stared into the fire at the end of yet another day's journey, watching the flames dance around the cooking pot. In the gathering dusk by the river, men moved about their business in preparation for their night's rest. Recognising the now familiar behaviour pattern,

Will Clarke was aware that their leader was about to make another critical decision, the flames seemingly helping again to crystallise his thoughts.

The young Scot withdrew his journal from its oiled leathern wrap and scanned the pencilled entries. 'Today's been the thirty-second day. If our estimates have been anywhere near correct so far, we've covered over three hundred miles, perhaps nearer three hundred and fifty.' He waited for his companion to go on. 'Have you something on your mind?'

The Englishman nodded. 'Let's say three hundred an' twenty miles, which is only ten miles a day – against the fifteen I originally aimed for when I said we might get to Port Jackson in around thirty odd days. At this rate, an' depending on just how far we've still to go, we might yet be two or three weeks away from the settlement.'

He rose to his feet, Will Clarke following, and strolled slowly down towards the river, continuing the dialogue as he went. 'We haven't reached Bateman Bay yet, which Cook recorded as a pretty deep coastal indentation. It ought to be fairly well unmistakable when we get there. The chart shows Botany Bay, which lies just south of Port Jackson, to be about as far north from Bateman Bay as Cape Howe is to the south of it. As I said, we're not even at Bateman Bay yet, an' how long have we been walking since Cape Howe?'

'Nineteen days,' answered the supercargo, checking the journal again.

'Aye, nineteen days. Three weeks, near enough, an' likely to take all o' that an' maybe more, allowing for reaching Bateman in a day or two. Then the same again at least for the last stretch from there to the colony. Another month, with some of the men in poor state.' It seemed almost as though he was talking to himself. 'An' as they get weaker, slowing down the rest of us, it could take even longer.'

He paused, staring at the flowing waters while he re-assessed his thoughts. 'Because of the longboat mishap, rescue for the people on Preservation Island is nigh a week overdue – an' they won't know it, of course. I'm thinking of splitting the party, Will, an' moving the faster group on more quickly to reach Sydney and get the rescue underway sooner.'

'If the slower group follows on as far as Bateman Bay in a few days an' waits there in a permanent camp,' he reasoned, 'we can pick them up from there, as prominent as it is, on the way back to the island to bring off Captain Hamilton an' the rest o' the crew. What do you think? We need to move a lot faster if we're to give the Old Man the chances he deserves. You could say the same for those of the lads who'd need to stay behind here.'

Will Clarke considered the plan, which reflected his own feelings of apprehension, and finally nodded. 'Finding food for a party as many as seventeen will never be easy, Chief, an' certainly no' tae sustain us as long as you're suggesting. I think we both know some o' the men aren't going tae last the full distance, anyway. I'd agree. It's perhaps better tae leave them as a group now, able tae fend for themselves collectively among friendly natives, rather than have them drop out one by one later.'

'As ye said yourself just now, we could easily pick them up at a place we'd recognise, knowing they'll be there, rather than having them scattered where they can't be reached, or lost all over the coast. Who are you thinking of leaving?'

Hugh Thompson told him, acknowledging the additional point about the friendliness of the local tribesmen. 'With nine or ten left here,' he went on, 'we could leave some of the load with them too. We'd only need one o' the water casks since the water hasn't been too bad, an' we could leave them the swords ...'

A sharp cry from the campfire followed by a shout of rage interrupted their conversation, and they turned to see Pochari sprawled on the ground from a blow by the carpenter, and the oldest of the lascars being shoved angrily away from the steaming, part-extinguished fire. The pair strode rapidly across to the crimson-faced Irishman, who was busy righting the upset cooking pot. He stood up defensively as they approached.

'Jus' look at all o' this, will ye!' the man declared, glaring at the fallen boy and Hugh Thompson together. 'Our dinner almost spoiled, such as it was, an' all because o' this shiftless little brat! Can't we even trust one of 'em t' be left in charge o' the fire now, without spillin' half o' what's on it? Why, an' I've a good mind t' give the young larrikin a real thrashin' an' all!'

He made a dive at the weeping youngster who was holding a bruised ear, but Hugh Thompson caught the man's arm and heaved him away, staggering, even as the boy squirmed aside with another cry.

'You'll keep your hands to yourself, Job Duggan! I'll do any chastising of the lad! More trouble from you, remember, an' you're very likely to end up left behind in the bush! I haven't forgotten your last exhibition, although it seems you might have!' The chief officer stared warningly at the Irishman as he backed away, but the man was not inclined to let it go easily.

'Ah, you an' your favourin' these bastards,' he muttered, scowling sullenly. 'We should see a few of 'em off, an' then there'd be more for the rest of us. We're gettin' nowhere near enough as it is without waste the likes o' that!' he flung out.

Hugh Thompson leapt at the man with a growl of fury, and seizing him by the shoulders shook him so violently that his head rocked, his teeth rattled, and he stumbled awkwardly to his knees when finally released and thrown bodily aside. 'Ye'll belay talk o' that sort around here, Job Duggan,' he grated angrily, 'or you'll be the one seen off, that I promise! Don't get me riled up! What's spilled'll pick up an' wash, an' no-one'll go hungry, d'ye hear me?'

The carpenter cowered under the lash of the chief officer's tongue, remaining where he was even as the leader stalked back to the fire. The old man and the boy were blowing the embers back to life where they had been dampened by the spillage, and carefully feeding small sticks to rekindle the blaze. The old man looked up.

'Mr Thompson, sah – please. Most sorry I am – for the cause of all this, but I – I have to say the – the accident was not the fault of – of your servant here. I wish that you should know, the – the cooking fell from the fire only after I had put on – more sticks, and for that I am most regretting. Therefore, if anyone is to – to be punished, I am the one, and so – it is my share that is lost, I think.'

The chief officer's anger had evaporated. He looked down at the old man who had spoken with such grave dignity, and shook his head. 'No-one'll go without, I've already said. 'Chari can wash the sand away from what was spilled an' put it back into the pot. There wasn't much, an' that way we'll lose nothing – but thank 'ee for telling me, anyway.'

He wandered down to the beach and along the shore for a few minutes, letting the wind purge him of his irritation. The incident served to further cement his decision to split the group. For all the wrong reasons, even Job Duggan had been right about the adversity in their numbers. A smaller group would indeed move faster, with fewer mouths to feed. If it would avoid further unpleasantness through hunger, sickness and ill-temper, and most importantly speed their ultimate rescue, then so be it. It would be done, tomorrow.

8

ASSOCIATES
IN MISFORTUNE

17TH APRIL, 1797. *With weather and seas abat'd somewhat, we
begun this day to save what little else we might from the wreck,
now much reduc'd, before worse sets in. We are grown anxious on
our rescue prospects in the face of prolong'd foul weather, continually
wond'ring of the Chief Officer's fortunes in scanning the north
horizon. We shall await the month's end then consider fully our
options, one of which may be our own voyage in the ship's jollyboat.*
FROM THE SHIP'S LOG

Choosing the nine most incapacitated to be left behind had not been
easy, and there had been some protest. Of the men selected for the
slower party, all of them lascars, only the most exhausted and trail-
weary showed any signs of relief.

Mareshi Patel, who had coughed his way from beyond Cape Howe,
was spitting blood from the rigours of the walk and his dark skin showed
an underlying deathly greyness. The old man, Patnaranji, was close to the
end of his tether, his fatigue being manifest more each day in longer
pauses which punctuated a faltering progress.

Three others had limped painfully during the last few days as a result
of dirt-encrusted cuts and unhealed cracks in the thickened soles of their
feet, including one man who leaned heavily on a stick. All of these slumped
gratefully, thankful in the knowledge that their ordeal was almost over.

There was vociferous opposition, however, from the other four, in that
they were men who showed little physical damage or ailment. They carried
no scars nor other impediments, but the perpetual hunger showed most

gauntly on these four, who had walked much of the way with dull eyes and lacklustre expressions, like men already devoid of life. Their constant failing was slowness, and on this count the chief officer was unwilling to have them as a continuing burden on those still more fleet.

They protested loudly and vigorously on hearing their names amongst those who would wait at Bateman Bay, and for a few moments Hugh Thompson was assailed by a barrage of angry and emotional pleas in Bengali.

Azim Prakash forced his way into the hubbub, trying to restore order and respect as the chief officer strove to control his rising anger, whilst seeking to understand their cries and pleadings, and at the same time quell the rising dissent. They ignored his shouted English and feeble Bengali, and it was not until Azim had dealt the leading pair enough smart clouts to assert his own authority that his superior was able to understand their demands and offer some reassurances.

'They are thinking you are leaving them here to die, sahib,' Azim explained, 'now they are feeling we have no more use for them. They are saying the sick are being left to starve, or to – to be butchered by the wild tribesmen, and – and all are being – being abandoned, just as yesterday the carpenter was heard to say.'

The men looked sullen and rebellious even when Azim translated the plan to establish a camp at Bateman Bay. Some further doubts and protests brought a storm of exasperated anger from Azim.

'Hah! Sometimes I am having no times for these people!' the lascar foreman exclaimed when at last he had berated the dissenters into cowed submission. 'They are so much ignorant men, who are seeing no further than their noses and bellies! Most of us – we are understanding and accepting what it is you have said we will do, Chief. But them – it is as well they are being left behind, having not the spirit, nor courage, still to be going onward!'

Patnaranji approached Hugh Thompson as the reduced party was about to leave. 'With most respects, sahib,' he said, 'we wish it to be known that you have made – the most wise decision on our – our behalf, and

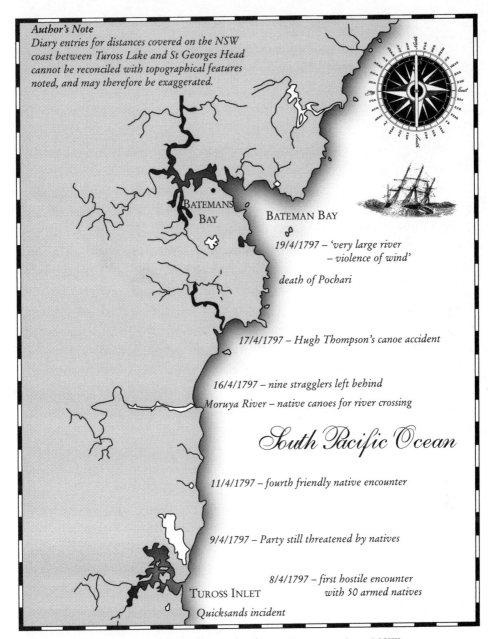

Author's Note
Diary entries for distances covered on the NSW
coast between Tuross Lake and St Georges Head
cannot be reconciled with topographical features
noted, and may therefore be exaggerated.

BATEMANS
BAY

BATEMAN BAY

19/4/1797 – 'very large river
– violence of wind'

death of Pochari

17/4/1797 – Hugh Thompson's canoe accident

16/4/1797 – nine stragglers left behind
Moruya River – native canoes for river crossing

South Pacific Ocean

11/4/1797 – fourth friendly native encounter

9/4/1797 – Party still threatened by natives

8/4/1797 – first hostile encounter
with 50 armed natives

TUROSS INLET

Quicksands incident

MAP 11. *Present-day Tuross Lake and Inlet to Batemans Bay, NSW.*
Approximates journey of 8–20 April 1797.

are about to take the only way possible to save us. Not one of us left here could have – have completed the long journey to your destination, but this way – we are feeling it is better for you to bring a ship, if this is to be. Before you go, please to have – little concern for us, while you are travelling. We shall make what friends we can, amongst the people here, and we – we shall be at this Bateman Bay when you return. In the meanwhile – may your God look well upon you.'

They had thus set out amidst an atmosphere of calm acceptance tinged with smouldering distrust. Freed of their encumbrances, the remaining eight pushed on along the sea coast at a forced pace, as if to demonstrate to themselves the rightness of the decision.

In justification, they did indeed make good progress until, after five miles or so, they came upon a narrow but deep river offering no immediate crossing. There were no sand bars such as they had used to cross so many similar barriers. The beach and banks were clear of any dried timbers from which they might have built a raft. And the weather, water depth and temperature made the prospect of a cold swim uninviting.

In order to find a way around the obstacle they turned upstream, expecting to find a place where the river narrowed or shallowed sufficiently to create a ford. They had not gone more than 300 yards, however, when a cry from Fran Gilbaert at their head proclaimed an unexpected find.

'Look what we got here,' he shouted, pointing into the scrub. 'How easy it would have been if ev'ry river had one of d'ese!' He was kneeling by the slanted trunk of a stunted, windblown tree, extricating an upturned native bark canoe from amongst the undergrowth. 'It looks to be an old one,' he said, as the others gathered round, 'but it might easily have been left here for us, all d' same. Is it jus' what we need?' His beaming grin brought its own answer.

Together they hauled the roughly-fashioned craft from its hiding place, then examined it for soundness and leaks. 'Aye, it should suit,' Hugh Thompson agreed. 'It's not exactly built like a longboat,' he observed, fingering its thin and seemingly brittle sides, 'but it'll do for now, so long as we handle it carefully. That was well done, lad. Do you want to be the first one over?'

Tying a retrieving line to the canoe's stern, they helped the Dutchman gingerly inside till he found his balance, then gently pushed him out into the stream. For a moment the flimsy shell rocked alarmingly and the pole they handed him did little to help him. The river at this point was neither wide nor swift, and within a few minutes he had worked his way to the far bank. On the next trip Azim Prakash ventured across, with the same teetering precariousness and lack of expertise.

'It might be easier wit' two people aboard for even balance, Chief, an' wit' a paddle each, 'stead of d' pole, if you can make some,' Fran Gilbaert called over as the canoe was hauled back by its tether. 'Sitting low in d' boat, instead of standing as d' natives do, d' extra weight in d' bottom maybe will keep it more steady!'

Heeding this advice, Hugh Thompson motioned Job Duggan and Tenby Read into the bobbing craft, the latter eyeing its thin skin and rude assembly with some hesitation. 'Is – is it going to be safe, Chief?' the youth asked anxiously. 'It – it doesn't look any too strong to me, with two of us to get in. I'm not – not such a good swimmer like, if – if it sinks.' His features were pale, and a cold sweat stood on his brow, notwithstanding the coolness of the day.

'You'll be all right, son, don't you worry,' the chief officer declared encouragingly. 'Chippie here'll help you. Just remember you've been in one of these before, an' it got Azim and Fran Gilbaert across just now. Two in's a better way, as you've just heard. If the natives are able to use these things with two or three aboard, I'm sure we can!'

With some awkwardness, and more than one frightened yell from the young seaman which brought threatening growls from the carpenter, they reached the other side safely, paddling with a split branch. Tenby Read wasted no time in scrambling ashore.

'When the next lot are over, ye might as well start moving on instead of waiting around,' Hugh Thompson shouted across the stream. 'We'll be across ourselves shortly.'

After drawing the boat in once more, it became the turn of the lascars Cuttagee and Pochari, who needed the same kind of assurances as Tenby Read. By now a measure of water had seeped into the canoe, but it was emptied by turning it upside down. Set again on the river, Will Clarke and Hugh Thompson lifted their single water cask into the rear of the canoe to make up for the slight weight of the young Indian.

The pair were almost halfway across when Will Clarke's glance was caught by a movement in the nearby scrub. Instantly alarmed, he turned to see two of the four lascars who had stayed behind under protest observing the crossings from the edge of the bush. They had obviously been trailing at a distance, though their reason was unclear.

As he watched, the other two came up behind, their bundles proclaiming they were prepared for travelling. There was nothing to show that the rest of the crew were following. The newcomers stayed away from the two officers, however, and Thompson did not attempt to remonstrate with them for leaving their lame comrades.

Hugh Thompson shrugged. 'What do you do, Will, short of kicking their arses or beating them about the head?' he asked in a tone of exasperation. 'They obviously don't mean to hang about. Leaving the canoe on the far bank may slow 'em down 'til the rest catch up, or at least give 'em something to puzzle over. They'll stay on at Bateman Bay, though, even if I have to cripple the buggers myself!'

When the canoe was returned the fourth time there was much more water in the bottom, and one or two cracks were evident. It was clear that the old, weather-worn material would not last much longer.

'You'd better go across alone this time, Hugh,' Will Clarke offered. 'It's looking pretty doubtful now, and might not make another trip with two of us in it. If it's still in one piece next time round, I'll use it last, otherwise I can always swim. That's something I could easily spare myself on a day like this, remember, so away ye go an' try not tae be puttin' your foot through it!' A chill wind and a heavy grey sky added feeling to his words.

His comrade laughed as he stepped carefully inboard and placed the chart container in the bow, away from the obvious leaks. 'Well, sooner you than me, matey!' the Englishman retorted. 'You've heard me say before, I'm much more at home on the water, than in it! It's already swilling round my backside, an' I can fairly vouch it's too cold for any kind o' swim!'

It took Thompson a moment or two to get the hang of the flexing hull before being able to keep its nose pointing towards the opposite shore. His efforts were regarded in silence by the group of lascars whom Will Clarke could see were edging closer, apparently intent on taking their own turn. Just over halfway across, Hugh Thompson's cry jerked his attention back to the canoe's progress.

'There's a split starting, Will, and water's pouring in! I'll have to try stuffing something into it!' Sudden uncharacteristic anxiety tinged his voice as he stopped paddling and knelt to wriggle out of his jerkin, while striving to maintain a precarious balance. Without forward motion the canoe began to swing in the stream, its trailing tether acting like a drogue, turning its tail towards the sea.

'No, Hugh! Keep paddling! Try to make the far bank! If you lose way you may upset it!' Inexpert as he was, Will Clarke could plainly see the need to preserve a forward motion.

His warning came too late. The canoe began to rock dangerously, catching the chief officer off-balance, half-in and half-out of his jacket. His effort to regain his trim was too violent and more than the ageing bark could stand. A ragged tear appeared along the length of the canoe as the weakened structure twisted under the strain, and in an instant the strength and support amidships was gone, and the canoe began to fold.

'She's going under, Will! The bark's breaking up, an' I can't ... ' His shout was cut off as he splashed sideways into the flow, still fighting to get out of his encumbering garment. It was a critical moment. He sank into the deep waters, struggling in a splutter of foam, already in difficulties. The young Scot looked around for some form of support. The four Indians stood impassively on the bank, obviously unprepared to help even though all were good swimmers.

Without a second's thought he flung aside the rope he was holding and plunged bodily into the cold river. Through a peaty-brown haze and bubbling spray his head broke the surface, the blurred wreck of their canoe looming downstream as he shook his vision clear. Of his companion's whereabouts, scarcely a ripple showed.

'*Hugh!*' His friend's name escaped his lips as he struck out swiftly towards the drifting canoe. Closing in, he gulped air and dived into the copper-tinted deep, straining amongst the rippling reflections to catch a glimpse of something, anything. A dark mass wavered into his vision. Surfacing quickly, he gulped a fresh breath and kicked deep again, straining desperately for sight of the drowning man.

The dark mass loomed distortedly, his hands reaching out to clutch at the drift of hair and clothing. With bursting lungs he fought his way to the surface, dragging the inert body up with him. The cold air and colder water struck him together as he gasped and coughed, but he barely paused before kicking out frantically for the nearest bank, knowing that even now it might be too late to save Hugh Thompson's life.

Rough gravel and pebbles stubbed his bare feet as he found ground, and he struggled ashore unthinkingly, hauling the drowned man by the shoulders from the water. He stumbled as willing hands reached out to help him, and instinctively he sought to lift the body across a group of boulders, head downwards, before his own mind succumbed to the effects of the debilitating chill.

'Hurry, sir, oh please, hurry! What shall we do? The master is so sick and still. Tell me what it is we must do, please! How we can help him?' Will Clarke was numbly aware that Pochari had appeared, or perhaps had never left when told to push on. While his own body shook in the creeping cold he could feel the boy's warmth, seemingly the only other living thing as they leant together over the deathly form of their leader. With the hope of gaining some further help he scanned the opposite bank for the lascars, but they were no longer to be seen.

'Let's get – get his head an' – and chest hanging d-down, s-so, with his – his legs highest', he stuttered through chattering teeth. 'M-m-must empty w-water out of him c-c-quickly and g-g-get him m-moving, s-soon as we c-can. B-both of us, n-now, p-push hard on his b-back, y-yes, that's m-m-.' His words stopped as he concentrated, seeing the lad grasp what to do, and conserving his own strength and sanity by clamping his jaws on the unnerving rattle of his teeth.

Copious amounts of water seemed to pour from Hugh Thompson's lips as he hung limply athwart the rock, but there was no sign of life. They worked grimly on his body for what seemed an age, forcing his chest against the rock, feeling the skin clammy and seemingly lifeless beneath their fingers, but unable to think of what else they might do. Their actions became automatic, their sensitivities assailed by the shrinking wind.

A groan, followed by a weakly gasping cough, was the first sign of a returning spark. Another groan issued from the upended figure as Will Clarke collapsed against him, relief flooding through his soul. For a moment he was gratefully aware of the transient warmth that his efforts had brought to his own numbed limbs. For the first time he peered consciously into the young brown face that had laboured silently beside his own, and was shocked to see the same haggard relief in its tear-stained expression.

'That's – that's fine, Pochari, just – just fine. We can stop now,' he gasped, his chest heaving from the sustained exertion and the shock of reaction. 'We've managed t-tae revive him, God be thanked, though I – I had begun to fear the worst.'

Together they slumped alongside the chief officer, drained of all energy by the sudden, near-death drama. Then as they listened to the feeble coughing sounds of Hugh Thompson's recovery, watching with concern the irregular rise and fall of his chest, Will Clarke became aware again of the creeping cold and its threat to the still comatose victim.

He looked across into the brown eyes, sharing the weary triumph. 'Can you start up a fire, 'Chari?' Will Clarke asked. 'If you've still got flint and tinder with you, we could all do with some warmth while we see how quickly Mr Thompson recovers.' The boy nodded and wiped away a tear with a weak smile. His voice was emotionally subdued, barely audible.

'Yes, sir, I – I have everything I am carrying. I shall set a fire going, very soon, now – now I know – .' He faltered, still with tears of relief unshed. 'Thank you, sir, for – for what you have done.' He bit his lip, blinking. 'Thank you, for the life of – of my master.' He bobbed his head and darted away, just as the first tremors of returning consciousness touched the big man's fingers and fluttered his eyelids.

All three of them sat close to the warming flames a little while later, Hugh Thompson leaning his back against a log, looking wan, but close to recovery. Hunger pangs gnawed at their bellies in a manner sharpened by their recently shared trauma, but there was no food, though they were grateful for the heat of the fire.

Hugh Thompson's voice was hoarse, and his hands shook a little as he held them towards the leaping tongues. Though the fire was warming limbs, the clothes they wore were still wet enough to carry a chill wherever they were turned away from the heat.

'Don't be blaming yourself, Will,' the chief officer was saying to a stricken-faced Will Clarke, who had just realised they had lost their precious chart. The urgency of pulling Hugh Thompson from the river's grasp had pushed any thought for the fate of the broken craft and its contents entirely from his mind. It was not until asked that he remembered seeing the bamboo container lying loose in the bow.

Immediately he had set out with Pochari to comb the banks for signs of the drifting tube, but without success. The wreckage of the boat had snagged in an eddy and from this he retrieved the rope, but the lost chart had been irreplaceable and he felt that their very lives might hinge on the vanished tracings.

'There wasn't a great deal of detail shown for the coast along here, Will, as you've seen for yourself,' Hugh Thompson went on encouragingly 'I'd reckon I've looked at yon chart so often now that every last line on it's etched on my brain! It'll be no hard task to score another onto a piece of bark or some such. You did all you could in pulling me out of it, an' for that I owe you my life, as well as my grateful thanks! Think no more about it, lad. You saved what was most precious, I can tell you!'

The heat of the fire was so welcoming that they cheerfully agreed to stay there for the night, building the coals higher to keep away the cold. There seemed little sense in walking but a few miles to set up the same kind of camp, as drained as they were from the day's events and the ravages of an unappeased hunger.

Furthermore, the chief officer was given to spasmodic bouts of coughing from the effects of his near-drowning. Seeking warmth and rest in lieu of food, for the shore was barren sand, they used the time before dark to build comfortable beds of cut vegetation, listening again to the derisive evening laughter of their feathered observers, and turning in by the fire as the light faded.

Hugh Thompson spent a restless night, troubled by persistent spells of coughing, and waking in a rash of sweat in the early hours, disturbed by a nightmare wherein the suffocating cold of the river again threatened to stifle his being. The fire had died, and the chill of his sweat led to fits of shivering. Next morning the nagging cough was no better and his limbs felt heavy and weak, though he decided to push onwards.

Before leaving, Will Clarke examined the river banks for signs of the lascars, but as they had neither seen nor heard anyone on their side of the river since the previous day's incident, nor fires on the southern bank, they assumed that the four crewmen had returned to their fellows.

For Hugh Thompson it was a day of trial and torment, racked by a harsh chest irritation, without food to soothe his dry throat, his pace a leaden-footed, light-headed plod. The coast was beginning to break into a series of crescent-shaped bays and rugged headlands, beaches backed by high dunes or low cliffs, with thick bush to the very fringes of the shore.

Though urged to stop and rest another day, he would not, even when faced with difficult traverses round a number of rocky promontories. Here and there they came across traces of their companions' recent passage, a set of footprints in the sand pointing the way ahead, a clutch of broken shells reminding them of their own hunger. Though Will Clarke and the young Indian boy scouted for food as they progressed, they found next to nothing.

'No doubt they're collecting everything they find, Will, in expectation of us coming up behind them soon,' the chief officer said, in response to the Scotsman's terse criticism of the others' apparent unthinking greed. 'After all, we did say we'd not be long behind them. That's why we need to press on if we're to eat soon. God knows, after that ducking I've got a windpipe full o' salt an' a bellyful o' sand, an' I'll not be right until I've eaten well of a *kanguru* stew, or at least supped long on a good meaty broth!'

They could only cover eight miles or so that day, though, despite Hugh Thompson's wish to continue at all speed. The nagging cough tore raggedly at his lungs in alarming spasms and his breathing rasped so audibly that, within sight of the bay they were looking for, he was forced to give in. They made camp again, this time in the notch below a wave-scoured cliff perched above the sea, between two fires to ward off a rising wind.

Snug beneath their overhang, it was Pochari who, entirely without bidding, devoted himself to relieving his master's sufferings and discomfort. With the drier leaves of the papery-barked coastal scrub he infused a hot, acceptably aromatic brew, a tea-like concoction they had tried once before, then commenced to scoop hot, moistened sand from near the fires into their headscarves and neckerchiefs, which he then applied to the chief officer's chest. There was little more he could do, without food to cook. As each of the hot packs cooled it was replaced by another, and before long the hoarse breathing had perceptibly softened under the constant soothing warmth and attention.

As darkness fell, Will Clarke watched the lad going about his ministrations, appearing certain that his simple remedy would help. Hovering a little later on the brink of sleep, staring at shadows dancing on the rough stone of their shelter to the sounds of wind and surf, he was aware that Hugh Thompson had been asleep for some time, yet his youthful servant still applied more of the hot sand packs by the flickering light of the fire. It was a vigil he was to maintain faithfully for most of the night.

Will Clarke awoke to a blood-red, chilly dawn. The banked fires had burned to low embers and the stack of driftwood they had gathered the previous evening was gone. The receding warmth was beginning to give way to cool invading fingers from the sea, pushed by the wind they could not wholly feel within their shelter, but which stirred the waves and rendered the whitecaps just visible in the rising light.

He shivered and eased his aching, ill-clad body. Behind closed eyes he tried to regain a measure of his earlier comfort, but there was no way of getting back to sleep. Hugh Thompson's breathing close by was soft and regular in sleep, with little sign of the irritation that had troubled him the day before.

As the sunrise waxed in glowing tints, its first rays revealed Pochari curled alongside the chief officer, adding his slim body heat to allay the morning chills while at the same time drawing warmth for himself from his master. Raking the coals into reluctant life, Will Clarke watched the crimson orb climb slowly above the sharp-lined horizon, its shifting beams bursting forth to caress the high clouds, then pale gradually into full and vivid brilliance.

The display had gradually transformed the early gloom of morning into a panoply of glorious colour that awed the senses, edging with pink the dark cloudmass on the southern horizon, lighting for a moment the higher horse-tail gossamer veils which foretold of stronger winds, and casting a rose-hued pall over the tumbling sea itself.

In such empty and ageless surroundings, it was easy to appreciate the magnificence of daybreak as part of a vast eternal cycle, a primordial sequence that had taken place since the very dawn of Creation. He left his companions sleeping as he wandered out into the warming sunlight. His thoughts carried him onto the beach, across rocks left wet and weed-strewn by the falling tide, over sands lying cold beneath his naked feet. He stopped to drink at a freshwater stream that bisected the shingle strand before mingling with the inward rush of the sea.

Stepping round yet another craggy bluff, a column of smoke some distance along the curving shore caused him to pause, wondering as to its source. Reluctant to face a native band alone, he was about to turn and retrace his steps when a figure moved out of the scrub along the beach and, without seeing him, proceeded to make its way down to the tideline.

The man was clothed! The supercargo's heart gave a sudden joyous bound as he realised that he had stumbled upon Fran Gilbaert and his party and, indeed, it was Fran Gilbaert himself who turned at the sound of the distant halloo and waved in response. Hurrying back to their overnight shelter he arrived out of breath to find a raw-throated Hugh Thompson only slightly the worse for his ordeals, thanks to his attendant's loyal ministrations, and within the hour they were reunited with the five who had gone on ahead.

As they approached the head of the deeply incised bay, the winds increased markedly. The steady march of the white-crested waves ended on the surrounding shores in fountain-bursts of pounding breakers. Every protruding rock tongue and headland wore a mantle of flung foam as the seas beat endlessly around them, filling the air with a suspension of spray. On the bluff where they rested, trees thrashed in restless torment and serried cascades of leaves, giving the men cause to withdraw from the bite of the wind while they took stock of their situation. There was more than a hint of rain.

'Well, I'd say this'd have to be the place that James Cook named as Bateman Bay,' Hugh Thompson declared. 'It's about where it ought to be, according to what I can remember from his chart. We'll know for certain in a day or two if we come upon no other of similar size. I doubt that Cook would mark one an' not another if he was this close in.'

His arm swept the triangular embayment. 'This is more of an estuary than a bay, an' probably deeper except for that bar, judging from the big river yonder. There haven't been too many like this along the coast so I'd say for certain it's Bateman Bay we're at.'

With a seaman's eye he mentally conned a ship past a cluster of islands into the inlet's constrained reaches. He spoke almost as if to himself. 'Not too bad a place from which to pick the others up, just as I'd thought. Though we'd need to come in cautiously with a lead, an' be wary o' the lee shore, anchoring before that bar an' then bring 'em off by boat. But it's not a bad place for all that. Plenty of natural shelter, timber for fires, an' both fish an' birds from the sea.'

Will Clarke also stared between the enclosing arms of land, his mind set on more immediate matters. Out beyond the bush the waves had begun to leap boisterously before the press of a freshening south-easterly wind. A line of creaming combers warned of shoaling waters. The islands to seaward did little to impede the march of crests towards the head of the bay, where they met and mingled in confused conflict with the outflowing stream.

'Crossing that river'll likely be a wee bit difficult in this wind, Hugh,' he said at length. 'Are ye thinking o' pressing on any further today, or maybe waiting until tomorrow for perhaps better weather? There's rocks an' pools all along here,' he pointed out purposely, 'and we might usefully use the time in getting oursel's a meal or two if we were tae bide here a while.'

Having listened to a marked wheeze in Hugh Thompson's laboured breaths, he felt he already knew what the answer would be. The chief officer coughed hoarsely in the blustering wind. 'I've had my fill of dodgy river crossings,' he replied, 'as ye might well imagine! This one's bigger'n any we've seen for quite a while, an' we can even see it's bad! So – yes, let's give it time to blow itself out, an' meanwhile catch the chance o' collecting whatever's goin' by way o' vittles round here. My belly's been certain me throat's cut these last couple o' days, an' I'll not be getting rid o' this blasted affliction until I've had something near reasonable to chew on! We'd best not stay hereabouts too long though, otherwise we'll be cleaning out what the others'll be needing to live on when they eventually get here.'

Somewhat surprisingly they had not been overtaken by any of the rear party. There was no sign even of the four lascars who had dogged them so closely at first.

While they talked and planned and took a spell in the shelter of the bush, Hugh Thompson's young servant slipped away, satisfied they were to stay on this side of the river and start collecting food. It had become part of his duties, along with others of the crew, to seek out anything edible, but as a personal servant he had a particular responsibility for the burly Englishman, who even now was suffering again from the effects of his recent near-death accident. The lad was therefore concerned to seek some special kind of treat amongst the rock pools at the foot of the bluff, driven as much by his own hunger as the needs of his master.

The way down to the pools was steep and crumbly and the sharp rock scored into his feet. By clinging to the scraps of vegetation, however, he was able to work his way carefully from the edge of the trees above until his feet touched the broken stones at the base of the descent. Safely down, he moved amongst the isolated ponds of the intertidal garden, peering into each, searching for the delicacies he hoped to find.

There were plenty of mussels but, heedful of Hugh Thompson's last caution, he left them alone for the men behind to discover. Instead he sought and found numerous sea anemones and the creature he knew as *trepang*, excising the one from its rock-hold with a sharp piece of broken shell, and squeezing the inky contents from the other.

His collecting cloth was almost full when a hail signalled an imminent departure. Pochari waved, acknowledging the recall, then bent to tie the corners around his precious finds. They would make a most welcome addition to their first real meal in two days.

Scaling the cliff proved to be more difficult than the scrambling descent. He needed one hand to carry the seafoods he had collected, and the bundle itself was a concern whenever he paused to lodge it somewhere in order to use both hands for the climb. The skin of his feet had also softened in the sea-water during his food-gathering foray, and the rocks therefore felt sharper. Before long he realised that his upward route was not the one he had taken on the way down.

He looked around fearfully, seeking secure holds, suddenly aware of the drop below, and of the angular sharpness of the rock surface to which he clung. Near the top the face became smoother, but also revealed a narrow ledge leading off towards his downward path. Almost in desperation, he took the bundle in his teeth and reached out to clutch at a crevice-held shrub, shifting his weight to wriggle his way across to the left.

Immediately the rock he had stepped onto dislodged with a lurch and a clatter, sliding away with others in company. Instinctively he flung himself forward, fingers gouging frantically amongst the fragments of stone to halt the threatened fall. While he clung fiercely to the root with his left hand, the front of his shirt snagged momentarily on a firmer projection under his dragging weight, allowing him sufficient respite to search for another toehold, his eyes shot wide in silent horror, the bundle clenched between his teeth muffling the frightened cry. In these same critical seconds, however, the shrub gripped in his left hand pulled away from its hold while the taut fabric of his shirt gave way with a rending tear, tumbling the luckless youth almost forty feet to the beach below.

On the cliff-top, four of the party had already started out towards the last long beach before the river when Fran Gilbaert heard the faint cry of despair. Cautiously he craned out as far as he could with safety, searching below but seeing nothing obviously amiss. He turned to call over his shoulder, finding only the young supercargo on hand.

'Mr Clarke! Mr Clarke! D' boy down here's in trouble of some sort! I t'ink he might have fallen! Where's d' Chief? I have to go down!' He ran back towards the cliff edge, stooping quickly to ease himself over the lip before being stopped by Will Clarke's answering shout.

'No, wait! Not that way! Hugh! *Hugh!*' Will sprinted down the track, catching sight of the chief officer who had set out last. 'Come back, Hugh! Something's happened to 'Chari!' He wasted no time in explanations. As his friend turned in a stumbling run he hurried back to the Dutchman, lifting the coiled rope from his shoulders as he ran.

'I'll go down on the end of the rope, Fran, while you pay it out behind me! You're the stronger and I'm the lighter, an' Mr Thompson's in no state yet tae go scrambling up an' down cliffs. I'll see tae the lad. Hold hard on that,' he said, thrusting the loose end at the seaman. 'I'll give you three tugs when I want ye tae haul in!'

Carefully he picked his way over the edge and down the eroding face, glancing up at the bar-taut rope as he descended. Part-way down he saw the fresh scar of the dislodged rock, and the mark of the pulled-out shrub close to a flutter of calico rag caught around a sharp protrusion.

It was a foreboding sign. The steepness of the cliff here was pronounced, and his apprehension mounted as he peered downward. It was not hard to imagine what had happened. His worst fears were confirmed by the still figure lying beside a clump of stunted bushes, out a little from the base of the cliff.

''Chari! *Pochari!* Are you all right?' He flung the rope away from him as he ran quickly over to the youngster, but he knew even as he approached that he would receive no reply. Although the boy lay face down, there was something ominously unnatural about the angle of his head. Where another time the soft sand might have broken his fall, his position now spoke only of a twisting impact which had given the youth little chance. His thin neck had snapped like the loose scatter of sticks onto which he had fallen. Close by lay the bundle of food from the rock-pools, its contents spilled onto the sand.

Though Will Clarke realised the futility of his gesture, he reached trembling hands out to the boy, cradling his head and gathering his slender limbs together before turning him over to search for a heartbeat. In the action of brushing sand grains away from a grazed cheek he paused, staring then as confusion and disbelief flooded his expression. Kneeling beside the still form, he shook his head slowly in disbelief, unable to grasp for a moment what fate and the youngster's torn shirt had chosen to reveal so cruelly.

He felt himself overwhelmed with a deeper sense of tragedy and needless loss. Tears pricked his eyes as his mind took in the poignancy of what he saw, an extra sorrow which he felt and shared, a heightened sadness now which lodged in his throat and there remained. While his numbed feelings were still slow to absorb and accept, yet somehow he had nevertheless known, and knowing thus, understood. So many gestures and actions were explained. So many half-questions, never crystallised, were answered.

He did not know how many minutes passed as he knelt there, but he found himself unable to answer the shouts of the others above when he finally became conscious of them. It was not until the rattle of stones from the cliff face heralded the hurried arrival of Hugh Thompson that he rose slowly to his feet. The two men stared at each other across the space of several feet, neither wanting to move, the chief officer breathing heavily from his speedy descent. He was the first to speak. The question was cautious, almost defensive.

'You know, then?'

'Aye', Will Clarke replied quietly. 'Though I did begin tae wonder a little, after the quicksand incident a few days ago.' He could still picture the bedraggled creature Hugh Thompson had pulled from the mire, whose sodden form had been quickly covered with his own shirt.

The older man looked down, unwilling to let his companion read his face. 'Is she dead?'

'Yes, Hugh. I'm afraid so.' His words seemed pitifully inadequate. So little could be said. An intruder, he just wanted to leave the chief officer alone with his feelings. 'If it helps, it – it would have been quick. I'm sorry, Hugh.'

A heavy sigh escaped the big man, and his stature seemed to visibly shrink. For a moment he stood as if uncertain. Then, collecting himself, he moved silently around his friend to kneel at the other side of the body. His face was still hidden.

He gazed down. The unbuttoned jacket had fallen aside, the thin shirt lying agape at neck and chest, ripped through by the spur of rock at the instant of the fateful fall. Its tattered edges stirred lightly in the breeze, the ragged tear revealing the unmistakeable swell of a small, youthful breast. The skin was grazed here too, and at the collarbone and along the length of one arm. Blood marked her dusty fingers, and her knuckles and knees were raw from lacerations. The disarticulated neck told its own story.

'Would you – just give us a few minutes, Will? I'd – I need a bit of time – you understand?' Emotion choked his voice, and Will Clarke nodded.

'Aye, Hugh. I understand.' In those few words he tried to convey all his compassion, but it still seemed inadequate. 'Is there anything I can do? Will you ...'

'Just throw me down a length of the calico, Will, that'll be all. I have to – I'll bury her here myself.' He shook his head slowly, as if still unable to accept the stark reality. 'I'll not be long. Won't need more'n a yard or two, either. She's – she never was very big.'

Later that evening, after setting up camp on the river near the point from which they might cross on the morrow, the pair walked off together along the cold moonlit beach, away from the campfire and the ears of their five remaining shipmates. For once their bellies were full, of shellfish from the rock pools and greenstuff from the bush. The waves still lapped rhythmically, though the wind had eased at dusk. The woods and the surrounding hills were dark silhouettes, relieved only by the fire-glow marking the site of their camp.

After their meal Hugh Thompson felt a curious need to tell Pochari's story, but whether in response to a close companionship which flourished in the face of adversity, or simply to talk away his servant's death as an emotional palliative, an alternative to brooding and introspection, he did not know. Sharing the burden, however, brought a measure of relief to the difficult feelings he had carried since the accident.

'After all this time, it – it seems hard to talk of Pochari as – as a girl,' he began as they tramped along side by side. 'I suppose, though, that must show something of the strength of our deception. There were times I wondered how long it could last, but I – I never thought of seeing it end this way.'

'I found her in Calcutta's back streets one day, begging,' he went on quickly, 'about three, three-an'-a-half years ago. God knows the place is full of such people, youngsters struggling on the absolute edge of existence. I can't say why I paid any particular attention to this one. Her hair was rough-cut, her clothes were ragged, an' she hadn't washed in days. Maybe all this made me see her as just another slip of a lad.' He shrugged.

'Anyway, about then I needed a lad aboard as cook an' cabin-boy, my last one having taken himself off on the coast. So, I took him – took *her* on,' he corrected himself. 'Maybe she seemed brighter than most. Somewhere she'd picked up a smatter of English. Enough to beg with, at least.'

'She had no home, no folks, an' slept in the streets,' he explained. 'An' as we carried a lascar crew aboard the *Cove* – she was called the *Begum Shaw* then – taking one more on the muster as a personal servant to work in my quarters wasn't a problem.'

'Did no one know about her at all,' Will Clarke asked, 'not even Captain Hamilton?'

The chief officer laughed at the memory. 'No. Even I didn't know early on, remember. It was a full six months, no less, before I realised she wasn't a boy! By then we were on another China run. And what was I to do? For her part she'd been glad of regular meals, some kind of roof over her head, a way out of what she'd been born into, an' me, I suppose, seen as some kind of protector. She built up a pretence, an' worked harder an' more willingly than any boy I'd ever known – to keep what she'd got, I suppose, in the time before I found her out. And in case I found out too, no doubt.'

For a moment they walked in silence, while Thompson relived the memory. 'If I'd known she was a girl,' he said at length, 'I don't think I'd have dreamed of taking her aboard. Some did, on other ships, but old Captain Hamilton was a fair stickler for right an' wrong. Probably why Campbell an' Clarke trusted him to carry all that liquor here.'

'What did you do then, when you finally found out?' Anything so unusual or irregular fired Will Clarke's curiosity, but he limited his questions discreetly.

The chief officer smiled into the darkness. 'What could I do?' he asked in response. 'We could hardly abandon her amongst the Chinese, an' I couldn't in all conscience turn her off the ship, back to the life she'd been leading, amongst the lepers an' the beggars an' all! I'm not a hard man. By that time she'd been with me too long, besides which I'd – I'd got to feel – well, fond of her. I realised – in an odd way, she'd begun to give me a little of what I'd never had, like – same as having something of a family around.'

His voice became distant, reflecting the unseen expression in his eyes. Presently they reached the end of the beach, then turned and walked slowly back, the campfire gleaming like a distant beacon in the darkness. 'She'd deliberately deceived me an' everybody else to keep her place in the ship. An' a fair pretence it had to be, too, as young as she was. Either that or starve, I suppose!'

'At the time I rumbled her,' he went on, 'she said she'd jump over the side before be put ashore. Imagine, *she* said that to *me*.' He shook his head in lingering amazement. 'An odd kind of spirit, that, in one like her. So we kept up the pretence. She looked after the Old Man then, as well as me, but I don't know whether he ever suspected. Sometimes I wonder. She naturally had a woman's instinct for caring in a way you never get in a manservant. I don't know if it ever showed. As little as she was, she – she looked after me an' was a real comfort, this last year or two. An' in doing that, now she – she's . . .' He could not go on.

They walked the rest of the way back in silence.

A long swell was still driving choppy waves into the bay next morning, and so they further traversed the southern bank of the river amongst reeds, trees and mangroves until they came to a sheltered neck. Debris high in the branches of the nearby trees indicated wild floods from time to time, but the waters now were dark and placid. Using driftwood logs as supports, they crossed without difficulty, despite the river's depth.

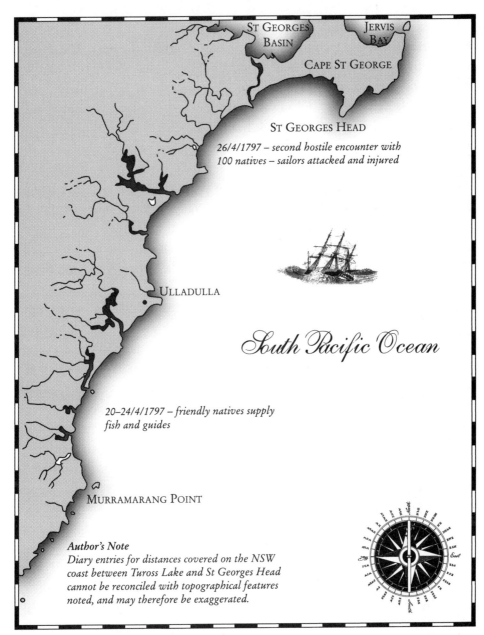

MAP 12. *Present-day Murramarang National Park to St Georges Head, NSW. Approximates journey of 21–26 April 1797.*

For six days then they moved along or parallel to the coast, pushing ever northwards, eighteen miles the first day, fourteen the next. The going was relatively easy and without incident. They passed through immense open woods which were dry and crackled underfoot, across plains that were high in long grass and occasionally burned in places, or along the fringe of alternating beaches and headlands, the weather holding fair except at night when fires had to be lit to keep the sea chills at bay.

With the assistance of a friendly native guide whom they met on the day of the river crossing they were able to avoid the worst terrain, cutting off high points and headlands, thus saving many needless miles of travel. This same fellow, seeing their evident hunger and distress, was able to obtain supplies of fish for them from a party of natives who accompanied them for several miles on the second and third days, finally leaving them with a further generous provision of fish.

The need to keep moving allowed little time to indulge in the patient pursuit of trapping fish for themselves, and none at all for seeking and bringing down larger game, even had they the means. Since there was little to be had from the bush that was truly palatable, they were glad of the friendliness and generosity of the local people, and rewarded them as best they could from their meagre supply of trinkets.

How far they had come to rely on native help was sharply demonstrated during the next three days when they met no local inhabitants and suffered accordingly, almost starving from their own efforts as they stumbled weakly and wearily over shorter distances, mostly across sterile beach sand, dry grasses or bare rock.

These were days of hunger and extreme privation such as they had not experienced before. Job Duggan's utterances of a month before were being vindicated as he had predicted, though he suffered with the rest and was as gaunt as his fellows. Even so, the eerie cackles from the surrounding bush in the early morning, and again at dusk, caused them to feel occasionally that someone was being cruelly amused by their plight.

Only the forceful drive of Hugh Thompson, and the ever-present knowledge that they carried the fate of all their other shipmates, kept them doggedly on the march. As it was, they lost the lascar Cuttagee five days from the river through exhaustion and starvation. Being unable to keep the pace of the others, he was perforce left to return either to the natives of the previous few days, or to his friends at Bateman Bay, while a vague and laggard Tenby Read, now the youngest of the party, was pushed along from behind by the chief officer.

To any observers the six would have seemed oddly assorted in age and appearance as they struggled along, half-starved, a seemingly impossible number of miles still in front of them. Azim Prakash most frequently led, his wiry figure bearing the strains of the journey unexpectedly well in light of the failings of the rest of the lascars. Fran Gilbaert was equally strong, changing places with Azim as they both strode without ailment, casting about for edibles or comfortable stopping points ahead of the rest.

Will Clarke was less hardened than the two seamen, but his youthfulness served him well and his spirit was buoyed by the progress, and his confidence grew as their numbers dwindled, the test he endured honing his physical body to the same keen edge as his strengthened self-dependence.

The oldest member of the party, the Irish carpenter, was the one most changed by their ordeal. While he pressed forward as gamely as the others, driven by a fear of both cannibal blackfellows and the chief officer's earlier dire declarations, his frame had shrunk, and his remaining hair was visibly whitening under the pressure of so many uncertainties.

Hugh Thompson forced himself on under the necessity of keeping the others moving. His place at the rear of the group was as much the result of his near-drowning, as the need to stir Tenby Read along. He felt the recent death of Pochari and his own failing in that regard far more than he had admitted to the young Scot. There were times when the appeal of remaining beside a quiet lagoon was almost irresistible, and he was already beginning to doubt his ability to see the entire journey through. The thought of old Captain Hamilton and the rest of the survivors on Preservation Island always drove such products of weak moments from his mind, but more than once he was thankful for the growing strength of Will Clarke to carry the party through to Port Jackson if, for any reason, he was himself unable to do so.

Thus they marched doggedly as the distances passed slowly, each mile now leaving its imprint indelibly on one or other. Their hair was long and lank, their beards unkempt, and their skins darkened from dirt, sun and wood-smoke. With their clothes also in rags they were brigand-like in the arms they carried and just as threatening in purpose, or so they may have appeared one morning to the horde of natives who suddenly appeared without warning, clubs raised and spears poised to throw, shouting and hallooing hideously in a frenzied mass attack.

In an instant, the six seamen were overwhelmingly outnumbered, and the first deadly shafts were being flung at them before they had any time to react.

9
TREACHEROUS
COMPANIONS ...

26TH APRIL, 1797. *The tempest that came on us the 23rd continues without let, and has turn'd our lives into an utter misery. Lightning storms, fierce winds and heavy rain have demolish'd almost all our shelters, and fires are barely supportable, everything being so thoroughly drench'd. We have seen nothing of our rescuers, nor might they hope to see us in such treacherous weather and shorten'd visibility. Tho' it be of little help to us, for their sakes we pray they are not amongst these islands, in these wild waters, at this time.*
FROM THE SHIP'S LOG

The weight and swiftness of the unprovoked assault was so sudden and so heavy as to give no time for defence. The shore was backed by rising dunes and the thick bush from which their attackers had emerged, and terminated ahead at a bluff point. They were hemmed in with nowhere to run. Their unworkable weapons were long rusty and useless. Hugh Thompson's instant decision needed little consideration with such scant options.

'Stay where you are *an' stand your ground!*' he yelled, lunging for Tenby Read whom he caught in the act of fleeing, so short was the time since the natives rushed upon them. 'Stand fast! There's nowhere to run, an' you're targets if you do! Stand fast, but don't cluster. Move apart!'

He picked up two or three of the few spears that had been thrown, none of which had caused injury. Their fate balanced on a knife-edge. Brandishing the spears back at the natives, he continued to shout to the others, but appeared to address his words to the wild mob. As usual they

197

had hesitated, seeming leaderless, uncertain what to do in the face of passive but unexpected resistance.

'We're in as bad a spot as we've ever been! We've got to bluff our way out, with lots of noise but no action, d'ye hear me? Don't make a show of threatening with the guns – just thinking they don't work might be enough to make 'em braver! For God's sake, no-one provoke them, but be ready to save yourselves as best you might!'

Will Clarke sidled closer, heart pounding, picking up two spears, but carefully keeping them low and non-offensive. 'Jesus, Will, there's at least a hundred o' the brutes, none of 'em too friendly, and not a workable arm among us,' the chief officer muttered to his companion. 'I'd give a lot right now for a cannon an' a troop or two o' stout marines! I can think of nothing to say that'll mean anything, though we're obviously going to need something fast. Have we anything left to give them?'

Tenby Read had also sidled closer, but with other thoughts on his mind. His eyes were fearful as he gazed on the ominously scowling warriors, some of whom wore painted body markings, and his mouth hung slackly as he sought for words. The involuntary whimper that escaped his lips reached Hugh Thompson first.

'Stop snivelling boy, an' stand fast!' he snapped harshly, turning and filling the tense lull with sound. Each heartbeat seemed like a week, each breath a month as both sides waited for something to happen. The charged atmosphere was unreal, the uncanny pause unnerving.

Tenby Read still gazed fearfully, his mouth working, his crushing anxiety breaking in a dry-throated wail. 'I'm – I'm frightened, Mr Thompson, s-sir. I don't l-like this! I – I think the-they're going to eat us! Oh, ohooo ...'

The chief officer's anger boiled over as his grip closed fiercely on the youth's trembling arm, the wail of fear being instantly replaced by a cry of agony. 'I'll eat you, ye miserable young bastard, if ye don't pull yourself together an' show some spine! The last thing we want them to see is one of us wailing like a demented girl!' The terrified seaman quailed before the chief officer's formidable bull-like roar, but the actions equally touched the puzzled warriors. The lull gained precious seconds in which Will Clarke made the only move he could.

'I've got a few trinkets left which I'll give tae them, Hugh, before they think o' making up their minds for another go at us. We've got them bluffed I believe, in not running, so let's keep it up! Give me your spears as well, but be ready tae run if needs be. I'm going tae hand their weapons back tae them along wi' their wee presents – an' I'll wager that's never happened before either!' His laugh was nervous, but resolute.

Hugh Thompson glanced at the young Scot in disbelief, but he passed over the crude weapons, nevertheless. As Will Clarke moved forward, the chief officer glanced warnings to the others who stood back, poised and alert. The supercargo had reached the group and was handing out buttons, nails and pieces of cloth to the nearest natives with elaborate pantomime, playing for enough time to soften their aggression, despite the fear which twisted in his gut.

With the spears he gestured northwards to emphasise their imminent departure and wish to move on, then laid the bundle on the ground before them. Their scowls being no less fierce, he was unsure whether they understood his gestures, and so he backed away, distinctly feeling that their lives were still in the balance.

His suspicions were fully realised as he turned to rejoin the chief officer. Almost instantaneously the uproar began again, and spears were caught up and flung from the midst of the clamour as several natives renewed hostilities.

'Hold hard, avast there! Don't run! Use the rocks around here, keep your faces to the bastards, an' fight!' Hugh Thompson's commands rang loud above the din, though he knew it was hopeless. The castaways were prepared to fight back, to battle for their lives, and Azim Prakash and Fran Gilbaert had already picked up large pebbles which they hurled at the milling throng, as well as returning some of the first spears they had swept up. Will Clarke bent with the same intent, but felt a numbing blow to his forearm after hurling a rock, turning then to grasp a spear that spiked the sand close by.

Despite their counter-attack they were steadily being pressed back. 'Keep together lads, as we give ground, but don't make it easy for them. Keep . . .'

Thompson heard a despairing cry from Tenby Read, and saw him fall beneath a spear, almost immediately feeling a sharp blow to his own side as another spear ripped the muscle and grazed his ribs. His reaction broke in a red fury. Without a second thought he seized up the weapon that had wounded him and snapped it across his knee, flinging the pieces back at the mob with a roar of wild anger.

'Stand your ground, blast ye, stand your ground! We'll not give way to these bleeding savages, by God, not while we've the strength to fight!' His determined shouts echoed in his ears as he seized other spears and snapped them across his knee, oblivious of his wounds, hurling the broken halves into the faces of their tormentors. He noticed the Irishman moving extraordinarily quickly, too, despite his age and previous fears, slashing at fallen weapons with his axe to prevent their re-use, and marked the other men still bravely throwing pebbles and some of the natives' own weapons with telling force and accuracy, sufficient to check the renewed onslaught. The rust-choked firearms lay abandoned in the sand, their feeble symbolism lost in the desperate struggle for survival.

The blackfellows were getting in each other's way, rendering their aims ineffective whilst offering a full target to the seamen. The expected conquest had not happened. The wreckage of their weaponry being flung contemptuously back at them or being chopped through with apparent disdain was not within their experience, any more than was the spirited resistance of the white men. They had expected to outnumber and run the strangers down like so many wingless birds, but the sea-rocks they threw so accurately hurt, and enthusiasm quickly faded as some of the men now stood weaponless.

The big man amongst the strangers returned their attack with his monstrous bellowing, enough for ten warriors, and hurled a throwing club back amongst them which several had to dodge. His own few warriors were still prepared to stand by him, even though one bled and another lay pierced by a spear.

'You miserable, ungrateful misbegotten spawn of a leper's whore! You murdering, shit-smeared God-forsaken savages! Would you expect to turn your treachery an' your cowardly designs on a bunch of unarmed seafarers, who only wish to leave you to rot in this accursed country, and to exploit us for anything more than you got?' The chief officer let his rage flow with all his force, as much to make enough abusive noise to cow the sullen multitude as he had subdued many another recalcitrant mob aboard ship, as to vent his fears and feelings.

Though his words were incomprehensible, the sounds he uttered and the violent gestures with the *wo-mu-rang* he had picked up left no doubt of his mighty wrath. Redness welled down the cloth of his torn shirt, but still he thundered his displeasures, finally hurling the *wo-mu-rang* as forcefully as he could at the nearest knot of still-glowering natives, to lay one senseless on the ground. Hoarse, exhausted and pained from the wound in his side, he felt he had finally made the desired impression.

As quickly as they could, the sailors removed themselves from the scene of the conflict, picking up Tenby Read to find the youth only superficially wounded in his shoulder, lying more in a paralysis of terror than in pain. As far as possible they wanted to be well clear of the blackfellows' treacherous company by nightfall, but were dismayed when, approaching a large and almost circular bay in the late afternoon, they realised that their late attackers were still following at a distance.

By now it was too late in the day to try to evade the native band, nor was the party in any fit state to try. The extensive bay kept them to its perimeter shores, its mouth by far the widest they had yet seen, and the sheer cliffs on the opposite side looked insurmountable. An island lying close inshore might have offered a temporary refuge, though equally they might starve there. There was nothing for it in their sadly weakened state but to make a virtue of necessity and spend the night close to their antagonists, who plainly would not let them from their sight.

With thoughts of nascent murder in their minds the castaways huddled close that night but did not sleep. They could read nothing of their neighbours' intent and so feared for their lives. Together they drew a plan to save themselves should they be attacked in the dark, but it was no more than a sop for their troubled minds, for there was nowhere to go.

'We'll lie close to the beach tonight,' Hugh Thompson had said, 'an' make for the water if there are further signs of trouble. Lord knows it's little enough, but we've seen none of them swimming, we've got three strong swimmers among ourselves an' the cask here for a float, an' they'd not be able to use their spears or other weapons too well in the darkness. Just keep together an' stay quiet, an' we might that way escape, God willing, if we could round that far point in the dark.'

He had shown them their chosen objective in the twilight without conveying their plan to the watching natives. They had lit no fire and made sure the near empty water-cask was handy, then settled to await their fate almost as men condemned, fearfully anticipating the inevitable.

But no attack came. After a long dark night of pain and relentless tension the travellers broke camp and left in the early light, followed shortly by their straggling pursuers. Then, inexplicably, mid-morning, the natives left them and disappeared into the woods beyond the point selected for the previous night's escape plan.

The relief in being rid of their unwelcome company was hard to contain, and for much of the rest of the day the small group pushed on as fast as their wounds and energies would permit, fearful all the while of some threatening reappearance at the edge of the bush. The beach aided their travels, however, just as much as the bush into which they had vanished would have impeded the progress of the natives, so that by evening they could breathe more easily, attend to their wounds, and take stock of their position.

Surprisingly they were only lightly wounded, despite the native numbers and the intensity of the attack. Perhaps their offensiveness had been more to keep them moving, more to menace than to kill? The natives' unexpected departure seemed to suggest this. Of the more serious injuries, Hugh Thompson's ribs were deeply scored and the torn flesh raw, but apparently clean. His shirt had matted to the wound and formed its own dressing, so the patch was cut round with a knife, though the discomfort remained.

The wound to Tenby Read's shoulder had penetrated completely through. Unnoticed dirt particles had been pulled into the pierced flesh as the spear was extracted, as a source of future trouble. Of all the sufferers he was the worst, not because of the severity of his wound, but because he resisted any efforts to tend it. Any suggestion of dressing it caused him to become wild-eyed and hysterical, so they quickly learned to leave him alone since the wound itself, covered by his torn shirt, seemed to trouble him less than the memories it evoked.

Will Clarke's arm gash was still weeping and attracting more than its share of flies. He had also sustained a ragged flesh wound to his right hand, now swollen and painful, in ducking and knocking aside another spear. He gained some relief by soaking both in the waters of the bay, bathing himself fully at the same time, then he tore the full sleeve from his shirt and had it bound tight about his injuries. As a simple treatment, it had to suffice.

'Could this be Botany Bay, Hugh?' The supercargo stood in the light of the campfire they had hidden amongst the dunes, but from where they could see onto the calm, moonlit bay. The distant cliffs loomed sharp against the horizon.

Hugh Thompson fed more driftwood into the flames while the others moved in closer, listening. 'No, Will, I'd say not,' he replied, picking up a stick with which to draw in the sand. 'I thought about it earlier, an' from what I remember of Cook's chart, this place'd have to be Jervis Bay.' He scored a rough coastline in the sand by the firelight.

'As I've told you before, there wasn't a lot of detail, but two of the points I recall south of Botany Bay, which is south of Port Jackson, were Cape St George an' Point Perpendicular.' He marked the four places on his sand sketch. 'Cape St George was where we had our brush with the blackfellows yesterday, though I was too preoccupied at the time to mention it.' The others laughed, the memory quickly becoming no more than a receding nightmare. 'Point Perpendicular is the vertical cliff you see yonder, at the entrance of the bay.'

They looked out into the moonlight, seeing the cliffs bulking dark against the paler horizon. 'So we still have a fair way to go d'en, Chief?' The question came from Fran Gilbaert.

'Aye, lad,' came the reply. 'That's the way of it an' it's as well we all realise it. We've a long way to go. By my reckoning there's still a hundred miles or more to cover, an' that's land miles – wrinkles, curly bits an' all.' He glanced across at Azim, seeing his grin bright in the firelight.

'If the natives'll leave us alone, an' if the weather stays fine, an' if we could just find the odd tavern or two along the way for food an' drink, an' soft beds an' softer attentions, then maybe we'd make it in another ten days or so. We know from experience, though, that we're not goin' to be that lucky. We're also not as fit as we were, even with fewer of us. So – let's turn in soon for an early start tomorrow. Even this far away we're still too bloody close to yon murdering bastards, an' I for one won't rest easy until I'm where I can see a long, clear way behind us.'

For days, drinking water had been a problem. They obtained some food from occasional native encounters or coastal finds, though it was never enough, even for their reduced number. However, drinking water was needed several times a day, and the brackish flows were barely palatable, doing little to quench their nagging thirsts as they pushed northwards.

The scant rain in the whole seven weeks since their stranding had been a blessing in one respect, making travelling so much easier but, with no rain to provide drinking water, and the rivers at their lowest levels – which had also been a blessing – their craving for clean, fresh water frequently banished all other thoughts from their minds save that of reaching the settlement at Sydney as quickly as they could.

Three days after their skirmish at Cape St George they came upon a wide river that wound its course through extensive salt marshes. After a considerable delay while seeking ways to cross, a party of natives helped them over in bark canoes, while their hopes were raised when the natives seemed willing to bring fresh water. However, they seemed wary, if not suspicious of the sailors, and never returned.

While they awaited the promised water, the two officers climbed part-way up a nearby hill, but they saw nothing to encourage them – just the need to stay on the coast to bypass the encircling band of high hills they were approaching. But at least they could also see they were no longer being pursued. It was an assurance that made their thirsts tolerable a while longer.

Such assurances did little to stay the growing realities of the journey for long. Within 48 hours of the last big river crossing at least two members of the party, Tenby Read and Job Duggan, began to flag. The carpenter still clung doggedly to his axe, steadfastly refusing either to lay it down or hand it to one of the younger men and so ease his burden. Beyond this he said little. His former truculence had vanished, and all he showed now was an intense weariness which had come upon him as fast as he had visibly aged.

Tenby Read, the youngest of the seamen, was as laggard as ever, constantly troubled by his injury, and rarely acknowledging the presence of the others except to refuse assistance. His seemed to be a half-world of pain and emptiness. The obstinacy of the pair was all Hugh Thompson could cope with in keeping the group moving. Given also their failure to keep up the daily mileage, it was becoming increasingly clear that they would soon have to rest for a day or two at some suitable spot, or split up yet again.

Thinking of a day's rest from their efforts reminded the Englishman that they had not enjoyed such a luxury since – he frowned in tracing the memory – since the day after they had caught the shark. Which was almost all of four weeks ago! The party had not separated at all then, and here he was thinking of splitting up the few that were left. Should he have kept them together? Should he have allowed more breaks for rest? Had he pushed them along too severely? He had driven his crewmen

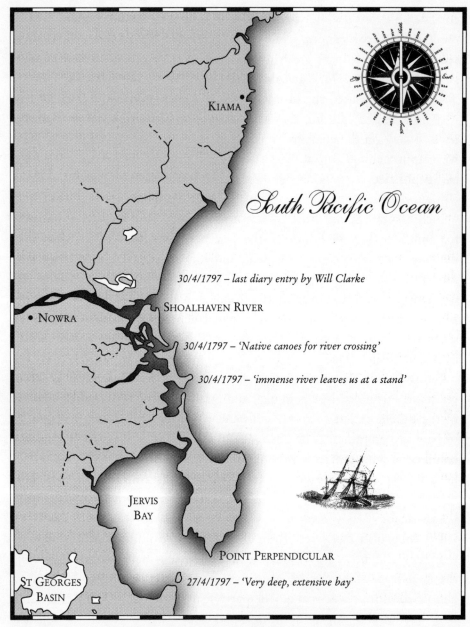

South Pacific Ocean

30/4/1797 – last diary entry by Will Clarke

SHOALHAVEN RIVER

30/4/1797 – 'Native canoes for river crossing'

30/4/1797 – 'immense river leaves us at a stand'

KIAMA

NOWRA

JERVIS BAY

POINT PERPENDICULAR

27/4/1797 – 'Very deep, extensive bay'

ST GEORGES BASIN

MAP 13. *Present-day Jervis Bay to Kiama, NSW. Approximates journey of 27 April to 4 May 1797.*

almost without complaint, and had heard pleas from some to remain with him when the group finally did separate. Had he been wrong? Was his judgement wrong?

He shook his head angrily, not used to such creeping self-doubt. He recognised quickly that he had had little option, that half the crew were becoming liabilities well before Bateman Bay, that there was little food along the way even for the six they were now, let alone the full seventeen ... They certainly wouldn't be where they were if they *had* kept together ... Nor perhaps would Pochari have died .... He sighed and shook his head, feeling a heavy depression stealing over him. For a moment he stopped while the others walked on.

Where was it to end? Could they truly hope to reach the settlement, in the state they were in? He had serious doubts about the carpenter and the lad. For Will Clarke and the others he held every confidence – they had been magnificent, real stalwarts, and young Will especially. Though a bit doubtful at first, he had grown quickly to share some of the leadership burden, and would grow further, too. These three would surely go on to Port Jackson, given the chance ...

He looked out to sea and heard the thunder of the surf, the cry of the gulls as they wheeled and swooped in the sun. Their flight seemed effortless compared with his own leaden-footed trudge. The sea and air were their natural elements, offering sustenance and freedom, whereas man had to struggle to conquer the sea, and sometimes even found the land alien.

Ahead across the coastal plain, a line of high bluffs crowded closely to the ocean and he remembered the vertical cliffs of Jervis Bay. Unless they could pass along the cliff-foot ahead, these would be a major obstacle to climb and already he could see the heavy bush. He glanced again at the winging birds, envying their liberty ...

Ten days he had said, only a day or two ago. Port Jackson seemed half a world away. Once he had suggested they might accomplish the journey in thirty days, by mid-April, but that was – nearly three weeks ago ... The pain in his side burned where the spear had torn the flesh, his lips were parched, while his mouth was never free of the cling of salt. At night he slept little . . .

How much further, and how long? He plodded forward, scuffing through the footprints that stretched out ahead. The burden of what he had to do was bearing heavily upon him. And would *he* push on to the settlement, if they left the Irishman and the lad behind? Could he honestly keep up with the younger men? Could he leave the lagging pair to fend for themselves? He shook his head again, perplexed . . . A day at rest would give him time to think, and then he would clearly have to decide.

They saw the lake glinting in the mid-afternoon sun from their vantage point on the high sandhills. From similar heights down the coast they had earlier surmised its existence from a large and open scrub-free area amongst the bush, and from the numbers of obvious water birds they had begun to notice. They could also see from a rocky eminence close to the beach that it would not be a bay or inlet, for the sands curved unbroken to a headland further north.

In all likelihood it would mean fresh water, edible roots, small animals or even another pelican, perhaps, if they were lucky. It seemed to be a heaven-sent place to stop and gather strength. Carefully they picked their way through the skeletons of an old extensively burned area until they came to the nearest point on the water's edge.

The lake proved to be providential. At the place where they chose to camp, two miles or so from its connection with the sea, as they later discovered, its waters were reasonably fresh. For the first time in many days they could drink their fill. Some distance away they cleansed themselves and, after some little exploration, found quantities of edible roots amongst the rushes along the shore and backwaters, with other welcome greens and some small fish they were able to trap.

For two whole days they foraged in their immediate vicinity for foodstuffs on which to rebuild their waning stamina, but they remained cautious in their movements so as to avoid further hostile confrontations with their neighbours. That they shared the lake with others was evident from the smoke of native fires to the north, with several others on the landward side. The large body of water was clearly home to a number of groups, many of which would need to be circumvented as their journey continued.

The chief officer had allowed them the extra day of comparative ease to avail themselves of what they could gather as edibles. He had no idea when, or even if, similar vittles would be as readily forthcoming along the coast ahead. The steep cliffs looming before them suggested little immediate possibility, and so it seemed both right and sensible to give the men a little extra time in which to rest and recover. As they went about their activities, taking care to minimise any signs of their presence, he judged each man afresh, assessing his potential for the last few days of the journey.

Will Clarke, Fran Gilbaert and Azim Prakash were as fit as he had previously noted, given the rigours by which they had been tested, and the young Scot's injuries notwithstanding. He felt certain he could send them ahead to Port Jackson at a faster pace. That it would be necessary was becoming progressively clear from the lassitude shown by the carpenter and the youngest seaman, who would remain as hindrances if they all stayed together. Both could be left with friendly tribesmen.

To give the best chance to the fitter, faster trio, he himself would also stay behind, to further ensure fair treatment of the ailing pair. Both men were fearful of the natives in their respective ways, especially the injured and increasingly vacant Tenby Read, and neither was capable of productive dialogue with even friendly natives. It would be necessary to test the attitude of the inhabitants to the north, towards whom they would travel on the morrow.

They had departed their lakeside camp early the following morning and were once more making their way back to the coast when, on traversing a belt of scrubby dunes, they were suddenly alerted to a commotion beyond some thicker bush ahead. Alarmed that this should presage yet another native attack, though sure they had seen no-one, the six men quickly dropped into the waist-high vegetation. Fran Gilbaert dragged down a bewildered Tenby Read while Hugh Thompson and Will Clarke wriggled forward to spy on the disturbance from the cover of the sandy ridges.

There were none of the sounds of a gathering attack, none of the blood-curdling howls, but the obscuring bush before them still waved and shook violently under the impact of charging bodies, and there was little doubt that soon the unseen runners would burst forth. The pair quickly turned to run back towards the others in deeper hiding when Hugh Thompson's hand on Will Clarke's shoulder checked them both, at the sound of a voice shouting clearly, but faintly, in accented English.

'Over here! Come across this way an' stay in the trees, will ye! The buggers'll not be finding us here! Over here, I say!'

The startled pair looked at each other in shocked surprise, then turned in their tracks and hurried back to their former lookout. As they did so two distinct reports like musket shots sounded away in the distance, bringing more excited shouts nearby and a quickened thrashing within the brush. Soon pounding footsteps could be heard distinctly on the muting sand, then an instant later first one, then another of two red-faced white men, breathlessly perspiring, broke out of the thicket to glance desperately right and left before rushing headlong towards the hidden observers.

Hugh Thompson stood up quickly, his mind already preparing to hail the fugitives, but the instant he appeared with Will Clarke alongside him, the others promptly vanished with a yelp and a curse, flinging themselves abruptly down amongst the scrub in a wild attempt to evade this new and unexpected threat. More thrashing in the trees warned the two friends now of hostile pursuers, and without a word they too sank back into the rough cover, a knife gripped in the chief officer's hand in anticipation of a violent assault.

'Michael! Shamus! Oh, where is it ye've gone to now? Saving yerselves it is ye'd be, without so much as a thought for others! Where are ye?'

The Irish tones of the speaker, sharp with anxiety and hoarse with exertion, struck the hidden listeners like a body blow, for as unexpected as this encounter had been, even more unexpected in these parts was the distressed voice of a young woman!

'Michael – ! Oh – Holy Mother o' God, what is it?'

The woman screamed, and for a moment held herself in terror upon being confronted by the pair of ragged-garbed, dark-visaged, wild-looking strangers who had arisen like demons from the scrub, not quite the threatening natives from whom she had just fled, but no less villainous in appearance and in a place she least expected them. Her eyes were wide in horror, just as those of the stocky youth with her were confused and uncertain, though not especially perturbed.

There came more faint shouting and sounds of pursuit from the rear. Hugh Thompson spoke up quickly, with little time to explain.

'Sorry to surprise you like this, ma'am, but we're seamen from the *Sydney Cove*, wrecked to the southward an' so passing this way. No doubt these are Michael an' Shamus,' he went on, nodding to the pair of heads now peering sheepishly out of the scrub, 'but all of ye'd better move back with us, smartly now, if we're to escape fresh trouble with the natives!'

His authoritative tone and quick decision were all they needed to pull together and hurry away with the big Englishman and the younger man. The others were already on their feet and waiting as the newcomers rushed up breathlessly, whereupon they all ran back towards the lake and a high point amongst the sprawling dunes before stopping to listen for sounds of further pursuit. They heard nothing save a distant calling of gulls, and the dull booming of surf off to the east.

No one spoke for several minutes, time spent in regaining their composure and taking the measure of each other whilst waiting for the chief officer to descend from his sandy lookout. At last he slithered down amongst them, seeing the strangers clearly for the first time, aware of Tenby Read staring vacantly at the puzzling addition to their numbers, of the sharp eyes of the young Irish girl, for she seemed no more than that, and of the expectation on all their faces.

'Well, have they gone? Did you see anyone coming this way at all?' The questions from the girl were direct and without deference, in tones no less sharp than when she had sought her lost companions.

Hugh Thompson took his time before answering, judging the strangers and guessing at their presence. Only the girl had spoken much, but he felt they were a close group. Her accent and their collective garb all seemed to suggest they were Irish convicts, and escapees at that. They had obviously been on the run for some time.

Given decent clothes and a bath, the girl would have been passably pretty. The youth she had been dragging through the bush seemed strong but dull-witted, while the other two, stirring uneasily beneath his gaze, were men in their early thirties, one short and sharp-featured, the other tall and broad-faced. Both of them looked furtive and shifty as if prepared to bolt should he so much as raise his voice. The men's torn clothing was a grey drab, while the smaller man's carried yellow patches, signifying he knew not what. This, he guessed, was Michael, and a type of fellow with whom he was familiar after long years at sea.

'An' what would you be doing in this neck o' the woods, Michael,' he barked, seeing the small man flinch at the suddenness of the question. 'Natives is it you were running from, or troopers mayhap? There's no-one near us for the time being, so for a while it's fairly safe. You'd be expecting others,' he said to the girl, 'though they're a long time coming. So what's going on?'

He stared at the more alert trio, his curt manner and commander's eye demanding the truth. After a brief hesitation and an exchange of glances, all three started to answer at once. He held up his hand to stem the rabble, then pointed to the little man.

'You, Michael. Tell me.' The man with the yellow patches licked his lips and looked quickly to the girl. Hugh Thompson felt he already knew the answers, that they were probably too far south for pursuit by troopers. 'How many of you?'

'Ye might as well be telling him, Michael,' the girl replied dully, not bothering to look up. 'We've nothin' to lose now, an' there's nothin' he can do anyway.' She appeared almost resigned. To what?

The little man appeared relieved that the decision had been hers, and he began to answer eagerly. 'Well now, y'see, there'd have t' be the six of us if the other two was here but – well, this mornin' early we saw this bunch o' natives makin' towards us like, hundreds of 'em they was ...'

'No more than a score, Michael, though thoroughly armed, I grant you,' the girl corrected. 'Go on.'

'Yes, well – well the fellers who've got the guns, see, Sean O'Riordan and Brendan Slattery, no less, well – they goes up an' tries to parley see, but these native blackfellers are forever asking for some kind o' presents like, which we don't have any of, an' so it's wanting the guns they're after. One of 'em, we see him grab at Sean's pistol, an' so Sean has to shoot at him ...'

He broke off, seeing his listener's grim expression as he learnt the local native attitude. So much for leaving Duggan an' the boy with them, the chief officer thought, abandoning any hope of a peaceful passage. The little man hurried on reassuringly.

'Oh, the fellow was only wounded, sorr, he wasn't at all killed. An' then off they all ran, away into the trees.'

'There were more o' them when they came back, though,' the girl added, 'which they did a short while later – by which time we'd got close to a little island by the mouth o' the lake. You can cross over on foot there since the water's not deep.'

'That's right, too,' Michael continued, eager to finish his tale. 'All hollerin' an' a'screaming they was, an' painted up like fiends.' The man's eyes grew wide. ''Tis said in Sydney Town that it's cannibals they are along this stretch o' coast! Well – Sean an' Brendan, being good men both, pushed us off to run for it, while they held 'em off near the island. Them it was ye heard firin' jist a little while ago. I expect they'll be here soon,' he added confidently, though the chief officer heard the girl sniff. The girl was more perceptive than her male compatriots it seemed.

For a moment Thompson considered their situation, then conceded the position. 'It looks as though we'll not be going past them this day,' he ventured, 'not if we want to keep our skins, so we may as well stay where we are until dark. There's a small chance the other two might turn up, though I've a feelin' they got more than they bargained for. If we stay down here as a large group we'll be less easy to spot than with everyone wandering all over the sandhills, supposing they're still interested, an' they might be less inclined to tackle a big number of us if they do find us. We can work our way past them later on. They seem a bit unwilling to move far from their fires at night, so after dark it should be easy enough to bypass them, and especially if we walk in the sea an' leave no tracks for them to follow.'

The chief officer was speaking for his own party, but immediately the two older Irishmen, Michael and Shamus, made it clear that their little group would continue south, with or without their missing leaders. Though Hugh Thompson and the other castaways tried to dissuade them, telling them of their own recent experiences of hostile natives, lack of food and water, and of all they had suffered on the way from the wreck of the *Sydney Cove*, they still meant to persist in their escapade. Mention of the wreck seemed, in fact, to egg them on, and learning of the cargo of spirits brought a gleam into Michael's eye that nothing in the Roaring Forties could have extinguished.

'It's rum there is now, ye're sayin', an' all on a little beach, waiting by the ship?' His expression was openly speculative, and vastly readable. 'Well then, isn't Shamus here just the handy carpenter, an' no better man to patch up a boat, an' isn't young Sean here a strong lad – slow, but strong y'understand,' he explained significantly, ' – an' just the sort to help a fellow at his work.'

The suggestion that the pair between them could achieve what the entire crew and Job Duggan had failed to do roused the old Irishman into a spate of angry abuse, the likes of which his crewmates had not heard for many a day, but the convict party already had notions of nothing more than a soundly repaired ship with its cargo of rum, bound for some uncharted earthly paradise.

Nothing would convince them of the impossibility of reaching Furneaux's Islands, the *Sydney Cove* and its amber cargo. Thompson cut angrily across the rising tide of bravado and ignorance to curb the nonsense, and for a while afterwards they simply sat in strained silence.

Before long Tenby Read fell into an uneasy sleep, and the old carpenter snored quietly in a rest that would serve them well in the night walk that lay ahead. At one point in the late afternoon, Azim Prakash and Fran Gilbaert slipped away to refill their depleted cask from the nearby lake. After some time, more to kill time than for any supposed interest, Will Clarke and Hugh Thompson drew from the others something of their experiences and the circumstances of their escape.

Though willing enough to tell their story, the Irishmen were at pains to point out that their 'crimes' were, in fact, political, like so many others of their countrymen, and that their transportation arose more from being a continual thorn in the side of the English than for any other misdemeanours that carried the penalty of transportation.

As 'politicals' they were regarded as troublemakers like the Luddites and the martyrs of Tolpuddle with whom they were incarcerated, and therefore to be especially watched. Fired by intelligent men, rather than by the lower classes of felons and misfits who were content to endure their lot in idleness and squalor, the Irish felt it necessary to keep up the fight even in prison, and so the acme of their struggles was to escape if possible, and make their way back to Ireland if a chance arose.

The man they called Michael had been a 'trusty', hence the patches on his clothing. In this capacity, with special privileges, he had been recruited by the more radical pair Sean O'Riordan and Brendan Slattery to help in their plan to escape. As well as securing the guns from a source he swore he would not reveal, Michael had known the girl Bridgit O'Keefe as a maidservant, usefully placed amongst certain of the officers and their wives, a gleaner of information snippets and the occasional keeper of coats, and the pocketed keys within them, at dinner parties.

Shamus and young Sean got involved as boatmen in the escape plan, and all five of the men would have cleared Sydney earlier had it not been for Bridgit's threat to expose their plot to the authorities unless she, too, was included.

Unsure to whom she may have spoken, and not being murdering men, they had played along rather than knock her on the head. And on a moonless night, with the officer of the watch suitably distracted and the guards bought with rum, they quietly slipped away from the Parramatta wharves to begin their run for home.

'But why south?' Hugh Thompson asked in puzzlement, knowing the lie of the land in that direction, and its forbidding emptiness. 'Where did you think you were heading, by coming down this way?'

Michael looked at Shamus, then at the girl and back to Hugh Thompson, as if the answer should have been obvious. 'Why, an' wouldn't it be to China o' course? Where else would ye be expectin' to catch a ship back to the old country?'

'China?' The chief officer stared back disbelievingly. 'You really believe you can get to China by coming this way – south?' Michael nodded, and Shamus smiled.

'Everybody knows this is the way to China,' Shamus declared, 'an' surely, as a sailor boy, ye'd be wise to that too, now wouldn't ye? Sure, an' every ship it is that comes in from England an' the Cape, an' one or two from India even, alwus comes up from the south 'cos it's the way we watch for 'em see, an' they're alwus leaving that way, too, as many a man's seen, some of 'em known t' be goin' off t' China. Stands t' reason then,' he added knowingly, 'that if ye wants t' get t' China, all ye have t' do is keep walkin' that way!' The man vaguely waved his hand the way the castaways had come. 'It's where we'll be goin' to, after t'night, 'cos it's the way right enough.' His words had an indisputable finality.

It was almost dusk and the light was beginning to fade, but Hugh Thompson felt he had to try at least once more to show them the error in their reasoning, to prevent them walking off into a measureless wilderness – though from other dealings with the Irish as shipmates he knew that he might be wasting his time. With the aid of a stick he outlined what he remembered of the charted coast in the sand, producing a rough inverted boat shape for what was known of New Holland, and a detached circle for Van Diemen's Land. On the coast of New South Wales he marked the settlement of Sydney.

'This is Sydney, an' here is about where we are now, an' that's where the *Sydney Cove* was run ashore,' he said, marking each point, then glancing up at the watchers as they strove to understand what he was showing them. 'Here, having crossed this stretch of water in an open boat, we think there's a wide strait, though no one knows for sure, except I can tell ye now you'll never reach that wreck on foot.'

'It's almost as certain as you'd be right in saying all shipping comes up from the south, this way,' he continued, 'but that's not because England, or the Cape, or India, China or anywhere else lies that way! Captain Cook found nothing but icebergs when he took his ships down there thirty years ago! Other ships come up this coast because that's the easiest way to approach Port Jackson, having come eastwards this way through the Roaring Forties, or down this way from China, or from India as we did.' He made bold strokes in the sand with his stick across and down the respective coastlines.

'Both China an' India are damn' near seven thousand miles away, give or take a few hundred miles,' he went on, 'about where Will there's standing. You'll never get there from here without a well-found ship, even if you were going in the right direction, which you're not. As we said before, there's nothing to the south of us but a lot of rough country, precious little by way o' vittles, an' natives who'd probably skin you alive for the clothes you're wearing, given the chance. If you want my advice I'd say, forget your idea, come back with us, serve your due an' sail out when your time's up. Ye'll not be leaving here any other way, that I can tell ye!'

His words were blunt, uncompromising, and final. For a moment there was silence as the two Irishmen tried to make sense of the lines in the sand, both of them looking dubiously at where Will Clarke was standing. Shamus scratched his chin in mystification, while Michael shook his head in puzzlement and disbelief. The boy Sean was drawing lines in the sand with his own stick. Only the girl seemed to understand what the Englishman had been saying.

'With all due respect, Captain, an' I'm sure you'd be meaning well,' Michael said at last, clearing his throat apologetically, 'but there's folks back in Port Jackson who're certain sure of what it is they're saying, an' they're saying this way's right, an' all we have to do is keep walkin' for a few weeks, an' we reach China. Others who got away before came this way also for certain, an' they must surely have got home since they didn't ever come back.'

Hugh Thompson forbore to comment on what might have happened to them. The depths of their ignorance and lack of understanding were becoming irksome. Instead he said with some exasperation, 'I'm telling you what it's like that way, since we've covered every last blasted inch of the four hundred miles from here to Point Hicks an' beyond, over the past seven weeks! If ye don't starve, drown or drop from exhaustion, you'll be run down by the blackfellows. The only civilised beings in this country are up around Port Jackson. China isn't part of it, an' ye won't find that it is if ye walk until Doomsday!'

Shamus spoke again after a pause, clearly unconvinced, his tone unmistakably defensive and mistrustful. 'There's those at Port Jackson, those as you'd be callin' civilised, Mister, with their orders an' their whips an' their high and mighty ways, who'd be for tellin' us exac'ly what you've just said, t' keep us in our place, an' under lock an' key for as long as it pleases them! Well, it's not pleasin' us, an' we're for getting out of it! We're sure where China is, an' that's where we're a'goin'! We know what it is we're about, an' besides, we've got ourselves one o' your sailor's clever toys that'll be pointin' us th' way. Here, jus' show 'em – show 'em the little machine, Michael, go on, an' mebbe then they'll be for believin' us! It's not been wrong so far!'

None of the watching seamen could imagine what the 'little machine' might be, and all craned forward expectantly while Michael withdrew a piece of worn and much-creased paper from some inner fold or pocket, and opened it out carefully. In the fading light he proudly revealed the drawn outline of an octant crossed by an arrow, with the letters 'N' and 'S' at opposite ends. His face was almost reverent.'Well now, bein' sailor boys an' all, I'm sure ye'll have seen one o' these little beauties before? 'Tis a compass, no less,' he exclaimed, answering his own question, 'though I'll never be for tellin' any, where 'twas I got it!'

Will Clarke and Hugh Thompson looked at each other in amazement, thankful that the gloom masked their expressions. Azim Prakash turned away to hide his white-toothed grin, while Fran Gilbaert stifled his snort of laughter in a spluttering cough. With an effort the chief officer swallowed his own mirth, though not knowing on reflection whether to laugh at the incredible innocence, or weep for the stubborn stupidity that might soon drive the escapees to their deaths.

'A paper compass,' he said at last, realising the total futility of arguing further. He nodded accedingly, in apparent recognition of the Irishman's forethought and preparedness. 'Keep it carefully, Michael, you never know when you might need it. If you're still intent on going south, just point the arrow that way and keep on following it, but always remember, if you change your minds, this letter 'N' at this end'll bring you back towards Port Jackson just as easily.'

'Sure now, an' I'm glad y' understand, Mr Thompson,' the little man replied, slowly refolding and stowing his precious paper back in its secret place, 'for it's good t' get real advice when it's going. We'll be on our way in a little while then, when it's good an' dark, an' after that – well, I wouldn't be thinkin' we'll need t' be seein' Port Jackson again!'

'I'm sure you're right, an' I wish ye God speed, for it'll be a cruel journey unless I'm much mistaken.' If their choice was to go on – and it clearly was – so be it. Thompson's greater concern was for his own people, not a band of wandering miscreants.

His tone hardened as he turned to the girl, aware that she had said nothing during the last exchanges. 'And what of you, Missy?' he demanded. 'I'm sure you know your own mind. You were never welcome on this trip. Do you go with your friends here an' likewise hope to get all the way to China, or do you go with 'em and simply starve? Do you go off and join the natives of your own free will, or do they get you eventually anyway, as a plaything? There aren't a lot of choices, an' all of 'em's bad! Ye might come back to dirty, miserable, safe Port Jackson with us if ye like, either, an' take your chances on freedom from there.'

He stared hard at her in the last of the light. The first stars beyond now framed the distant hills. 'You're young, an' the years'll pass soon enough, I daresay. Ye might do a lot worse, but make your mind up now, an' smartly! It's a fair push back to the coast while we can still see, so we'll need to be starting out in less than five minutes!'

10

NO ORDINARY SHARE
OF FORTITUDE ...

7TH MAY, 1797. *While the interminable winds have held moderate
since the start of the month, we are torment'd still by the harsh colds
and continual wetness. The people are so far reduc'd that nothing
further can be taken from the ship, which is now much broken down
by the weather's past inclemency. Any thought of a journey in the
jollyboat must await the turn of the seasons, all endeavour to be
given meantime to building a house or like shelter which might allay
our suff'ring. Tho' it be exceeding hard, we must consider Mr
Thompson's party lost, and so prepare to bear the winter before
us as best we may.*
FROM THE SHIP'S LOG

*I*t was dark when they drew close to the rocky islet which marked
the outflow from the lake. Though the sky was almost clear, there
was no moon. Hugh Thompson led his group and the girl slowly
through the scrub along the edge of the dunes in order to minimise their
tracks, while Will Clarke brought up the rear to ensure there were no
stragglers.

Tenby Read stumbled frequently over the broken ground and walked
as if in a dream, constantly needing to be pressed from behind. Both he
and Job Duggan moved reluctantly, but Tenby Read's hesitation was
more and more that of one almost lost to his surroundings and
circumstances. At a point where the waters of the lake cut across the
sands they descended onto the paler beach, and out into the knee-deep
stream.

The cold waters caused the young seaman to whimper loudly in bewilderment until he was grasped firmly on either hand and given quiet assurances. Held close thus, each of the men supporting him felt the lad trembling between them. They had long understood and made allowances for his nervousness, but these tremors seemed to augur something more than his usual nerves. Will Clarke frowned in concern, and peered closely at the youth as he plodded forward behind closed eyes.

The tide was ebbing. When they reached firm sand and surer footing at the edge of the receding waves, the supercargo and chief officer changed places in the column to enable the latter to superintend the laggards more closely. In this way they pursued their northward progress, leaving all marks of their passage to be extinguished by the next rise of the tide.

They had only travelled a few hundred yards when, from his place in the van, Will Clarke's alert attention was caught by a dark sprawl some little way ahead. The beach was otherwise flat and empty. From the events of the day the find was not unexpected and instinctively he knew, despite the darkness, that these were the remains of one of the missing Irishmen.

The girl knew it too, or had been looking more keenly, for she broke away with a cry and splashed across the swirling eddies to fall upon her knees beside the contorted form. When the others caught up she was huddled in anguish and racked by choking sobs.

Hugh Thompson dropped to one knee beside the girl. 'Who is it, Bridgit?' he asked gently. 'Do you know – can you see which of the two it is?'

Muffled sobs greeted his question, and he had to make his enquiry again and lean forward to catch her broken reply. ''Twas – 'twas Brendan Slattery who's – who's here. An' see there, see – oh, they – they've taken away his rings!'

Her trembling fingers pointing to an outflung hand from which two of the fingers had been cruelly severed, and she became convulsed once more with added agony. Mercifully, his other injuries and mutilations were hidden by the night.

'Maybe we were lucky after all, Will,' Hugh Thompson said aside to

222

his companion, 'but for the grace of God, this might have been us. Take the rest on before Tenby Read realises what's happened. We'll follow in a few minutes.'

There was little he could say to the girl that wasn't awkward and empty. He shook his head, measuring the depth of her grief and finally asked, as gently as he could, 'Was he a beau, perhaps, this Brendan?'

He knew immediately that he had made a mistake. Her tones were angry as she found an outlet for her distress in the crassness and stupidity of her questioner.

'Brendan Slattery? A beau? Oh, in the name o' God! In *Sydney Town*?'

She took a deep breath and faced him, and for a brief moment he was stung by the viciousness and hatred born of her captivity. In a cracked voice she launched her savage verbal assault. 'Holy Mother, man, don't you *know*? Sydney Town's a *prison*, don't you understand – a penal colony where your lot go to dump your problems! You – you're one o' the bastard English! Have ye no idea what it is you're going to? There's no picnics an' glitter, no fancy tidbits where we're bound! It's chains, iron bars, mud, sweat an' the lash, Mister, and half-starvation most o' the time an' filthy mongrels forever seekin' to have their way – not courtly entertainments, fancy folks an' the opera!'

Hugh Thompson found his voice. 'For Christ's sake, girl, take hold o' your tongue an' keep your voice down! Just remember where y' are!' The chief officer was quick to regret his clumsy thoughtlessness, but was just as keenly aware of the proximity of the late Irishman's murderers. Of the other fugitive there was no sign.

His sharp retort brought fresh sobs to the girl's misery as she stood up, wiping her hands across her eyes and sniffing loudly, spurred to get away from the man, but not knowing where to run. The lap of the waves and her stifled sobbing filled the strained silence.

'I'm sorry, but you – ye've no notion of what it's like,' she said at length. 'Two years of it I've had, one continual hell on earth, an' still another five, an' – an' all for a handful o' coppers, to keep away the hunger.' Her voice dropped bitterly as she went on. 'No doubt there'll

MAP 14. *Present-day Lake Illawarra to Port Hacking, NSW. Approximates journey of 5–15 May 1797, with rescue at Watta-mow-lee.*

be more to be served after this, or maybe a few dozen strokes o' the lash if – if I'm lucky.' She broke off, unwilling to face up to her fate, while Hugh Thompson again knew an unfamiliar helplessness and a sense of his own ignorance.

She shook her head and spoke into the dark. 'No, he wasn't a beau, as you put it, for there was never time nor chance. His keepers saw to that. He's the real reason I came away with the others, though. He was out to get back to Ireland and the cause, an' – an' I couldn't stand the thought of – of him not being there anymore. The only real man o' the whole rotten, randy mongrel pack,' she continued passionately, 'an' as true a patriot as ever there was!'

She stared down at his tortured body, struggling to hold back further tears. 'Oh Jesus, he – he was such a lovely man, an' – things might a' been so – so diff'rent if – if only ... And now ...' She choked on words she could not utter, on emotions she dared not admit. Her dishevelled head sank in grief, and she shook silently afresh.

It was time to leave. Will Clarke's party were long out of sight, and the tide was slackening, beginning to turn. 'We have to go,' he said.

'Aren't we – aren't you goin' t' bury him?' There was a rising anxiety in her voice. 'We can't just leave him here! He's – and where's Sean? ... Oh no, oh God!' Her hands flew to her mouth as she realised all the hideous possible fates of the other man.

Hugh Thompson thought fleetingly of the time he had taken to bury Pochari but this was totally different. This stranger was dead, butchered, as might his defenceless mourners be if they were spotted on this open beach, dark as it was. They could never expect to survive another attack like the last one, especially not from the gruesome evidence at their feet. The girl was looking around anxiously, sobbing anew. He steeled himself and took her arm.

'Burying him'd be no good, Bridgit, 'cept maybe to warn those who did this that others are still around. The tide'd soon uncover him, an' they'd see he'd been buried. We can do nothing for your other man, Sean. This is tribal territory, they're a barbarous people, an' they don't welcome

225

strangers. Let's be off before we're seen here and they come chasing after us.'

He knew this to be unlikely as native peoples often feared the dark, and rarely ventured abroad at night. He didn't tell her this, though, as he hurried her away.

Tenby Read's condition was fast deteriorating. They had walked for two nights and part of a third to reach the foot of the distant cliffs, though neither as fast nor as far as Hugh Thompson would have wished. Job Duggan was slow but constant, whereas the sickly youth was becoming difficult to rouse, was stumbling more frequently, and had collapsed twice in the last half-mile.

'If you ask me, Hugh, the lad's pretty far gone,' Will Clarke offered, having listened to the heaving chest. He was kneeling on the wide rock shelf they had been traversing for some time in the shadow of the soaring, bush-clad slopes. 'There's nothing we can do for him here. We'll need to carry him to where he'll be more comfortable at daybreak, and then ...' He shrugged in the darkness.

Hugh Thompson looked down at the young seaman, seeing reality where once was only suspicion, and therefore hope. 'Aye, it's all we can do now, until we can see. What then, I'm not sure. There seems to be an indent up ahead,' he said, staring along the starlit coast to where a change in the shades of darkness marked a place discernible only to his acute mariner's eye. 'A sandy cove with fresh water is what we need, though for how long ...' He left his comment unfinished, acknowledging his uncertainty.

Apart from the girl, Azim Prakash and Fran Gilbaert were the least scathed of their number. Between them they carried the comatose youngster almost two miles to the point Thompson had identified. In the darkness there was sand underfoot, and a broad gully offered shelter. Somewhere above the pounding of the waves they could hear running water, but a search would have to wait. Above the tide they made themselves and the boy as comfortable as they could, then settled down to sleep.

Early light the following morning brought several revelations. The first, occasioning an early rise for most of them, was the seeping cold wrought by a blanketing sea-fog which hung thickly against the cliffs. As exposed as they were to the elements, it chilled them to the marrow and beaded everything – rocks, clothes, vegetation – with a heavy dew. The dampness immediately caught at Hugh Thompson's chest, reviving the wheeziness he had first contracted on his near-drowning more than three weeks earlier.

To allay the cold, however, they found large quantities of driftwood washed high upon the nearby beach, from which they built a large fire, glad of the grey curtain around them in that it reduced any concern that the smoke might attract unwelcome attention from any natives in the area. The shape of the gully gave rise thirdly to a fast-flowing freshwater stream that drained from the hills and out across the sands. During a search for food which brought in a number of small, dark green crabs, the most unexpected discovery was coal.

At the previous day's camp they had seen quantities of rounded black pebbles amongst the rocks but had paid little heed to them. Now, however, Will Clarke and the two older seamen found a broad black seam of it in the scrub-covered strata above the beach, and in isolated pockets amongst vegetation. Though they would happily have traded its weight in bread, the trio carried enough back to the camp to add to their fire, which they were then able to sustain from what they could collect closer to hand.

Meanwhile the chief officer and the Irish girl had examined Tenby Read, and found nothing encouraging. While he shifted and moaned in his unconsciousness, the pair had listened to his irregular heart, felt his hot brow, moistened his parched lips and eased the torn and grubby shirt away from the swollen wound contusing his left shoulder.

Before this, Hugh Thompson had been unable to approach the youth without causing near-hysteria. What he saw now, though, caused him to purse his lips and frown deeply. The flesh was raised, hot and hard to the touch. Where the spear had passed through, there were dark, ugly-looking scabs with brightly inflamed edges. They found tight raised pustules in other places beneath his shirt, and became aware of an odd, rankly unpleasant smell that confirmed the insidious sickness they had begun to suspect.

The chief officer sighed, sat back on his heels, and gazed up at the bush-clad hills towering away into the mists. 'It's not good, Missy. It's one very sick lad we've got here, an' almost nothing we can do for him. Save perhaps for a bucket of leeches, I'd say nothing less than a surgeon'll mend his ills, an' the nearest's at least thirty miles away by my reckoning. I can't think of anything else that might help, can you?' He turned and looked at the girl, noting that she had at some time that morning washed in the stream, removing some of the tangles from her hair. It was an improvement.

'An' what would I be doin' that you can't, may I ask?' She looked startled, surprised that he should think of needing her advice or assistance.

He shrugged and shook his head, assailed by a recurrent feeling of galling inadequacy. 'I don't know, I just asked – you bein' a woman, an' all, ye just might ... who knows?' What else she as a woman might do, he could not begin to guess at.

'An' it's mother's milk I'm supposed to feed him, I expect, is that it?' There was a hint of scorn in her words. 'Well, I'm tellin' ye, at barely nineteen an' precious little schoolin', I probably know a lot less than you, Mister, who as a man o' the world must surely a' seen more sick men in his time than I've had hot meals these past few years!' She gazed down at Tenby Read, her tone perceptibly softening. 'Still, the boy's in a poorly way, an' that shoulder o' his looks an' smells worse than it ought to.'

They both looked up as Will Clarke joined them, fresh from washing away coal-dust in the stream. Hugh Thompson answered his look of enquiry with a negative shrug.

'The lad's injury's turned him sick, Will, an' there's not a lot we can do to help him.' His brow creased with a concern sharpened by his own nagging debility. 'Broken limbs an' bruised bodies can oft be put to rights shipboard with bandages an' vinegar, or a generous helping o' rum,' he remarked, 'but I own to knowing very little of bodily distempers an' like ailments.'

He stood up and looked about him, up into the misty green gully and out along the shrouded coast. The fog persisted and the cold had a polar quality away from the fire. ''Tis said Captain Cook cured the scurvy hereabouts, with fresh greens and herb tea, but with none o' those, an' no other alchemy save brine an' a man's spittle, there's really not much to be done but look after him here, an' wait.' It seemed pitifully insufficient, a mere token care, though no more than a measure of the straits they were in.

Will Clarke stretched out his forearm, showing the fresh purple scar from his own wound. 'This seemed tae heal well enough with a daily soak in salt water, except it was ne'er as bad as the boy's. Perhaps if we were tae treat him that way?'

'Nay, it's a bit late for that, I'd say.' The chief officer was pessimistically emphatic. 'Maybe if we'd attended to it earlier, or cauterised it soon after it happened, we'd have less of a problem. It's easy to be wise afterwards, but you remember how the stupid little bugger wouldn't let us near it! He's got a fever now, so we'll just have to wait it out unless you, Azim and Fran Gilbaert want to go on ahead later today, or tomorrow?'

The idea of splitting the party had little appeal to the young Scot. He shook his head. 'We'll wait, since we'll know soon enough. If it's a fever we should know tonight or by early tomorrow, for he'll either recover or – or …' He hesitated, but the alternative remained clear. 'Let's leave that decision until then.'

They waited, but no more certainty was forthcoming. Throughout the day they watched where the youth lay in a scoop of sand on the rock shelf, between coal fires they had lit to counter the cold and dampness from the persisting fog. There was no colour to the day, and not much was said. Showing little change, the invalid regained consciousness after a time but seemed unaware of where he was, not recognising his companions. He took water thirstily and grimaced his discomfort like a wounded animal, afterwards sleeping fitfully.

In cooling his feverishness, the young girl cleaned away most of the dirt from his thin face and chest using strips torn from her petticoat, but they left his wound alone. Through all these ministrations his condition neither improved nor worsened. When not attending him they walked the shores seeking shellfish and crabs. It was a long and tedious day.

The night seemed longer still. They pulled in firewood and collected more coal to keep the fires alive, and though Hugh Thompson arranged a nominal watch to tend both the fires and the restless youngster, it was the girl who kept vigil throughout most of the night. At intervals she could be seen against the flames, bathing away the fever that seemed reluctant to come to a head, or huddled in a doze, always close to hand. At other times she stood out beyond the firelight gazing over the darkened sea, a prisoner even within her mind, suffering her own kind of torment.

Early next morning she appeared blear-eyed, tear-stained and much dishevelled from more than the rigours of the night. She confronted the chief officer as soon as he was awake.

'I'll be leavin',' she announced abruptly, staring down at him. 'The boy needs good attention, an' there's only one place it'll come from. I'm going back t' Sydney Town, like y' said y' self. It's the only way.' She seemed agitated and not entirely sure of herself, and for a moment Hugh Thompson doubted that he'd heard aright.

'I have to go. The sooner the better. That's no fever he's awaitin', I feel certain. All last night, I was thinkin' o' one o' the prisoner boys who died after cleavin' his foot with an axe. They said he was the same as the boy ye've got there, sick an' a long time a-dyin', but when he did they said his blood was bad. Ye were right, as well, about the others,' she added, 'an' about not walkin' to China. If – if that were so, then – then why would we be brought here by ship I'm askin'? They'll surely perish out there, like so many others whose bones they've found. I'm goin' back.'

Hugh Thompson rubbed the sleep from his eyes and drank deeply from the cask. The grey haze persisted still, he was cold, his side ached abominably, and it was too early to take in everything she said. Lately he had not been at his best first thing in the morning.

Others had been lost, she said, in answer to his questions, having also escaped custody and taken to the bush. Judge Collins had been notified of the finding of upwards of fifty skeletons since the early days of settlement, which had clearly once been white men, she informed him, more than a few of whom had equally clearly been knocked about the head. Some were thus known to have been killed by blackfellows, while others had walked until they perished of starvation and thirst. Others were simply not seen again, though she hardly believed they reached China. That never did seem right, she considered, though she had occasionally wondered about the colony of white folks said to live in the same direction.

The missing ones had likely been murdered in the same way as Sean and Brendan, she ventured, driven by an ideal or a dream for which they had eventually died. Here she began to weep again for their tragic demise, as well as the feeling of a personal loss. Too many lives were needlessly wasted through greed, brutality and indifference, she concluded. Someone had to go for help for the boy.

The chief officer tried hard to dissuade her from her chosen course, pointing to the dangers, the security in numbers, and the limit to their remaining days of travel if they stayed together. She would no more accept this as a reason for staying, however, than she would consider waiting to return to Port Jackson with the three younger men.

For all their youth and normal masculine superiority in strength and endurance, they were obviously tired and decidedly gaunt. The way was long, rocky, and much cut by the sea, she insisted, having already passed along that route, and they would only slow her as she was the least trail-worn of any, and so would get back sooner, alone. Furthermore, she was intent on leaving them then and there.

With mounting frustration she listened to all Hugh Thompson's arguments until she saw him as only one more cursed, overbearing

Englishman trying to tell her what she should or shouldn't do. She became incensed at the slur cast on her ability to make the journey alone. Will Clarke was roused during one heated exchange of vain persuasion versus tearful obstinacy, and promptly added his own concern to his friend's objections. When at last they gave in, unable to deny Tenby Read's obvious need for assistance if he was to recover, she promptly threw their expressions of gratitude back in their faces.

'Keep your thanks, if ye please,' she sniffed, 'for I can do quite well without 'em! I'm doing this just as much for me as I am for him,' she admitted bluntly, 'for they may look a mite less severely on my return if – if I'm carrying news o' your lot, an' o' this poor creature's condition.' Her tone then changed. 'I'd ask no favours,' she said compassionately, kneeling to lay a hand upon the pale forehead a last time, 'for I might one day get out o' this place simply by bidin' my time, just as ye told me. Time's – time's a thing this boy hasn't got a great deal of, though. So – make sure you'd be lookin' after him properly now.'

So saying, she brushed aside a tear, gathered up her damp skirts and walked quickly away. They watched her cross the sands until she was cloaked and lost in the mist before either spoke.

'A prickly customer, yon,' Hugh Thompson mused. 'But one worth knowing better, I'd wager, despite all she is. Either that, or she'd make a man's life hell! Were I your age, laddie, I'd have something more'n a passing yen to find out which.' He grinned across at the young Scot, who laughed in response.

'Ah, now, after listenin' tae the pair o' ye earlier, I'd be having strong doubts that ye ever would, Hugh, for all your sailor's ways,' he retorted. 'Your trouble is being an Englishman. She was arguing rings around ye first thing this morning, and so much did she fret she might soon a' throttled you on the spot, had I not intervened! With a Celtic sympathiser such as masel', though, well – things could a' been quite different, I daresay, in other circumstances. It's all a question o' temperament – an' not being English, o' course.'

Thompson laughed, thinking how his companion had grown over the past four months. 'Aye, it may be you're right, Will. Part o' the price of greatness. She's a spirited lass, all the same, an' showing no mean courage in going off alone into this wild country, that you've got to admire. Many's the man who wouldn't. She deserves some credit for what's she's trying to do, so – be sure you see her treated right when you get to Port Jackson.' He broke off in a fit of hoarse coughing that made his head swim, another tiresome legacy of their trials.

Will Clarke watched with some concern. 'Is this tae mean you're thinking of not going on yourself, then? An' if you don't – where will you stop? We must be so close now that we could finish this together in a few days. Didn't the girl say herself she'd be taking only three days or so about it?'

The chief officer looked back at him, flush-faced from his coughing, and the youngster could see that the decision had already been made. 'Nay, Will, face facts. The lad here's sickly an' may easily not recover, for all the girl's good intent. Chippy's game enough, or stubborn enough, but getting slower by the hour. With two of us already ailing like this, we have to see the truth of it, an' call a stop.' He looked about him, then shrugged resignedly. 'This is probably it. There's water here, the gully behind us for shelter, coal an' driftwood for fuel, an' food on the rocks. I've given it a lot of thought.'

He drew a breath and hurried on. 'If we were to keep on going – but no, we can't keep on going, not with the lad half-dying on his feet. So you see, he couldn't make it, an' I seriously doubt that Job Duggan would, either. For myself, well – I don't seem to have the wind nor the fortitude I used to, to be honest, not since that ducking, so it makes sense for me to stay on here with these two while you push on with the others.'

Another bout of coughing shook the older man, each one reminding him of his lacerated ribs. Ignoring them, he continued, 'We're long overdue, the Captain must surely have given up hope for us, or be close to it. These are no waters for an open boat now. Mid-April was the time they expected rescue, an' it's now a month beyond. We must reach Port Jackson soon. Tomorrow morning, if the lad's no better, I'll be trusting the three of you to go on through to the settlement as soon as you can.'

With that accepted, Hugh Thompson turned away and walked over towards Tenby Read, passing Job Duggan as he did so. The Irishman looked up with a quaint, gap-toothed grin, and waylaid him with uncharacteristic *bonhomie*.

'Sure, an' it's a fine mornin' this mornin', I'm thinkin', Mr Thompson, sorr! So fine is it now that maybe I'm even thinkin' it'd have t' be St Patrick's Day an' all, for wouldn't it just start as such a good day for all the Irish?'

Hugh Thompson had no idea what the man was rambling about, although he was clearly in better spirits and a decidedly unusual mood. 'I always thought St Patrick's Day was in March. This is May,' he pointed out with a frown, wondering if the other was becoming in some way touched.

The carpenter continued to grin smugly, like a cat in cream. 'Well now, St Patrick's, St Christopher's, or St Bridgit's even – where's the diff'rence, I'd be askin'?' He wagged a finger roguishly at the chief officer. 'That little colleen was a rare one for havin' the true Irish spirit an' no mistake, aye, an' a ready tongue t' go with it. I'd have t' say, it did me old heart a power o' good t' hear her up t' givin' you a fair old trouncin', Mister! Got the better of ye' she did! An' doesn't that make it a great sort of a day for the auld Emerald Isle an' all, t' be sure, for niver did I expec' t' see yer lordship here bested at last by a slip of a thing such as her!'

Thompson's curses did nothing to stifle his old adversary's glee, and he could still hear the man's chortles as he strode away angrily, irritated by the stupid taunt and the nagging pains in his chest and ribs. It was only later he realised that this was the first time he had seen the cantankerous Irishman without his customary glower.

The day passed tediously while they watched over Tenby Read, waiting for the predicted fever to manifest itself with more certainty. The sick youth's condition nevertheless changed little, except for his being in a more natural, albeit uneasy, sleep, and less comatose. It appeared to be a small improvement.

They were themselves restless, chafing at the enforced halt, none more so than the younger three. Will Clarke was still reluctant to see the party broken further, however, unless it became absolutely essential, for this would inevitably mean abandoning his friend in this forbidding spot. So many men to find again, so many places to remember. He glanced up at the frowning hills, noting the shifting mist tinged rose from the late afternoon sun behind the coast. It was becoming noticeably cooler, and he shivered involuntarily, though not just from the cold. Hugh Thompson fished a pinkish crab from the simmering pot with a stick, cracked it open while blowing on his fingers, and pronounced their meal ready.

It was meagre enough. The shellfish yielded little, plump though they appeared. Judging from the heaps of discarded shells, the mussels were harvested regularly by the natives, so none were especially large. The numerous periwinkles offered more labour than nourishment as they prised the contents loose with sharpened twigs, while the crabs were all legs and shell, with no more than a thin morsel of meat. The latter were always quick to hide at human approach so there were few of them, and the seaweed they added was vapid and without substance, but at least the meal filled in time, if not their bellies.

'Not much for a starving man, Chief,' Fran Gilbaert grumbled, swatting at a hovering mosquito. 'Even d' blasted flies are better fed d'an we are!'

The chief officer was philosophical, not inclined either to argue or reprimand. The Dutchman had a point, and little could be done to assuage it. Their search for food had taken most of the afternoon, they were still hungry, and he nodded agreement.

'Aye, you're right, lad. But occasional starvation's nigh universal, affecting most of us at some time or other, except mebbe among the gentry. Even then, those in Port Jackson have had to pull in their belts with the rest on occasion, as I've heard. Things haven't been easy these past few years or so, with what's grown being dry or burned, an' all the rest having to be brought in from abroad. It's not a plenteous country we've come to, as we've already discovered.'

Will Clarke agreed, tossing away a handful of shells. 'It certainly keeps the blackfellows thin and hungry-looking,' he concurred. 'Hungriest of all are the poor beggars in chains up in Sydney, by Bridgit's account. Sourdough and water, an' fish and occasional rum if they can get it. Fare that'd canker any constitution, in no time.'

Hugh Thompson added more wood to the fire, staring into the flames. 'Be that as it may,' he said feelingly, 'I'd give a lot for a pound or two o' sourdough myself right now, an' I wouldn't be saying no to a measure o' rum for comfort, either! Those "poor beggars", as you call them, are better off than we are just this minute, an' at least get some kind o' meal once a day, without riskin' being speared for it.'

He paused in reflection, studying the land about them. 'Them "poor beggars" are probably better off here than they've ever been,' he continued thoughtfully, 'considering Newgate, Bedlam or Tyburn as options, along with any floggings they might earn for themselves anywhere. A man could do a lot worse than straighten his record here, I'd say. Though it's hard enough now, this'll be a fine country one day when some real farmers find a place in it an' make it produce. You only have to look to North America or around Table Bay to see what can be done in the lands of a new country. With coal here such as we've seen ...' He paused, unable to imagine fully the changes that might be wrought. 'It's early days yet for this place.'

The young Scot took up the thought-provoking discussion. 'One o' the reasons I was sent here was tae try and see how far things might develop, with an eye tae trade and needs,' he said. 'Campbell, Clarke and Company are canny enough tae feel there may be good prospects – which is why they want tae be in early, without the kind o' monopoly the East India Company might be after.'

'They're looking tae the future,' he continued, 'and more o' those land-hungry people who've been colonising America an' the Indies, an' parts of Africa. That kind o' starvation's a fair drive in a man, especially where he might make up in strength and courage what he lacks in capital. I'd agree with ye, Hugh, this'll likely be a far different place in a hundred, or maybe fifty years even, once the country's opened up.'

This was the kind of company and conversation which made the chief officer wish he had a pipe to light up, and a pot of ale to help it along. He realised then how infrequent had been the chances, or how preoccupied he had been with other matters, to get to know those with whom he had come so far.

'Aye, there'll be places here for a lot o' people, an' work to be had, an' plenty o' living space as well.' In his mind's eye he saw again the teeming streets of London, Canton and Calcutta with their cripples and beggars, and the hordes of poor and homeless, and those forlornly seeking paid employment in the crowded thoroughfares. 'Many's the tale I was told as a boy of how things were in Cornwall's tin mines where my father once worked, an' where men were treated little better than slaves. The dark, the wet, the terrible accidents, the food riots ...'

He stopped and shook his head as he recalled the unfaded memories. 'It's still bad, an' there are one-time miners in Sydney now, gaoled an' transported simply for trying to stay alive, but it was worse then. Ever on the verge of starvation, to hear my folks talk, always people dying young – but here perhaps, yes, it could be different.'

He glanced across at the Indian who had listened in silence, and saw, too, that here was a man with his own tale to tell, familiar perhaps, but different, also. 'You've been a tough little bugger all this time, Azim,' he declared. 'What is it that's kept you going, while the rest o' your shipmates have been dropping behind?'

The man flashed his seemingly irrepressible smile, lifting his shoulders in mystification. 'That I am not to be knowing at all, Mr Thompson, sah, for – for all this time, I have been walking, eating, drinking and sleeping just the same as they did. What I have more than them, now they are not here, I cannot – cannot be saying, except maybe some little of what you would be calling luck, I think, or – or better fortunes.'

'I also have known hunger, many times, and – and so perhaps I am less troubled by so little food – even so than you, I am thinking. But, still the others have been dropping out and they, also, have been as hungry. So why, I am asking, are they not still with us? One thing I do have, which they do not,' he stated, holding up a thin finger and pointing back along the coast to the south. 'You will remember, please, that my younger brother, Rajendra as he is called, is still with Captain Hamilton on Preservation Island? So – being the most older, I have the – the ...' He floundered for the word, smiling apologetically at his inability to express himself more clearly.

'Some responsibility, perhaps?' Hugh Thompson prompted with a guess.

'Yes, yes, most certainly, sah, the responsibility,' Azim echoed, savouring the word as he repeated it. 'I have the responsibility for this brother Rajendra, indeed yes, to see him safe from the shipwreck, if I can. Our family, in Bengal, is most large with many children, and so are needing both of us to help them in living. They also have known famine, many times with – with so little food, you see, and so we have been sailing as *lascari* in your ships. Now that I am myself walking with you instead, I must be doing whatever is possible to bring my brother from the island, together with the captain. I have a duty to them both. So many re – responsibilities, for which I must be reaching Port Jackson, even on foot!' His listeners nodded understandingly.

'There is, also, one other cause for why – for why I may still be with you, sah, and the others not, for which you are perhaps to be less – less believing?' He paused with a slight frown, wondering how far he could explain. It had never been necessary before. 'It is perhaps my *karma*,' he said simply, 'which we Hindus must take as the path by which our lives will be travelling.'

'You would, I think, be calling it another name, sah – which I am most sorry to forget, but which we also call *niyani*. This it is that makes the – the way of each of our lives, like the course a – a ship must be sailed across the oceans. Perhaps – perhaps my own ship, my *niyani*, is set to take me to Port Jackson, but none of those of my fellows. This alone may be why I am here. Or perhaps all of which I have spoken. Whatever it is,' he concluded, 'I am most sincerely grateful for,' and he beamed his bright grin in evident thankfulness.

The others pondered his words in silence, thinking of their own *karmas*, and how far and in which direction they might be set to travel. On reflection, they seemed little different from the watchful eye and ready hand of their Christian God, but understood and expressed in quite different ways. Will Clarke was about to raise a question, as ever, but it died as they heard a cry that brought an instant shock of relief and mingled disbelief.

'A sail! A – *a sail!* Th-there's a *ship! Sail ho!*' The hoarse excited cry caused the five men to start in unison, jerking suddenly alert to the waving figure up on the rock platform. Some time during the course of their discussions, unnoticed by the others, Tenby Read had roused himself enough to visualise a swell of canvas in the shifting sea fog, and he had struggled erect, his hair blowing in the wind, to make himself heard.

They quickly rose to their feet, straining their eyes seawards, but seeing nothing except wraiths of mist as the sun gave way to evening. The grey ocean pounded and swirled mockingly in its stark emptiness, but the illusion remained sufficiently clear in the mind of its beholder for him to start moving unsteadily towards it.

'The lad's off his head an' started seeing things!' Thompson called after Will Clarke's flying heels. 'Keep him back from the edge, before . . .' His shouts were lost in the boom of the surf as the supercargo scrambled up the rocks towards the staggering seaman. The latter's broken words were clearer now, though telling only of a disordered mind.

Tenby Read broke into an unsteady run across the wide rock platform, finding a desperate strength from some hidden reserve, and a will that subdued all his pains. He appeared not to feel the cutting, barnacled surface that scored his feet. Such was his imagined purpose that he somehow managed not to fall upon its sea-carved roughness either, for all his unsteadiness.

'Wait! Wait for me! Please, I want to go home! *Don't leave me!*' The frantic words were shrieked as he ran blindly on, oblivious to the roar of breaking surf below the pitted shelf, and the warning swirls of foam sluicing across the bulk of half-submerged rocks, spurred by the ghostly vessel fading before his distraught vision. The surface was treacherous with green slime and the young Scot following some way behind, his heart pounding in his ears and the sharp rock tearing at his own bare feet, was painfully aware that his pursuit would very likely be in vain.

'Wait, wait! Don't go! *Wait for me!*' Again the anguished cry reached him over the thundering might of the crashing combers before the fleeing youth stumbled, slipped – and in an instant was gone. The broken cleft wherein boiled the awesome surges of an entrapped tide yawned dizzyingly as Will Clarke reached the sea-licked edge, his heart and mind in similar turmoil. Tenby Read had vanished.

'Will! Will! Don't! Come back, Will, come away! You'll never get him out o' there!'

Through the wind, spray, and slop of leaping waves, Will Clarke slowly became aware of his friend's anxious calling and the sound of other voices as they hurried across the weed-clad expanse towards him. He could still feel the cold air blast of the booming waters on his face as he realised with a shock how perilously close he had come to flinging himself unthinkingly in search of the hapless youngster.

He turned and edged away from the brink, shaking and pale-faced as Fran Gilbaert and Azim Prakash joined him breathlessly, securing him on either side as though he might still change his mind. Together, they could see nothing below them but a sea alive with a mass of kelp-weed, then the seething, broken swell.

'He's gone, lad, he's gone.' The chief officer's hoarse words urged into Will Clarke's benumbed mind as he was carefully led away. 'You could have done nothing for him, an' you might easily have been lost yourself! 'Twas a fearsome spot, to be sure. He's gone, an' maybe 'twas for the best – a blessing ye could say, with him as sick as he was. Maybe it was his *karma* to end it all here, one way or another, just as Azim had been saying, so don't be blaming yourself for not catching him in time.'

Approaching the camp fires once more, they stopped and looked back at the restless, hungry sea. 'Maybe now we can all get to Port Jackson.'

Had Hugh Thompson known anything of the way ahead, he would not have spoken so hastily. Though they set out next morning feeling that an immense burden had been lifted from their shoulders, they discovered before long that the narrow path at the foot of the cliffs was as testing as any they had passed along thus far, and it soon reminded them that their strength and fitness was still diminished by hunger and fatigue.

Compared with the extensive beaches soon after the wreck of the longboat, when they had marched long and easy distances each day, the jumble of rocks they were forced now to clamber over and amongst was irksome and wearying in the extreme, demanding an agility they no longer possessed, and energies that were long since short-lived.

In places where vertical rock slabs denied them easier passage they were obliged to climb high above the sea, clinging precariously to scanty herbage as they inched their way forward across crumbling slopes. As an alternative to more energy-sapping climbing, they decided at one spot to wait for the tide to recede sufficiently to let them through, since both the carpenter and the chief officer were badly affected by the exhausting scrambling.

In other places they picked their way through thigh-deep shallows, meeting with gritted teeth the occasional slopping embrace of an unexpected wave which chilled them thoroughly, making more than one regret leaving the sheltered gully they had occupied so recently, and the comforting fires.

It was a day in which they covered less than three miles, in stark contrast with their earlier travels. They spoke little as they moved slowly forward, each of them suffering stoic discomfort in his own way. Several times they had cause to wonder how the nineteen-year-old runaway might have circumvented certain obstacles, but saw no signs of her passing.

She had warned them that the way was steep and rocky, and their progress that day was finally such as to concern them about the remainder of the journey. Hugh Thompson therefore resolved that, at the next suitable spot, he and Job Duggan would set up camp and allow the others to proceed as best they could in order to avoid further delays, thus giving the three younger men the greatest hope of reaching Port Jackson more quickly.

Later that evening they huddled together in an exposed undercut without the luxury of a fire to keep the cold at bay, while the wind swept intermittent rain into their shelter. They slept little on its hard rocky floor as they waited for the dawn, their damp, salt-impregnated rags chafing harshly, heightening their misery. The chief officer's decision to stay behind at the first convenient campsite was reinforced during the course of the following day with a continuation of the same unrelenting shore.

Their progress was again agonisingly slow, frustration mingled with exhaustion as they drove themselves forward, the chilling winds and sweeping rain rendering them speechless. The wet rocks became increasingly treacherous underfoot, and when finally the carpenter fell heavily, venting his rage in a spate of bitter curses, all of them knew they must find a stopping place soon. And for once they were lucky. Within a short time the rock-bound coast gave way to a series of smaller beaches. At a point where one of them furnished a tiny rivulet they halted – cold, wet, ill-clad and utterly weary.

'This is it, Will. This is where we have to part company.' Hugh Thompson faced the younger man and for the first time Will Clarke appreciated the deep-etched lines of fatigue no longer hidden by a generous beard, the drawn expression behind the eyes, and a hint of something more in the wheezing which accompanied each breath. The long march had left an indelible mark on them all.

'You'd never be mistaking it as paradise, but it'll have to do us for the time being, until you can get a boat back to us,' the chief officer went on, 'and at least you'll be able to get one in here, not like some o' the other stretches we've covered.' He attempted a grin. 'We've also got drinkable water, a goodly supply o' greens to chew on, Chippy there to keep me amused, an' a beach that might easily grace a tropic isle – with a bit of imagination!'

His subsequent coughing belied the levity, however, as they rested briefly. The trio learnt as much as possible of the likely way ahead. Two days, or three at the most, Hugh Thompson had said. With rain to fill the streams, the Port Jackson group would have no need to carry water, nor the useless weapons, so these and the cask were left with the chief officer and the carpenter. Shortly, Hugh Thompson held out a hand to his friend in farewell. It was time to send them on their way.

'Be sure you hurry back before too long, Will, or we might get to like this place. An' that'd never do, not when there are plenty of real tropic isles still to visit.' His expression changed as he recalled with a curious sense of *déjà vu* some other recent parting words. 'Strange, but that's exactly what old Captain Hamilton said as we left Preservation Island.' He smiled and shook his head at the odd coincidence and the stark contrast, but to the young Scot the whole thing seemed bleakly foreboding.

Perhaps it was the atmosphere of the place, he thought, as he turned away with the two seamen, a brooding gloom not relieved by the leaden sky and misty hills. It was a place of ghosts, a notion lent credence by the traces of earlier campsites they had noticed at the edge of the bush. He shivered in spite of himself.

From a small rocky foreland the three waved their last farewells before dropping out of sight. But they remained clearly in view of a party of observers hidden within the fringe of a wooded knoll above, whom none of the castaways had seen, as their dark shapes blended readily into the sombre backdrop. From their eyrie the natives continued to watch as the strangers below slowly gathered up the weapons and the water barrel. One of them limped painfully as they headed towards the thicker bush, while the coughing of the other could be distinctly heard above the sounds of the surf.

When the three men walking the shore could no longer be seen, the watchers began to move quietly down to the beach.

For as far as they could see, the rocky path seemed to stretch interminably, a tortuous narrow strip leading ever onwards between bush-topped bluffs and the blue-green ocean. They had little idea how long they had been walking that day or, indeed, if their stumbling, clambering, zigzag progress along and around the countless misshapen boulders could truly be called walking. It was also difficult to know the approximate time of day, their stomachs having long ago ceased to remind them of hunger and of impending meal breaks. Since Will Clarke had ceased his regular recording of events, they had no clear idea of either day or date – and hunger had long been a constant companion.

The fog lifted, the rain eased, and before long a fitful sun shone weakly on the joyless shore for the first time in many days, but it did nothing to ease the growing lassitude of the trio, nor even to lift their spirits. Their very attitudes bespoke a thorough, bone-weary tiredness, though they continued to push themselves doggedly forward.

In truth they were fast approaching the point where they would scarce be able to walk. Their lips were cracked, their throats dry, they had found so little to drink that they had even sipped sea water to ease their ever-constant thirsts, and they had not eaten for days. On reaching a cluster of relatively flat rocks they sat down yet again in unspoken accord, a study of listless dejection.

Will Clarke had woken that morning cold, stiff, aching in every joint and feeling forty years older than he was. With no cover for comfort and the creeping chill of the returning coastal fog, not even the exhaustion of the last few days brought him more than intermittent sleep. They had left the firelighters with the carpenter and the chief officer, and so would not know that small comfort again until they reached Sydney.

Without Hugh Thompson's strength and comforting presence, Will had begun to feel more vulnerable and uncertain, and for the first time he also felt the burden of his responsibilities. The lives of close on fifty men lay in his keeping, but in the shivering early morning cold he had felt barely able to stand, let alone continue the thirty or so miles towards Port Jackson. The distance could just as easily have been 300 again for all the strength he could muster.

It would have been very easy to give up. The insidious chills and the effects of near starvation stealthily drained bodily reserves. Hunger now was just another focus of discomfort. They had become too weak to forage, their remaining energies too precious to chase the elusive darting crabs, while the smoother rocks they were traversing yielded fewer shellfish. Everything had seemed cold, grey and utterly without hope in the early dawn. The maniacal laughter they had heard so often amongst the trees near their camps sounded especially shrill and mocking now, driving home the depth of their misfortunes.

One of his companions had coughed and turned restlessly, groaning in his slumbers. Fifty other men, just as restless as he, waiting, not knowing ... He thought again of the responsibility ... Somehow, they would have to go on.

Hunched upon the warming rock, he found himself thinking of the Irish girl, who must also have come this way, stepping across their resting place, perhaps pausing a while herself. Where was she now? Had she fared any better? She at least knew what to expect, whereas he ... Without Hugh Thompson he felt curiously exposed, and yet the girl had gone, against their advice. It was indeed a rare undertaking – but would she, *could* she, make it?

'Is it *our* fate to make it, either? Shall *we* succeed?'

With a start the young Scot realised he had spoken his thoughts aloud, and looked up to find the other two staring keenly at him. 'I'm sorry, I – I wasn't thinking – I ...' He stammered at the unintended betrayal, and flushed in his confusion.

'Do you have any doubts d'en, d'at we shall make it?' The Dutchman sounded slightly surprised, as if the thought had not occurred to him. It had the effect of making the younger man feel smaller, but neither of the others appeared to notice.

'No, no, I . . .' He stopped to gather his wits, to try to appear confident while at the same time easing his nagging anxieties. Leadership was infinitely harder than he had imagined. 'Sometimes – like the time we were attacked by the natives ourselves,' he explained, 'and then later, when we found the Irishman on the sands – well, sometimes I have wondered, if we really could get all the way tae the settlement.'

'At first – it seemed an awfu' long way, but we all came through so far, an' – an' Mr Thompson kept us going. Then we found there was'nae much tae eat and – an' people started falling behind . . . After that we split up, and then wee Pochari died – and now we've just seen Mr Thompson himself drop out.'

He hesitated, not wishing to imply any weakness in his friend. 'I suppose we don't think of ourselves as not being able tae get there, but – well, once there were seventeen of us – and – I just wonder, sometimes. I don't think I'll believe it until we finally do get there. The whole thing is beginning tae seem – unreal. It's like – it's like looking for a needle in a haystack. At least Mr Thompson knew every line on the chart he once had, knew whereabouts he was going, but what about us . . .? Will we know the place when we get there? And what will we do if we go too far? How – how will we know even that?'

They were questions only time could answer, but he drew strength from the greater resilience of the two seasoned sailors. Azim had expressed a sure confidence in his particular destiny. For all their trials, his white-toothed smile was no less ready, and though he must have suffered just as much as his countrymen, he nevertheless seemed to radiate certainty.

Fran Gilbaert pointed out again, as he had done so long ago in the longboat, that others had made much longer journeys and survived. 'I can remember Mr Thompson in d' longboat talking of d' English Captain Bligh, while I told you, I think, of Pelsaert an' d' *Batavia*, yes? D'ere was one oder ship d'at I heard of, was also wrecked on its way to our port of Batavia, *Zeewijk* by name, or *Sea Witch*, as you would say. D'is happened about seventy years ago, perhaps, in d' same place as *Batavia*, on New Holland's westernmost shores.'

'D'ey say over two hun'red people was saved at first,' he told them, 'some of d'em going off in d' ship's boat same as we did, to get help. When d'ey didn't go back, d' oders began to build a smaller boat from d' timbers of d' *Zeewijk*, a sloop I t'ink it was, from how she was called. And in d'is nearly a hundred people got d'emselves t'rough to Batavia, maybe a year later. Is possible y'see, if you're prepared for to try hard enough.'

The supercargo listened wearily, appreciating the efforts of the others to boost his flagging spirit, but a short way forward he could see the bluffs begin to rise steeply again to a cliff head, with another one beyond. And here, Will Clarke could see, was the difference between their own venture and those of earlier shipwreck survivors.

He nodded acknowledgement of all Fran Gilbaert was saying, and knew they must make a supreme effort, no matter what the outcome. There was, after all, no alternative. 'Aye, Fran, I mark well all ye say,' he said, 'an' we have tae show the same kind o' resolution an' endeavour. We owe it tae all o' the others, whom we cannae be letting down now, not when we're as close as this, an' they've no other hope of rescue.'

'Say a prayer then, an' hope for a miracle,' he concluded, struggling to his feet and preparing to move on, 'for we can still use all the Divine help that's going. But I'm minded of one thing in all o' this, that may one day mark our journey apart from all those others,' he said. 'We mayn't have travelled the distances of either Captain Bligh, or your Dutchmen – but, with sound boats at their disposal, none o' those people were ever called upon tae walk!'

They found to their dismay that the bluff they had been approaching marked an extensive cliff-fall, and for some distance the raw face plunged sheer into the sea. A remnant of bush hung raggedly from the rim to mark the nearest point of the collapse, but there was nothing where the waves were breaking to assist their passage. The rock spoils had evidently tumbled out into deeper water, or had been removed by the age-long encroachments of the waves. With the sea surging sullenly at the base of the cliffs, there was no other way but to climb.

It was necessary to backtrack from their vantage point to find a way to scale the bluffs. The effort required to haul themselves up the smooth slabs and through scrubby vegetation was more taxing than they would have imagined as they pulled each other up, hand over hand. At the summit of the scramble their dismay was heightened by the denseness of the guardian bush, a thick screen of which they were forced to push through to reach easier going beyond. The tangle was still dry, abrasive and totally trackless, however, unpenetrated even by animals. Not even the natives had seen fit to burn it, knowing easier access to the sea.

They sweated and groaned, and spoke little against their raging thirsts, pushing blindly through the endless clinging thickets. So great was their want of water that they could not even afford tears of vexation. Only by keeping close to the cliff-top could they see an end to their miseries.

Only by keeping close to the clifftop could they see an end to their miseries . . .

When at last it came though, their relief was shortlived, for in front of them lay the most formidable gorge they had yet encountered, a wide gulf several hundred yards across incising the coast so deeply that they could not see its end from where they stood. The three bore their dejection in silence, for words could not adequately convey their disappointment, their feelings of utter hopelessness.

The girl had warned that the sea cut across the way ahead in places and for them this was the first evidence, an impassable chasm into which the sea rode majestically, deep and without impediment to break the swell. How far did this one extend? How many extra miles for its circumnavigation? How many more of these seemingly impossible barriers? And how extensive was Botany Bay, which they knew for certain still lay ahead of them?

The girl's claim of being able to reach Port Jackson in two or three days from the coal beach began to look like a fantasy. Even the chief officer's extension to four days seemed a wild improbability. At the limits of their endurance the anticipation of any further time or effort being added to their ordeal seemed an intolerable, impossible burden.

Oh God, how much further, how much longer? How much more? For the first time, the extent of their deepening exhaustion and shrinking fortitude was sharply brought home to them in the face of such forbidding obstacles as the one stretching now at their feet. Even Fran Gilbaert would have acknowledged the reality of their plight and the harsh truth in the supercargo's earlier remarks, could he have trusted himself to speak. He swore briefly and incomprehensibly in his own language instead.

'We'd better go on.' After a short pause, this was all Will Clarke felt able to say to the others.

Below them they could see rocks, and so they began to pick their way down to avoid further association with the bush. At least this way they would be free of the tangled scrub for a while, and ...

'*A boat!* See! *D'ere*, below d' cliffs! It's a boat!' Will Clarke jerked his head round to where Fran Gilbaert was pointing. His words choked in obvious emotion as his hand shook, almost incoherent in thirst and excitement. 'Look, look – can't – can't you see? D'ere's – d'ere's men over yonder, fishing! It's a fishing boat!'

His seaman's eye had lost nothing of its sharpness in picking up a familiar shape against unfamiliar ground, but Will Clarke had to search hard against the blue-green sea and grey-brown rock to see for himself. His heart surged in an immense bound of relief as he saw it in the shadow of the cliff, but then it seemed so far away that its crew might easily leave before seeing their presence. Together they waved and called, but to no avail.

'We must go down and get closer, for they'll never see us against the trees here,' Will Clarke declared, feeling his knees tremble at the appalling possibility of missing this providential delivery. His whole body shook with mingled relief and anxiety, and apprehension fumbled his senses as he slipped on the sea-washed boulders at the water's edge.

Again they yelled and waved until their dry throats croaked and their legs threatened collapse. It was as if they were using their very last scraps of life energy. Failure to draw the men's attention and rising concern caused them to shift their position twice more, but it was impossible to be any closer to the bobbing craft than they were.

So late in the day the fishermen might leave anytime, with thoughts only for their homes in Sydney, and the bounty they had caught. Will Clarke's mind seemed to throb in desperation of ever attracting attention to their presence, for the alternative now was unthinkable.

Their looks were rapidly becoming haggard and their efforts feeble when one of the men in the boat looked in their direction, stared, then turned again to his lines. It seemed the brutal end.

'Oh, dear God, dear God, can they no' see us for what we are?' Tears started with the younger man's cry as he clenched his fists in choking supplication and slumped despairingly to his knees, devoid now of hope. Azim Prakash looked stunned, and for once his smile failed him. That boat seemed to represent their final hope; so near, and yet so despairingly far.

'We're natives! Look at us! D'ey're out d'ere t'inking we're natives!'

Realisation dawned on the Dutchman's face in the last reserves of his sanity as he stared at his two companions, and no wonder. They were dark, dirty, wild-looking and unkempt, and distance would have rendered their croaking calls meaningless, were they to be heard at all. He leaned over and shook the young Scotsman roughly, his voice urgent.

'Get up quickly, man, an' take off your shirt! Wave it around and – and let d'em see we're – we're white men!' His words were feverish. 'You also, Azim, show d'em – show d'em we have clothes, for God's sake! From where d'ey are, d'ey mus' surely see us only as – as blackfellows!' And so saying he struggled out of his own shirt and jacket, baring his pale torso and jumped and shouted with the others as if, as was the truth, their very lives depended on it.

And then, 'They've seen us, they've seen us! Oh, thank God, thank God they've seen us!' Never were more heartfelt words spoken. Never were more earnest thanks uttered. As the boat pulled strongly across the narrowing waterway and they knew they were at last to be saved, all of them felt such rising emotion that other words were impossible.

The whaleboat ground onto the pebbly foreshore and the man in the bow took them in at a glance. From the style of their ragged clothes and the Indian with them, he could see they were neither the natives he had first taken them for, nor convict escapees. He was a man rich in healthy vitality compared with themselves as he jumped from the boat, his rich Scottish brogue heartening, emotionally overwhelming.

'John Thistle, Bos'n of His Majesty's Ship *Reliance*, now in Sydney! An' who wuid you be, oot awa' on these wild shores, might ah ask?' The fellow's accent and broad welcoming smile were unmistakable.

'Is – is it far now, tae Sydney?' Will Clarke spoke with difficulty, unthinkingly ignoring the man's question to satisfy the more pressing realities of their plight.

'Och, no. No more'n fifteen miles alang the coast here, an' thru' the Heads. But who are ye, mon, an' where're ye frae? Ye're in a rare state tae be sure, that ah can see!'

Lending credence to the man's observation, Will Clarke slumped down on the sand once more, shaking his head in disbelief, unable to stand further. The others stood motionless, equally unbelieving and still unable to speak. The bos'n himself filled the void.

'By the *Great Harry*, but you laddies have been through it, ah'd hazard, an' wi' a fair tale tae tell frae the looks o' ye!' He spoke encouragingly, waiting for a hint, a clue, looking from one to the other as they struggled to collect themselves.

Will Clarke replied first from where he sat, though his words and mind were still distracted. 'Aye, ye could – ye could fairly well say that, Mr Thistle.' The youngster's eyes were distant and unseeing, his head still too full of mental images of long, tortured miles and lost comrades, and of aching leg-weariness, near-starvation and almost unendurable thirst. He choked again in his relief, speaking with difficulty as he gazed through tear-misted vision at the pebbles by his calloused feet.

'Aye. Ye could indeed say that!'

EPILOGUE

The three survivors from the wreck of the *Sydney Cove* were taken overnight from the place known as *Watta-mow-lee*, to Sydney, where they arrived early in the morning of 17 May, 1797. There they told their story to Governor John Hunter, who immediately arranged to have his personal whaleboat equipped and sent off on a search for Hugh Thompson and the carpenter, the boat's crew being accompanied by Bos'n John Thistle to the place described by Will Clarke. Though they remained in the search area for three days, they were unable to locate either of the two men, finding only one or two trifling items covered in blood, from which the boat-party surmised that the defenceless pair had been murdered by natives.

In the meantime the colonial schooner *Francis* was being prepared for sea to make the journey down to Preservation Island, together with a decked longboat, the *Eliza*. The latter was commanded by Archibald Armstrong, master of HM armed tender *Supply*, who volunteered his services to help in the rescue of Captain Hamilton and his men. Both boats were to set forth on 27 May.

While these craft were being made ready for their errands of mercy, Will Clarke and his companions recovered well under good care and sustenance, so much so that Will Clarke himself volunteered to go with Dr George Bass, surgeon of the *Reliance* (and soon to be joint explorer of Bass Strait with his friend and colleague, Lieutenant Matthew Flinders), on a voyage southward to the place where he had reported their coal discoveries.

Once again Governor Hunter's whaleboat was made available, well-manned and armed. The party was away eight days, during which time they collected a large quantity of coal samples which were eventually delivered to Sir Joseph Banks in London, as President of the Royal Society and former explorer of the eastern coast of New Holland in company with Captain James Cook.

Sadly, at the beach where Hugh Thompson and Job Duggan had last been seen, the party was led by a native to the remains of the two men. One of them had his skull so badly fractured that their murder at the hands of local tribesmen was beyond doubt. Though they scoured the area thoroughly, however, they could not find the murderers, one of whom was actually known by name to George Bass from a previous encounter during his voyage along this same coast, fourteen months earlier in the *Tom Thumb*.

The rescue boats meanwhile made their way to Furneaux's Islands, carrying Azim Prakash to be reunited with his brother. The *Eliza* was spotted by lookouts on Preservation Island on 8 June, but although the jollyboat was quickly launched, those aboard the *Eliza* sailed on, ignorant of their pursuers, and were soon out of sight, to the total dismay and consternation of the islanders.

Next day, with colours hoisted and a large fire set to burn, watchers saw the schooner *Francis*, but the surf ran so high as to prevent any attempt to launch the jollyboat. It was not until the 10th that the *Eliza*, again approaching the island, was hailed from the cockleshell craft. The rescuers found Captain Hamilton and many of his crew alive and in reasonable health, though a number had died and were buried on the island. The old captain and a seaman by the name of John Bennett were the only surviving Europeans.

As soon as possible, efforts were made to begin loading the cargo onto the two rescue vessels, but it quickly became apparent that their combined capacity would accommodate little more than half of what had been saved, including the surviving livestock. The rest would have to be left until another voyage could be arranged. William Clarke had anticipated this, and so had recruited six of the Port Jackson rescuers specifically to stay behind on the island to look after the remainder of the cargo. It soon became clear to the captain, however, in his own judgement of men, that these six were unsuited, and that the rum would soon prove to be too much of a temptation. Six of his own crew, including Azim and Rajendra Prakash, therefore volunteered to remain on the island with what was left of the cargo until such time as Captain Hamilton could return with a larger vessel.

Thus arranged, the two craft set out to return to Port Jackson on 20 June, the captain and some of his lascar crew on the schooner, others with Mr Armstrong aboard the little *Eliza*. The two boats soon separated to sail off in different directions – and this was the last that was seen of the *Eliza*. After a stormy passage of fifteen days, the *Francis* arrived safely back at the colony, but without news of the *Eliza*. Fears grew for the safety of the longboat and her passengers as the days went by until, after a severe storm on 17 July which damaged parts of the settlement, she was formally given up as lost.

In the same two months, from the time of the castaways' rescue south of Botany Bay, nothing was heard of the return of the Irish runaway, Bridgit O'Keefe. In these early years, so many convicts attempted escapes or went missing in the bush that searches were minimal, and subsequent concern even less. Though a handful eventually returned to give themselves up, most either starved, or died at the hands of natives. Of the dozen crewmen who had dropped out of the survival march that followed the strandings of the ill-fated *Sydney Cove* and her longboat, nothing was ever found either, and they too were presumed to have perished. In September 1797, William Clarke and Fran Gilbaert embarked together on the *Britannia* for China, thence to India.

It was not until six months after his first departure that Captain Hamilton returned to Preservation Island aboard the *Francis*, no other suitable vessel having been available meanwhile. On his arrival, he found that five of his six men had survived tolerably well on a variety of fish, seal meat and other wildlife, and had even found time and energy to explore several of the neighbouring islands from the jollyboat. Leaving Sydney at the end of December, 1797, the return trip with most of the remaining cargo was completed on 20 January 1798.

During the period since her beaching the effects of local storms were such that the wreckage of the *Sydney Cove* was entirely washed away. When Lieutenant Matthew Flinders visited the island, however, in company with the still energetic Captain Hamilton on the third voyage of the *Francis*, he found many signs of the year's occupation. This particular trip was commissioned to carry out survey work which lasted from 1 February to 9 March 1798 – the time when George Bass was making his well-known whaleboat voyage along the coast of New South Wales to what afterwards became known as Westernport Bay.

Each of these respective ventures helped to pave the way for a joint circumnavigation of Van Diemen's Land by Flinders and Bass in the colonial sloop *Norfolk* later the same year, a momentous voyage which was to prove the claim of Captain Hamilton, and confirm the suspicions of Governor Hunter and others, that Van Diemen's Land was indeed an island. It confirmed also that the islands of the Furneaux Group were rich grounds for sealing, an industry which then rapidly developed.

Upon his return to Bengal, Will Clarke's story and diary of events after the longboat wreck were published in the *Asiatic Mirror* of Calcutta, on 27 December 1797 and 10 January 1798. One hundred years later it was reprinted in the *Historical Records of New South Wales*. His equally detailed observations to his business partners on trade prospects with the infant colony soon had the House of Campbell, Clarke and Co. preparing for yet another voyage of speculation to Port Jackson, notwithstanding their loss of the *Sydney Cove*.

The snow *Hunter* thus arrived on 10 June 1798, carrying with her one Robert Campbell, another junior partner, who later wound up his affairs in Calcutta to become one of the first merchant settlers of New South Wales, and ultimately one of the most prosperous of the early colony.

His name is commemorated now in Sydney's Campbell's Cove and in the settlement of Campbelltown, just as the names of William Clarke, Captain Hamilton and Mr Armstrong of the *Supply* are perpetuated in some of the landmarks and channels close to Preservation Island in the Furneaux Group. Even the lascars are remembered at a point across the channel from the island.

Soon after his rescue Captain Hamilton formally recorded the loss of the *Sydney Cove* in a Public Instrument of Protest, which is held today by the Archives Authority of NSW in Sydney. Thereafter he stayed almost a year in Sydney, during which time he twice returned to Preservation Island. All this continued to take its toll, however. Already an old man at the start of this adventure, Captain Hamilton survived the arrival of his employer Robert Campbell by only a few days. Worn out by the hardships and privations of five months on the gale-swept eminence he had called Preservation, and the worry and distress which he suffered at the loss of his ship and so many of his crew, he died in Sydney on 20 June 1798 – according to Judge-Advocate Collins, 'exceedingly regretted by all who had the pleasure of his acquaintance.'

Captain Hamilton was buried in the cemetery later known as the Old Burial Ground on George Street, Sydney, beneath a tombstone erected by his employer, Robert Campbell. Here his remains lay until the early months of 1869 when the cemetery, unused for 45 years, was cleared for the building of the present Town Hall. Robert Campbell's son, the Hon. John Campbell MLC, took particular care over the grave of the old sea captain. Captain Hamilton's remains were re-interred in the Church of England portion of the new Necropolis at Rookwood on 7 April 1869, where his tombstone can still be seen today as the only one removed from the old George Street cemetery.

New

Great Australian Bight

PA

N